ERRATA

page 60:	Open square brackets in front of the species heading "Scarce Swallowtail".
pages 76 and 80:	The photographs of the White-letter Hairstreak and the Brown Hairstreak have been transposed. Thus, the White-letter Hairstreak should appear on page 80 and the Brown Hairstreak on page 76. The captions are correctly placed: the photograph of the Brown Hairstreak was taken by Michael Hammerson and that of the White-letter Hairstreak by Paul Thompson.
pages 132 and 136	The photographs of the Gatekeeper and the Marbled White have been similarly transposed. Thus, the Marbled White should appear on page 132 and the Gatekeeper on page 136. The captions are correctly placed: the photograph of the Gatekeeper was taken by Stuart Holdsworth and that of the Marbled White by Michael Hammerson.

THE BUTTERFLIES OF THE LONDON AREA

by

Colin W. Plant

David Wright,
19th February 1988.

With coloured plates by various members of the
London Natural History Society

LONDON NATURAL HISTORY SOCIETY
1987

British Library Cataloguing in Publication Data
Plant, Colin W.
The Butterflies of the London Area
1. Butterflies – England – London
2. Insects – England – London
I. Title II. London Natural History Society
595.78'9'09421 QL555.G7
ISBN 0 - 901009 - 03 - 2

Published by the London Natural History Society from the Passmore Edwards Museum, Romford Road, Stratford, London E15 4LZ.

Passmore
Edwards
Museum

Printed in Britain by The Woodgrange Press Limited, London, E7 0EW

CONTENTS

FOREWORD

by Paul Whalley, DSc, FIBiol,

Department of Entomology, British Museum (Natural History)

The study of butterflies seen in and around London has a long and distinguished history. Many accounts of our butterflies have appeared in the literature, documenting changes in their occurence round the capital. Colin Plant's book is a tribute to all those who have collected and studied butterflies within a 20 mile radius of St Paul's Cathedral. .

In the 18th and 19th centuries London was at the centre of the study of butterflies and this association is reflected in the names of some of the societies. The premier entomological society in Britain, although for many years now an international society, still has as its full title, The Royal Entomological Society of London. It is only a few years ago that the South London Entomological Society was renamed the British Entomological and Natural History Society. Many newer associations have been formed now to study the butterflies and other insects of the area.

London may not be the first place to come to mind when you think about butterflies but how many other capital cities have a butterfly named after one of their districts. The Camberwell Beauty, named after Camberwell, where one of the earliest specimens was collected, is a rare migrant to Britain. As a migrant it might one day again be seen in Camberwell. However, it is not forgotten and art work depicting the butterfly is used as a decoration on the outside of one of Camberwell's buildings.

Another butterfly whose name has a London connection is Albin's Hampstead Eye, sadly not now believed to have come from the area, while the infamous Charlton's Brimstone butterfly, caught in London, subsequently proved to be a common butterfly with the hindwings painted to deceive, and perhaps defraud. Two specimens of the common Brimstone butterfly, with carefully painted hindwings were figured by the London-based entomologist, Petiver in 1767. They were even given a scientific name by the great Swedish naturalist, Linnaeus, before the fraud was discovered and the specimens discounted. The original painted specimens are now in the safety and decent obscurity of the strong room in the Linnean Society of London.

One of the more surprising results of the study of butterflies in the London area is the discovery that the number of species of butterfly has changed very little over the last 100 years, although undoubtedly their individual abundance has altered.

Whether for scientific study or for their beauty alone, butterflies have never been as popular as they are today. In 1981-82, *Butterfly Year* was launched to increase awareness of butterflies and to highlight the state of the fauna. Butterfly Year attempted to publicise them as part of an overall theme that the environment was in reasonable shape if butterflies were common and diverse. There is need, particularly in cities, for conservation of butterflies in order to keep what is there, and perhaps to encourage more to become established. Colin Plant provides a thought-provoking account of both the conflicts and values of collecting as well stressing the need to conserve butterflies.

Why do we want butterflies? Even if we ignore the variety of ways that they are important in weed control and pollination or of their part in the food chain of the animals and plants around, we cannot ignore their sheer beauty. The aesthetic appeal of butterflies and the pleasure they give is surely worth the effort of conserving them. You plant your garden, park or even window box to add a splash of colour. If you put in some of the right plants as indicated in this book, although you may spend money on the plants, the butterflies will come, free.

This book is the result of the work of a large band of dedicated enthusiasts. Their studies, and many of his own, are brought together with enthusiasm by Colin Plant in this fascinating study of the butterflies of the London area.

PREFACE

CONTINUITY AND CHANGE

by Ian G. Robertson, MA. FMA.

Curator of the Passmore Edwards Museum and President of the Museums' Association

Looking back twenty years after becoming Curator of the Passmore Edwards Museum in Stratford in 1967, it is interesting to reflect that amongst the very first part of the collections to come to my notice were eight drawers of butterflies, mostly from South Essex, which formed a part of the much larger forty-four drawer Lepidoptera collection of William Cole: Cole was the first Curator of the Museum when it was run by the Essex Field Club in the early years of this century after its official opening in 1900, and his collection was one of our earliest entomological acquisitions.

With the Cole collection, attention was also drawn to that of A.W. Mera, a twenty drawer cabinet of some 2,500 butterflies, still in excellent condition, collected between about 1900 and 1925; all British species are represented with many examples from south-west Essex localities as well as from Surrey, Kent and other parts of the area served by the London Natural History Society.

Thinking back to 1967, it was impossible then to envisage how things would have changed twenty years on. True, there is continuity with the students of the nineteenth century in the sense that the Essex Field Club, although long since having given up any direct management role in the affairs of the Passmore Edwards Museum, nevertheless has an important influence on policy through its representation on the museum's governing body. Similarly, through the London Natural History Society, a link is maintained with the distinguished entomologists of the past. Indeed, the LNHS began its life in 1858 as the City of London Entomological Society, producing its first *Proceedings* in 1892. Combining in 1914 with the then North London Natural History Society, it has gone from strength to strength, collaborating fully today in its eastern sector with the Passmore Edwards Museum to the mutual benefit of both.

But the continuity thus demonstrated by the vigorous existence of the Passmore Edwards Museum, the Essex Field Club and the London Natural History Society is but a background to the most profound of changes not forseen, and hardly forshadowed, in 1967. This change was centred upon what the 1980s had been pleased to label "the new technology". This facility to computerise data has revolutionised the role of the museum biologist and Society member alike. Indeed, writing in 1987 as President of the Museums' Association, it is clear that the establishment of Museum-based Biological

Records Centres is one of the more significant museum successes of recent years. So far as the Passmore Edwards Museum is concerned, the development of the Biological Records Centre at the Interpretative Centre at the Museum Nature Reserve in East Ham has transformed the quality of service which may be provided not just to other researchers, but to planning authorities also, thereby conferring a public benefit far beyond the confines of the Museum building itself.

The much closer liaison between museums and societies is also a feature of recent years. In the late 1960s it seemed that both types of institutions might well go their respective ways, both looking for new roles. In the event, the movement towards conservation in all its forms, and the need for detailed knowledge upon which further research, recording and conservation programmes could be based has led to a very much closer mutually beneficial association. In the case of the London Natural History Society and the Passmore Edwards Museum both have compatible computerised recording systems using programmes prepared by Museum staff. Similarly, there is a useful link in terms of personnel with Colin Plant, the author of this book and a valued member of the staff of the Museum, being actively involved in the affairs of the LNHS, particularly by being its President during the years 1985 and 1986.

Looking back over twenty years, the changes have been nothing if not beneficial for both museums and societies; a new role in promoting conservation has been very much to the public good, new technology has established paramountcy of biological recording, and a new generation of enthusiastic researches have maintained the necessary exacting standards in a way which would, no doubt, have earned them the approval of the great nineteenth century entomologists.

THE LONDON AREA

The recording area of the London Natural History Society is based upon a circle of twenty miles radius, centred upon St Paul's Cathedral. The boundary itself is a stepped polygon which follows the lines of the Ordnance Survey's National Grid along the circumference of the circle. This is shown in Fig. 1, in which the boundaries of the London boroughs are shown by solid lines and the boundaries of the Vice-counties by dashed lines. The River Thames flows from west to east. Marginal numbers relate to the numbers of the National Grid and here indicate ten kilometre squares and tetrads. Boroughs 1,2,3,4 and 7 all lie within the Vice-county of South Essex. A small part of borough 10 lies in Hertfordshire, the remainder, and all other boroughs north of the Thames, lie in Middlesex. Borough 22 straddles the Thames and is thus partly in Middlesex and partly in Surrey. The boundary between West Kent and Surrey more or less follows the boundaries between boroughs 30 and 31, and 28 and 29. Thus boroughs 29, 31, 32 and 33 are all in West Kent, and the remainder of those lying south of the River Thames are in Surrey. There is no overlap between Buckinghamshire and the London Boroughs. These Vice-counties bear no relation to any administrative county divisions and remain constant in spite of any political boundary changes.

A HISTORY OF BUTTERFLIES AND BUTTERFLY RECORDING IN LONDON

Largely as a result of the way in which human society was structured, London was the effective centre of entomology in Britain throughout the period of its birth and early development as a serious science, in the eighteenth and early nineteenth centuries. Indeed, it was here that the Aurelian Society, the first organised assemblage of British entomologists, was established as early as 1738, holding regular meetings at the Swan Tavern, in Change Alley, Cornhill until the disastrous fire which destroyed the collections, books, and very nearly the Aurelians themselves during the new year celebrations of 25 March 1748. Many

Figure 1. The London area. See text for details.

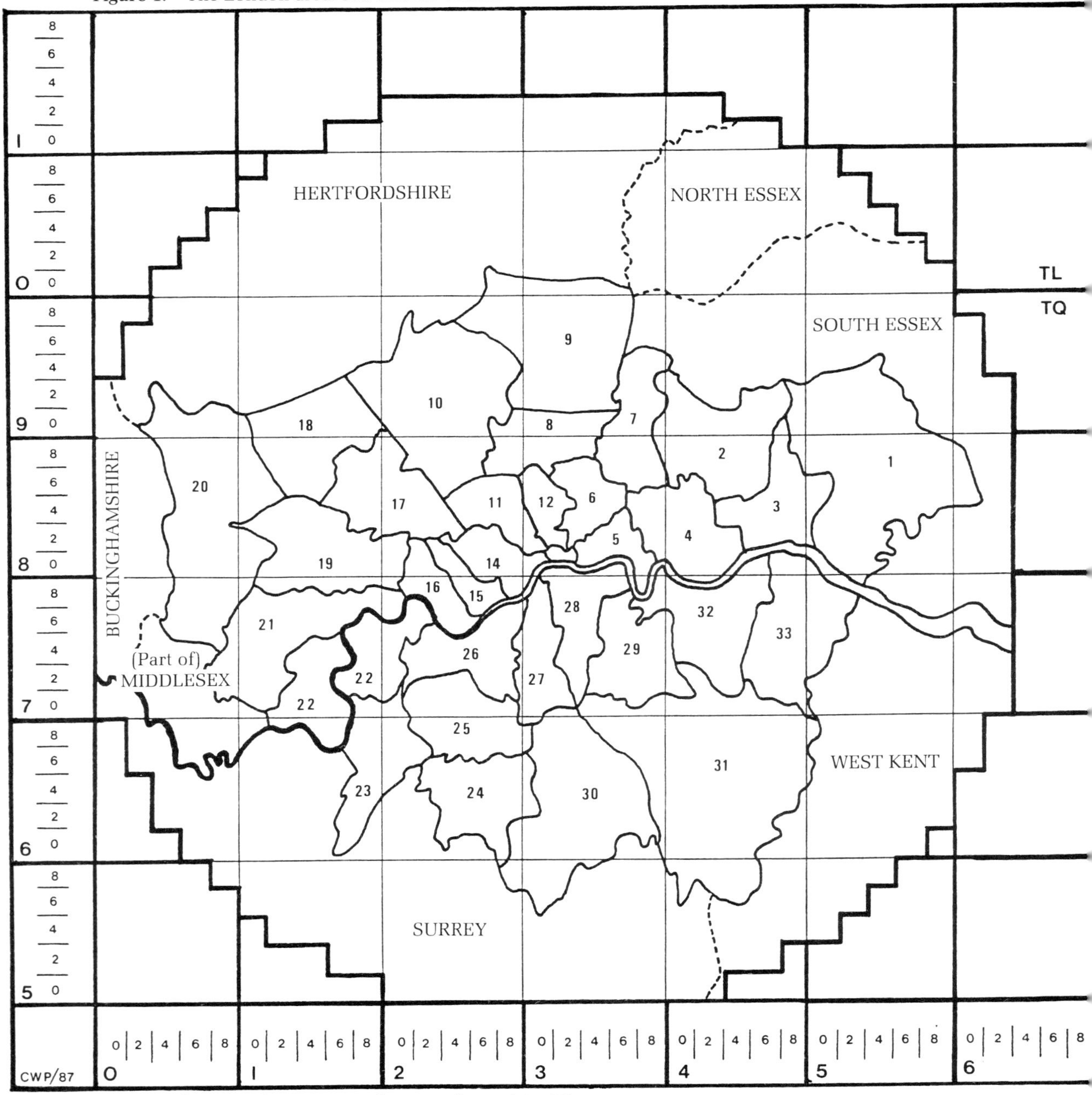

Key to the London Boroughs numbered in Figure 1.

1 Havering
2 Redbridge
3 Barking and Dagenham
4 Newham
5 Tower Hamlets
6 Hackney
7 Waltham Forest
8 Haringey
9 Enfield
10 Barnet
11 Camden
12 Islington
13 City of London
14 Westminster
15 Kensington and Chelsea
16 Hammersmith and Fulham
17 Brent
18 Harrow
19 Ealing
20 Hillingdon
21 Hounslow
22 Richmond
23 Kingston-upon-Thames
24 Sutton
25 Merton
26 Wandsworth
27 Lambeth
28 Southwark
29 Lewisham
30 Croydon
31 Bromley
32 Greenwich
33 Bexley

famous entomologists, including Petiver, Albin, Lewin, Wilkes, Moses Harris, Curtis, Haworth, Stephens, Newman, South and Tutt were active in what we now refer to as the London area, and there are very many references to the butterflies which existed here in classic works from these and author authors, including, by way of example, Jacobus Petiver's *Muse Petiveriani Centuria Prima* in 1699 and then later his *Papilionum Britanniae* in 1717, Moses Harris' *Aurelian* in 1766, Edward Newman's *British Butterflies* in 1871 and A.H. Haworth's *Lepidoptera Britannica* in 1803. The establishment of such specialist entomological journals as the *Entomologist*, and the *Entomologist's Record and Journal of Variation*, together with less specialist organs such as the *Zoologist* presented a further medium for communication of sightings, and most, if not all, of the London entomologists availed themselves of this facility. During the last ten to twenty years of the nineteenth century these journals regularly contained notes, communications or longer papers on the insect fauna of various small parts of the London area, and butterflies featured regularly.

It was during this same period that the earliest specific listing of insects, including butterflies, covering any significant part of the present day London area, appeared. This was T.D.A. Cockerell's *Preliminary List of the Insect Fauna of Middlesex*, published in twelve separate parts in the journal *The Entomologist* between 1890 and 1893. The butterflies appeared in the 1891 volume, and numbered just thirty-five species. It is evident from reading through the list that the coverage of that particular vice-county area, even allowing for today's higher standards, was poor to say the least, and largely placed on record the author's own observations, supplemented by additional details from other entomologists of the time. In addition, there is little resemblance between Cockerell's area of study and the presently defined London area - the latter now entirely consuming the former. During that same year however, on 5th November, Dr F.J. Buckell, a leading London entomologist of the day, read a paper entitled *The Lepidoptera of a London Garden* before the learned gentlemen of the City of London Entomological and Natural History Society. This account, in fact of two gardens in Islington between 1881 and 1891, listed sixty-three species in all of which only four were butterflies. The significance of this apparently minor contribution to the science lies in the fact that Buckell clearly intended his account to be a stimulus to others, for it is reported (*Transactions of the City of London Entomological and Natural History Society* volume 1, page 35 1892), that "*Dr Buckell incidentally called attention to the need that existed for the compilation of a list of the fauna of the London district. He expressed an opinion that the task was one which might very properly be accomplished by the Society, and urged The Council to take the matter in hand*". Clearly, the Council, under the leadership of their President J.A. Clark, were moved by Buckell's suggestion and reported in the *Transactions* volume 2, page 23 in 1893 that "*The Council of the City of London Entomological and Natural History Society have decided to compile a list of the fauna of the London district.*

The departments of birds, Lepidoptera and Coleoptera were already in hand". The report continued by defining, for the first time, the area from which records were to be gathered – "*a circle of about ten miles from Charing Cross, that is, lying within the following points:- Enfield Station, Ponders End Station, Chingford Station, Woodford Bridge, Ripple Castle, Abbey Wood Station, Pope Street Station, Chislehurst Station, West Wickham Station, South Croydon Station, Carshalton Station, Sutton Station, Worcester Park Station, Kingston Bridge, Twickenham Station, Hounslow, Station, Southall Station, Harrow Station, Edgeware Station and New Barnet Station*". The use of railway stations to define the boundary seems to have been a matter of convenience more than anything else, since the train was the fastest and most suitable mode of transport available at the time to those residents of central London anxious to reach the suburbs in pursuit of natural history.

Dr Buckell reportedly threw himself whole-heartedly into the task of preparing a list of the Lepidoptera, a statement which present-day readers, free of the protocol of the Victorian era, will doubtless realise means that nobody else volunteered! By the end of 1893, the first part of the list was ready for publication, but funding was not available and publication was delayed for six years. During this period Buckell, for various entirely honourable reasons, was forced to give up entomology, and the records were kept up to date by Mr L.B. Prout, President of the City of London Society from 1899 to 1902 and, in 1914, the first President of the London Natural History Society. The first part of the list finally appeared in the *Transactions* in 1899 (which volume covered the year 1898, and for which reason the work is referred to as "*the 1898 list*" by several later workers, including Baron de Worms) under the joint authorship of Buckell and Prout, and a further three parts followed in 1900, 1901 and 1902 under the same authorship. It is however, the first of these four which contains the butterflies, listing a total of thirty-nine for the area during the period from 1880 to publication.

In 1899 the National Grid had not been invented, and the now familiar method of indicating presence in a given area by a dot within an Ordnance Survey grid square on a map was quite unknown. Neither was it deemed appropriate to list the species recorded under the headings of the Watsonian Vice-counties, in existence since 1852 when Hewett Cottrell Watson so divided the country in the third volume of his work *Cybele Britannica*. At that time this would have included only West Kent, Surrey, Middlesex and South Essex in our area. Instead, the London area was split into four divisions: north-eastern, north-western, south-eastern and south western, and the presence of a species was reported under these headings, together with a note of the localities from which records had been received and, in some cases, an indication of abundance. This distribution is analysed in Table one. It should be noted that whilst nowhere are the boundaries of the four divisions stated, it is evident by implication that they lie more or less on the north-south and east-west lines

TABLE 1. Butterflies recorded by Buckell and Prout (1899) in each of the four divisions of the London area (see text page 12).

SPECIES	I North-east	II South-east	III South-west	IV North-west
Small Skipper	X	X	X	X
Large Skipper	X	X	X	X
Silver-spotted skipper		X		
Dingy Skipper	X	X		X
Grizzled Skipper	X	X		X
Clouded Yellow	X	X	X	X
Pale Clouded Yellow		X	X	X
Brimstone	X	X	X	X
Large White	X	X	X	X
Small White	X	X	X	X
Green-veined White	X	X	X	X
Orange tip	X	X	X	
Green Hairstreak		X		
Purple Hairstreak		X		
Small Copper	X	X	X	X
Small Blue		X		
Chalk Hill Blue		X	X	
Adonis Blue		X		
Common Blue	X	X	X	X
Holly Blue	X	X	X	X
Long-tailed Blue		X		
Brown Argus		X		
Red Admiral	X	X	X	X
Painted Lady	X	X	X	X
Purple Emperor	X			
Comma	X			
Peacock	X	X	X	X
Small Tortoiseshell	X	X	X	X
Large Tortoiseshell	X	X	X	X
Camberwell Beauty	X	X	X	X
Dark Green Fritillary		X		
High Brown Fritillary	X			X
Silver-washed Fritillary	X			
Speckled Wood		X		
Wall	X	X	X	X
Meadow Brown	X	X	X	X
Gatekeeper		X	X	
Small Heath	X	X	X	X
Ringlet		X		
TOTAL IN EACH	**26**	**35**	**23**	**23**
	GRAND TOTAL = 39 SPECIES			

Figure 2. Numbers of naturally occurring butterflies recorded in each tetrad of the London area during the survey period, 1980 to 1986

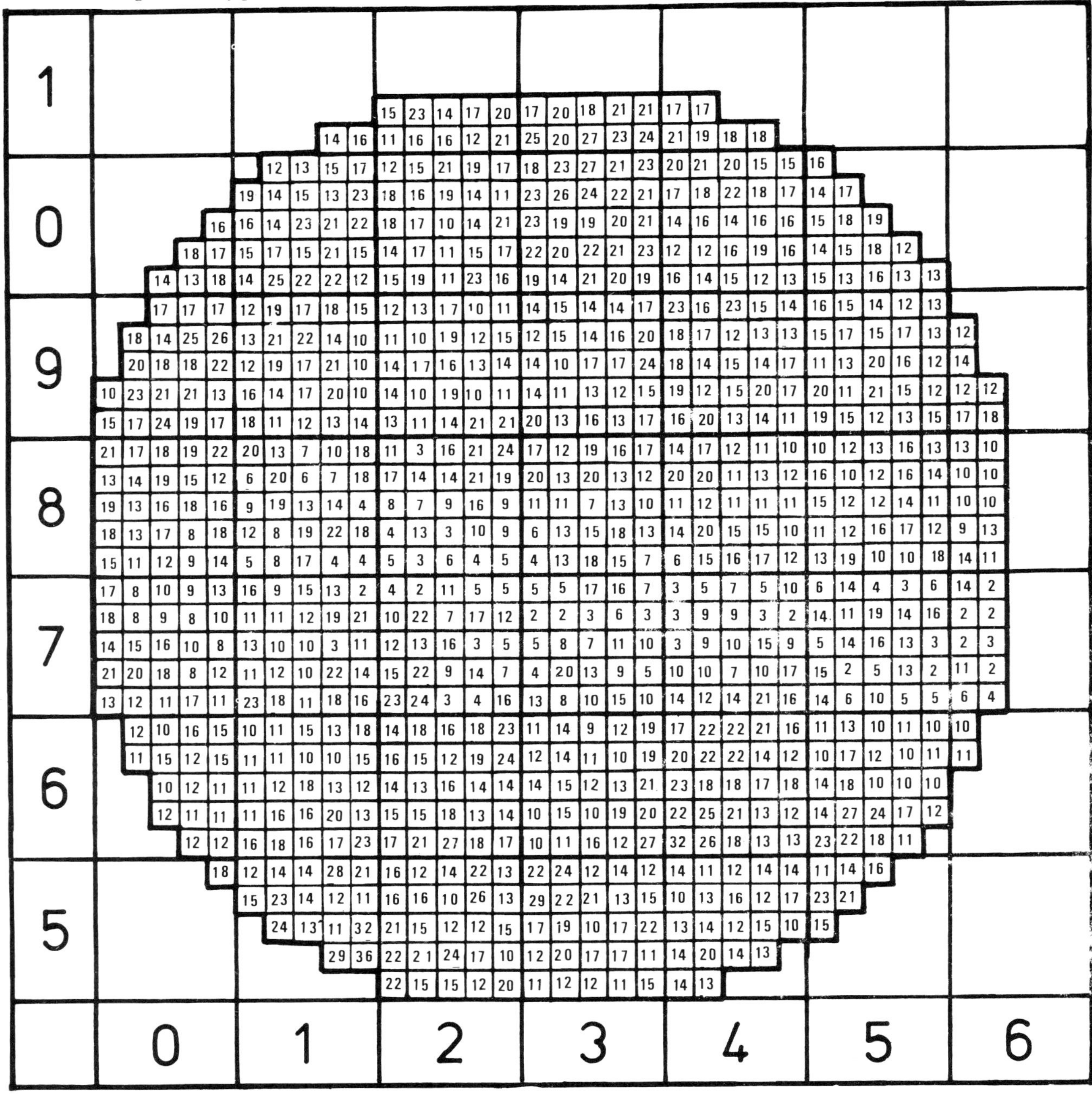

joining the points of the compass based upon what we today refer to as "grid north". Hence, division II, the south-east, contains not only West Kent, but also a part of Surrey, whilst the north-east division would also contain two vice-county areas. Five species reported from the south-east division were found nowhere else in the London area at that time. These were the Silver-spotted Skipper, Green and Purple Hairstreaks, the Speckled Wood and the Ringlet. Particularly noteworthy occurrences included the Grizzled Skipper at Wood Street, Walthamstow, in the north-east, Silver-spotted Skipper at Croydon and single specimens of both Silver-washed and High Brown Fritillary at Hackney!

Just over fifty years elapsed between Buckell and Prout's 1899 list and the next major work, when the Baron Charles de Worms produced his paper *The Butterflies of London and its Surroundings* in the 1949 volume of *The London Naturalist*, (published in 1950). Taking due account of a number of local lists which had appeared during the interim, particularly the South Eastern Union of Scientific Societies' *A survey and Record of Woolwich and Kent* (1909), and the major work on the Lepidoptera of Hertfordshire by Dr A.H. Foster in the 1937 *Transactions of the Hertfordshire Natural History Society and Field Club*, de Worms listed fifty-six species reported from 1900 to 1948 in the London area (now newly defined as a circle of twenty mile radius from St Paul's Cathedral) and compared this with the then accepted British total of sixty-eight species. Of the total for London, some forty-seven were noted as resident breeding butterflies (although in this total was included the Red Admiral which present evidence suggests has always been purely immigrant in the London region, and the Large Tortoiseshell, for which evidence that it existed in that date band as a breeding species is highly suspect) and nine as immigrants of which three Painted Lady, Clouded Yellow and Pale Clouded Yellow, were of regular occurrence. Two extinct species, the Large Blue and the Black-veined White, were also noted as having been recorded in the area in years gone by.

Seventeen species listed by de Worms therefore were absent from the 1899 list, but an examination of the records indicates that of these only four residents – the Grayling, Small Pearl-bordered Fritillary, Silver-studded Blue and the Essex Skipper, together with a single record of the immigrant Monarch were within the confines of the ten-mile circle which was the earlier study area. The remaining twelve – Swallowtail, Wood White, Bath White, Brown Hairstreak, White-letter Hairstreak, Duke of Burgundy, White Admiral, the Heath, Marsh, Pearl-bordered and Queen of Spain Fritillaries, and the Marbled White were all beyond the circle in the newly annexed outer zone which in practice had quadrupled the size of the recording area to approximately 1,260 square miles.

Broadly speaking therefore, the overall butterfly fauna of the "London District" had undergone no significant change, and this conclusion was indeed reached by de Worms himself. However, whilst this general statement about the overall fauna is true, there are a number of apparent alterations in the status of a few species between the two works, though how many of these are actual and how many are a consequence of a greater number of field workers covering a period two and a half times as great in the later work is difficult to say. De Worms noted, for example, an expansion in the range of the Speckled Wood which was probably actual, as too was beyond doubt the far greater spread of the Comma. Wider reports of other species, such as the Brimstone for example, probably resulted from greater coverage.

De Worms devoted the next ten years to writing about the moths of the same area, which work he concluded in 1958. Then, in 1959, ten years on, he published, again in *The London Naturalist*, "A Supplement to the Butterflies and Moths of London and its Surroundings – Part 1", which contained the butterflies. One new species, the Apollo, was added, and valuable additions made to the records for thirty-seven other species. In concluding the next and final part of the Supplement, de Worms added that "*the conclusion . . . does not by any means write* Finis *to the study of Lepidoptera of that area.*" His intention was to produce short annual reviews in *The London Naturalist*, but for various practical reasons these reviews were published biennially, the first, covering 1960 and 1961, appearing in 1962. These summaries of the more noteworthy records continued to 1978, (covering 1976 and 1977) adding a single species to the list in the form of the Brown Playboy (a tropical African species accidentally imported) in 1974.

It is appropriate to mention at this point a parallel study on the Lepidoptera of Kent. J.M. Chalmers-Hunt's mammoth work *The Butterflies and Moths of Kent: A Critical Account* was commenced in 1960 as a supplement to the journal *Entomologist's Record*, and the butterflies were completed at the end of the 1961 volume. Many valuable additional records for the London area are to be found in the pages of both this work and its 1979 *Supplement*.

After the death of the Baron in 1979, the present author was asked to carry on the task of recording the Capital's Lepidoptera, and has endeavoured to continue the biennial reviews to date. Upon accepting this task, however, it soon became apparent that there was a need for an expansion of the existing recording programme, and that there was a companion need for a modern system of data storage and interpretation. In order to assess the range and status of any given species, for reasons of conservation or whatever, it was necessary to read back through the many works already referred to here, a somewhat onerous task. There had never been produced, in any form, maps of the distributions of any of London's Lepidoptera and thus, with the entire Lepidoptera firmly in mind, the launch of the Butterfly Atlas Project was announced in 1981 (*The London Naturalist* **60**:104).

The decision to employ tetrads (two × two kilometre squares) as the basic recording unit was fairly easily reached.Ten-kilometre distribution maps would have been quite valueless, for they would impart little knowledge of a species' true distribution in the urban area. Identical comments were felt appropriate in relation to five kilometre squares. To go the extreme of using monads, (one

Figure 3. Comparative distribution of butterflies in the tetrads of the London area during the years 1980 to 1986.

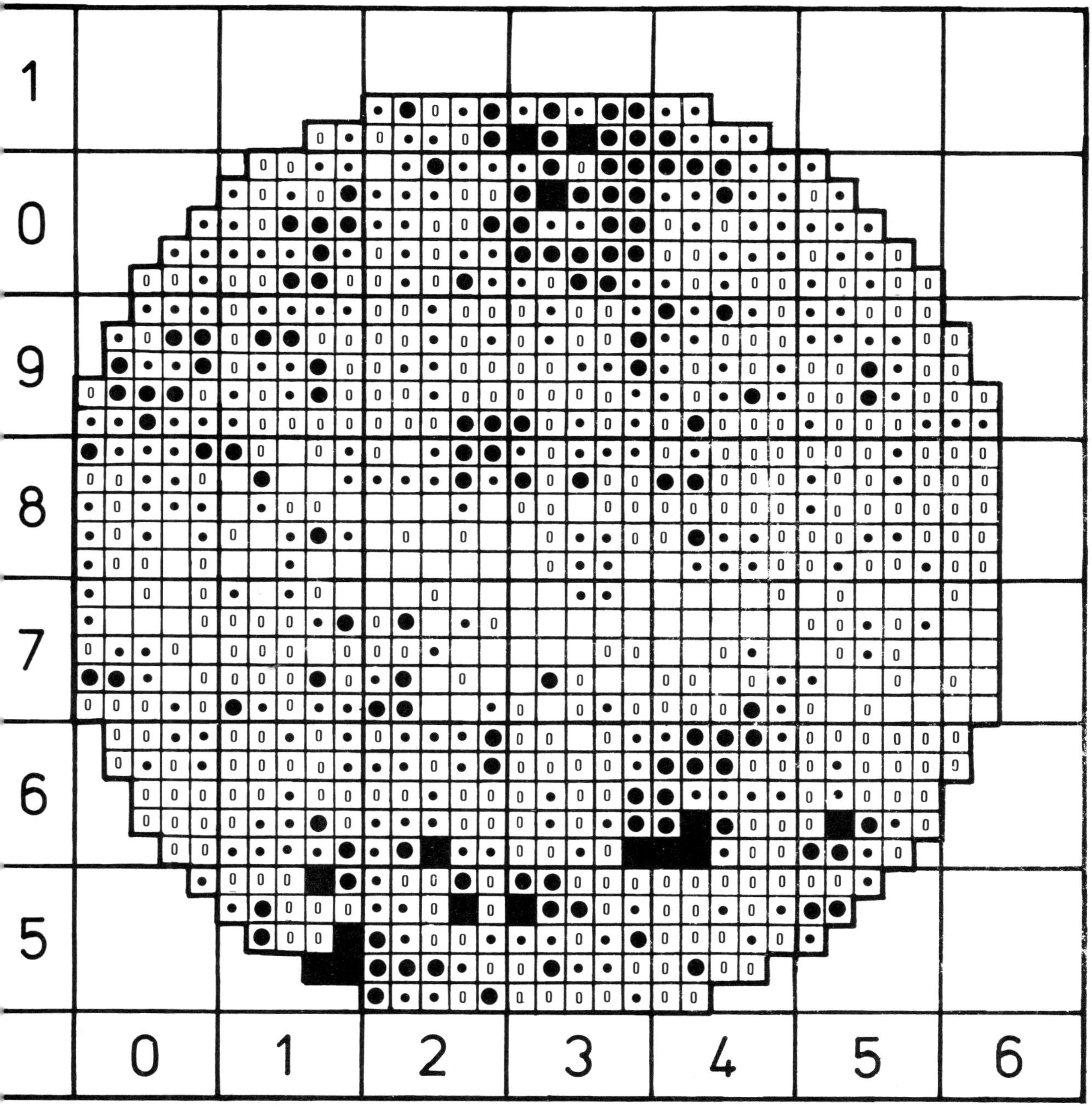

■ > 25 species recorded
● 20-24 species recorded
• 15-20 species recorded
0 10-14 species recorded
□ < 10 species recorded

TABLE 2. Complete list of butterflies which have occurred naturally in the London area, analysed by vice-county. X = record made 1980-1986. (X) = record made prior to 1980 only.

SPECIES	**VICE-COUNTY NUMBER**							
	West Kent (16)	**Surrey (17)**	**South Essex (18)**	**North Essex (19)**	**Herts (20)**	**Middx (21)**	**Bucks (24)**	**Inner London**
HESPERIIDAE								
Small Skipper	X	X	X	X	X	X	X	X
Essex Skipper	X	X	X	X	X	X	X	X
Silver-spotted Skipper	(X)	X			(X)	(X)		
Large Skipper	X	X	X	X	X	X	X	X
Dingy Skipper	X	X	X	(X)	X	X	X	
Grizzled Skipper	X	X	X	(X)	X	X	X	
PAPILIONIDAE								
Apollo				(X)		(X)		
Swallowtail	(X)	(X)	(X)			(X)		
PIERIDAE								
Wood White	(X)	(X)	(X)	(X)	(X)	(X)	(X)	
Pale Clouded Yellow *	(X)	(X)	(X)			(X)		
Clouded Yellow	X	X	X	X	X	X	X	X
Brimstone	X	X	X	X	X	X	X	X
Black-veined White			(X)			(X)		
Large White	X	X	X	X	X	X	X	X
Small White	X	X	X	X	X	X	X	X
Green-veined White	X	X	X	X	X	X	X	X
Bath White	(X)	(X)			(X)	(X)		
Orange tip	X	X	X	X	X	X	X	X
LYCAENIDAE								
Green Hairstreak	X	X	X		X	X	(X)	X
Brown Hairstreak	(X)	X		X				
Purple Hairstreak	X	X	X	X	X	X	X	
White-letter Hairstreak	X	X	X		X	X	(X)	
Small Copper	X	X	X	X	X	X	X	X
Long-tailed Blue	(X)	X				X		
Small Blue	X	X	(X)		X	X		
Silver-studded Blue	(X)	X	(X)	(X)		(X)		
Brown Argus	X	X	(X)	(X)	X	(X)	(X)	
Common Blue	X	X	X	X	X	X	X	X
Chalk Hill Blue	X	X	(X)		(X)	(X)		
Adonis Blue	(X)	X						
Mazarine Blue		(X)						
Large Blue					(X)			
Holly Blue	X	X	X	X	X	X	X	X
NEMEOBIIDAE								
Duke of Burgundy Fritillary	(X)	X	(X)		(X)			

TABLE 2 continued

SPECIES	VICE-COUNTY NUMBER							
	West Kent (16)	Surrey (17)	South Essex (18)	North Essex (19)	Herts (20)	Middx (21)	Bucks (24)	Inner London
NYMPHALIDAE								
White Admiral	X	X	(X)	X	X	X	X	(X)
Purple Emperor		X	X		(X)	(X)		
Red Admiral	X	X	X	X	X	X	X	X
Painted Lady	X	X	X	X	X	X	X	X
Small Tortoiseshell	X	X	X	X	X	X	X	X
Large Tortoiseshell	(X)	(X)	X		X	(X)		(X)
Camberwell Beauty	(X)	X	X	X	X	X	(X)	(X)
Peacock	X	X	X	X	X	X	X	X
Comma	X	X	X	X	X	X	X	X
Small Pearl-bordered Fritillary	(X)	X	(X)		(X)	(X)		
Pearl bordered Fritillary	(X)	X	(X)		(X)	(X)	(X)	
Queen of Spain Fritillary	(X)	(X)			(X)			
High Brown Fritillary	(X)	(X)	(X)	(X)	(X)	(X)		(X)
Dark Green Fritillary	X	X	(X)		X	(X)	(X)	(X)
Silver-washed Fritillary	X	X	(X)		X	X	(X)	(X)
Marsh Fritillary	(X)	(X)	(X)		(X)	(X)		
Glanville Fritillary	(X)	(X)						
Heath Fritillary			(X)	(X)		(X)		
SATYRIDAE								
Speckled Wood	X	X	X	X	X	X	X	X
Wall	X	X	X	X	X	X	X	X
Marbled White	X	X	(X)		X	X	X	
Grayling	X	(X)	X		(X)	(X)	(X)	
Gatekeeper	X	X	X	X	X	X	X	X
Meadow Brown	X	X	X	X	X	X	X	X
Small Heath	X	X	X	X	X	X	X	X
Ringlet	X	X	X	X	X	X		
DANAIDAE								
Milkweed	(X)	(X)	X		(X)	(X)		
TOTALS	**55**	**57**	**51**	**35**	**50**	**54**	**36**	**28**

* Pale Clouded Yellow includes Berger's Clouded Yellow, only reliably reported from West Kent.

kilometre squares) would have considerable practical difficulties – indeed some squares could probably not be visited at all either through inaccessibility or by virtue of the sheer number of monads in the area. The only logical scale available therefore was that of the tetrad, a system already proven useful by ornithologists and botanists in the publication of *Atlas of Breeding Birds of the London Area* and *Flora of the London Area* respectively. There is also the added advantage of being able to compare directly the distributions of butterflies not only with their larval foodplants, but also with the regolith, rainfall, air pollution and habitat maps published as overlays in *The London Naturalist* by Deacon and Sandford, and reproduced in print in *Flora of the London Area* by Burton. This work will hopefully also be of value in that it can be put together with similar maps for Essex, Suffolk and Hertfordshire to provide an authoritative overview of a major portion of the south-east of Britain.

THE CURRENT SITUATION

The present work lists an overall total of 72 species of butterflies recorded in the London area. This figure includes ten which are either deliberate releases or escapees of non-British origin, namely Oberthur's Grizzled Skipper, *Papilio bianor*, Scarce Swallowtail, Large Copper, Brown Playboy, Blue Pansy, Small Brown Shoemaker, Woodland Grayling, Hermit and the Tiger. They have only been included here because they have already been published elsewhere. The many other exotics which have been reported as escapes or releases over the years, but which have never made it to the literature, are excluded. Two species which have been published as having occurred in the London area are excluded from the totals here, since it is now certain that they were not in fact captured in London. These are Albin's Hampstead Eye and the Scarce Tortoiseshell. A third species, the Turquoise Blue, was an incorrect identification of the Adonis Blue, and it too is therefore not included. There is left a balance of 62 species which have occurred naturally, either as residents or genuine immigrants in the London area. These are shown against the vice-counties from which they have been recorded in the London area in Table two. Of these, 47 (comprising 39 residents and 8 immigrants) are recorded in the post-1979 "recent" period, and are analysed in Table 3. The boundary of the current area remains the same as that employed by de Worms in 1949, although it is now more precisely defined along the tetrad lines, describing a "stepped polygon" rather than a circle (see Figure one).

TABLE 3. Vice-comital analysis of the 47 butterflies occurring naturally in the London area during the period 1980 to 1986.

SPECIES	**VICE-COUNTY**							
	West Kent (16)	**Surrey (17)**	**South Essex (18)**	**North Essex (19)**	**Herts (20)**	**Middx (21)**	**Bucks (24)**	**Inner London**
Small Skipper	X	X	X	X	X	X	X	X
Essex Skipper	X	X	X	X	X	X	X	X
Silver-spotted Skipper		X						
Large Skipper	X	X	X	X	X	X	X	X
Dingy Skipper	X	X	X		X	X	X	
Grizzled Skipper	X	X	X		X	X	X	
Clouded Yellow	X	X	X	X	X	X	X	X
Brimstone	X	X	X	X	X	X	X	X
Large White	X	X	X	X	X	X	X	X
Small White	X	X	X	X	X	X	X	X
Green-veined White	X	X	X	X	X	X	X	X
Orange-tip	X	X	X	X	X	X	X	X
Green Hairstreak	X	X	X		X	X		
Brown Hairstreak		X		X				
Purple Hairstreak	X	X	X	X	X	X	X	
White-letter Hairstreak	X	X	X		X	X		
Small Copper	X	X	X	X	X	X	X	X
Long-tailed Blue		X				X		
Small Blue	X	X			X	X		
Silver-studded Blue		X						
Brown Argus	X	X			X			
Common Blue	X	X	X	X	X	X	X	X
Chalk Hill Blue	X	X						
Adonis Blue		X						
Holly Blue	X	X	X	X	X	X	X	X
Duke of Burgudy Fritillary		X						
White Admiral	X	X		X	X	X	X	
Purple Emperor		X	X					
Red Admiral	X	X	X	X	X	X	X	X
Painted Lady	X	X	X	X	X	X	X	X
Small Tortoiseshell	X	X	X	X	X	X	X	X
Large Tortoiseshell			X		X			
Camberwell Beauty		X	X	X	X	X		
Peacock	X	X	X	X	X	X	X	X
Comma	X	X	X	X	X	X	X	X
Pearl-bordered Fritillary		X						
Dark Green Fritillary	X	X			X			
Silver-washed Fritillary	X	X			X	X		
Speckled Wood	X	X	X	X	X	X	X	X
Wall	X	X	X	X	X	X	X	X
Marbled White	X	X			X	X	X	
Grayling	X		X					
Gatekeeper	X	X	X	X	X	X	X	X
Meadow Brown	X	X	X	X	X	X	X	X
Small Heath	X	X	X	X	X	X	X	X
Ringlet	X	X	X	X	X	X		
Milkweed			X					
TOTALS	**38**	**43**	**33**	**27**	**36**	**34**	**27**	**22**

Ignoring both the importations and the genuinely immigrant species, (including Red Admiral), it is clear that there are six fewer species recorded as London butterflies in the 1980 to 1986 period than during the 1900 to 1948 span covered by de Worms. These losses are the Wood White, Small Pearl-bordered Fritillary, High Brown Fritillary, Marsh Fritillary, Heath Fritillary and the Large Tortoiseshell, the latter being one of the species recorded by all the early entomologists, including Petiver who indicated it to be widespread in 1699. The declines of these species in our area are discussed under the individual species accounts, but it is perhaps not coincidental that all these extinctions, for that is what they are, have affected woodland butterflies. Woodland is a habitat which has suffered terrible losses over the last fifty years or so, particularly through the cessation of coppicing as a woodland management method.

Today, it appears that our grasslands are under threat too, particularly those chalk grasslands of the North Downs in Kent and Surrey, and species such as Silver-spotted Skipper, Silver-studded Blue and Adonis Blue are candidates for extinction in our area during the remaining few years of the present century. In the meantime, the long overdue re-introduction of coppicing in some areas, thanks to the efforts of assorted voluntary conservationists, has at the same time heralded a return of certain woodland species.

As far as immigrants are concerned, the Large Tortoiseshell is most certainly relegated to that category today, in spite of what its status once may have been. It is in fact a particularly rare immigrant in the London area nowadays. The Pale Clouded Yellow was certainly more regular in de Worms' day too than it is now. Since his paper was published there have only been five individuals recorded, one in 1956 and four in 1964! Evidence for the successful hibernation of Red Admirals is suspect in London, and lacking for the 1980 to 1986 period, so there are, in this same period, still three common immigrants – namely the Painted Lady and Clouded Yellow (as before) and the Red Admiral. The Pale Clouded Yellow (here taken to include Berger's Clouded Yellow) is not on the "current" list, nor is the Bath White, not seen in London since 1946, leaving just four scarce immigrants recorded, in the form of the Long-tailed Blue (one in 1980) the Queen of Spain Fritillary (one in 1982), the Camberwell Beauty, (eight records – two in 1981, and three each in 1983 and 1984) and the Milkweed (one in 1982). Of course the description of an immigrant as scarce is purely relative. During 1976 for example, Camberwell Beauties were seen all over London. A fuller account of immigrant butterflies (and moths) in London can be read in *The London Naturalist* number 65 for 1985, published in 1986.

... AND THE FUTURE?

The author would be pleased to receive additional tetrad records, and repeat records for the less common and less widespread species, at the publication

TABLE 4. Analysis of the resident butterflies and two regular common immigrants (labelled*) occurring in each of the thirty-three London Boroughs during the period 1980 to 1986.

SPECIES	London Boroughs in which each species has been recorded during the period 1980-1986.																															
	1	2	3	4	5	6	7	8	9	10	11	12	13	14	15	16	17	18	19	20	21	22	23	24	25	26	27	28	29	30	31	32	33
Small Skipper	X	X	X	X	X	X	X	X	X	X	X	X					X	X	X	X	X	X	X	X	X	X	X	X	X	X	X	X	X
Essex Skipper	X	X	X	X	X	X	X	X	X	X		X					X	X	X	X	X	X	X	X	X	X	X	X	X	X	X	X	X
Large Skipper	X	X	X	X	X	X	X	X	X	X	X	X		X		X	X	X	X	X	X	X	X	X	X	X	X	X	X	X	X		X
Dingy Skipper																				X										X	X		
Grizzled Skipper										X											X										X	X	
Brimstone	X	X		X			X	X	X	X								X	X	X	X	X	X	X	X	X	X	X	X	X	X	X	X
Large White	X	X	X	X	X	X	X	X	X	X	X	X	X	X	X	X	X	X	X	X	X	X	X	X	X	X	X	X	X	X	X	X	X
Small White	X	X	X	X	X	X	X	X	X	X	X	X	X	X	X	X	X	X	X	X	X	X	X	X	X	X	X	X	X	X	X	X	X
Green-veined White	X	X	X	X	X	X	X	X	X	X	X	X	X	X	X	X	X	X	X	X	X	X	X	X	X	X	X	X	X	X	X	X	X
Orange-tip	X	X	X	X	X	X	X	X	X	X	X	X					X	X	X	X	X	X	X	X	X	X		X	X	X	X		X
Green Hairstreak		X																	X					X	X					X	X		X
Brown Hairstreak							X																		X								
Purple Hairstreak		X					X			X							X	X	X	X	X	X	X	X	X	X					X	X	
White-letter Hairstreak									X											X	X				X	X					X		
Small Copper	X	X	X	X	X	X	X	X	X	X	X	X				X	X	X	X	X	X	X	X	X	X	X		X	X	X	X	X	X
Small Blue																				X										X	X		
Brown Argus																														X	X		
Common Blue	X	X	X	X	X	X	X	X	X	X	X	X	X	X	X	X	X	X	X	X	X	X	X	X	X	X	X	X	X	X	X	X	X
Chalk Hill Blue																														X	X		
Adonis Blue																														X			
Holly Blue	X	X	X	X	X	X	X	X	X	X	X	X	X	X	X	X	X	X	X	X	X	X	X	X	X	X	X	X	X	X	X	X	X
White Admiral								X												X								X			X		
Red Admiral (*)	X	X	X	X	X	X	X	X	X	X	X	X	X	X	X	X	X	X	X	X	X	X	X	X	X	X	X	X	X	X	X	X	X
Painted Lady (*)	X	X	X	X	X	X	X	X	X	X	X	X	X	X	X	X	X	X	X	X	X	X	X	X	X	X	X	X	X	X	X	X	X
Purple Emperor																							X										
Small Tortoiseshell	X	X	X	X	X	X	X	X	X	X	X	X	X	X	X	X	X	X	X	X	X	X	X	X	X	X	X	X	X	X	X	X	X
Peacock	X	X	X	X	X	X	X	X	X	X	X	X		X	X	X	X	X	X	X	X	X	X	X	X	X	X	X		X	X	X	X
Comma	X	X	X	X	X	X	X	X	X	X	X	X	X	X	X	X	X	X	X	X	X	X	X	X	X	X	X	X	X	X	X	X	X
Dark Green Fritillary																									X					X	X	X	
Silver-washed Fritillary																									X						X		
Speckled Wood	X	X			X	X	X	X		X	X	X				X	X	X	X	X	X	X	X	X	X	X	X	X	X	X	X	X	X
Wall	X	X	X	X	X	X	X	X	X	X	X	X	X	X			X	X	X	X	X	X	X		X	X		X		X	X	X	X
Marbled White																				X										X	X		
Gatekeeper	X	X	X	X	X		X	X	X	X								X	X	X	X	X	X	X	X			X		X	X		X
Meadow Brown	X	X	X	X	X	X	X	X	X	X	X	X	X	X	X	X	X	X	X	X	X	X	X	X	X	X	X	X	X	X	X	X	X
Small Heath	X	X	X	X	X	X	X	X	X	X		X	X				X	X	X	X	X	X	X	X	X	X		X	X	X	X	X	X
Ringlet	X							X	X	X								X	X				X	X						X	X		
Total for each Borough	**22**	**22**	**19**	**20**	**20**	**19**	**22**	**23**	**22**	**25**	**17**	**19**	**12**	**13**	**11**	**15**	**20**	**23**	**24**	**27**	**24**	**22**	**23**	**23**	**27**	**23**	**16**	**22**	**18**	**30**	**34**	**19**	**22**

Key to the London Boroughs numbered in Table 4.

1 Havering
2 Redbridge
3 Barking and Dagenham
4 Newham
5 Tower Hamlets
6 Hackney
7 Waltham Forest
8 Haringey
9 Enfield
10 Barnet
11 Camden
12 Islington
13 City of London
14 Westminster
15 Kensington and Chelsea
16 Hammersmith and Fulham
17 Brent
18 Harrow
19 Ealing
20 Hillingdon
21 Hounslow
22 Richmond
23 Kingston-upon-Thames
24 Sutton
25 Merton
26 Wandsworth
27 Lambeth
28 Southwark
29 Lewisham
30 Croydon
31 Bromley
32 Greenwich
33 Bexley

address on the reverse of the title page in this book. There is still much we do not know about London's butterflies, and in a work of this nature is not possible to delve into the complexities of butterfly biology. It is very much hoped, however, that this work will set the scene for more intense local studies, both of the overall butterfly faunas of discrete areas and into individual species. Whatever works are undertaken in the Capital, the London Natural History Society would be pleased to receive copies of all results obtained to enable an overall picture to be built up for the area, making possible comparisons between floristically or geologically similar areas which are physically separated, as well as between areas which differ in these or other respects.

LONDON'S GEOLOGY

The London area is almost bisected by the River Thames, flowing eastwards from Egham in the west to reach Northfleet in the east. It lies at the centre of a shallow synclinal basin composed of Cretaceous and Eocene strata laid down by seas that covered the area between 40 and 140 million years ago, and folded into their present structure during the Miocene period about 15 million years ago. The London basin is bounded by two ranges of chalk hills, both with outward facing scarps; by the Chilterns in the north-west and, in the south, by the North Downs running from the south west to the east. These hills comprise almost all of the higher ground in the London area, the highest point being between Limpsfield and Woldingham on the North Downs, at 269 metres above sea level. In some places the chalk is overlain with later deposits of clay with flints. Beneath the chalk, outcropping to the south of the North Downs lie layers of Upper Greensand, Gault and Lower Greensand. Of these, the Lower Greensand reaches the surface as a line of hills along the southern margin of the London area between Redhill and Brasted Chart. Between these hills and the North Downs there is a narrow band of Upper Greensand and Gault, the latter forming a low-lying clay vale. Above the Chalk, on the margin of the London Basin, lie the Eocene deposits of Thanet Sands and Woolwich and Reading Beds; these consist of sands and clays. Together with the Blackheath Pebble Beds they form relatively small patches on the London Clay which forms the floor of the greater part of the London Basin between the Chilterns and the North Downs, extending eastwards over much of Essex. In places, on higher areas of the London Clay, Bagshot Beds provide a capping of fine sand and gravel, for example at Brentwood, Hampstead Heath, Harrow Hill and Esher Common. Discontinuous patches of drift deposits overlie the Eocene strata.

Figure 4. Tetrads of the London area containing chalk at the surface.

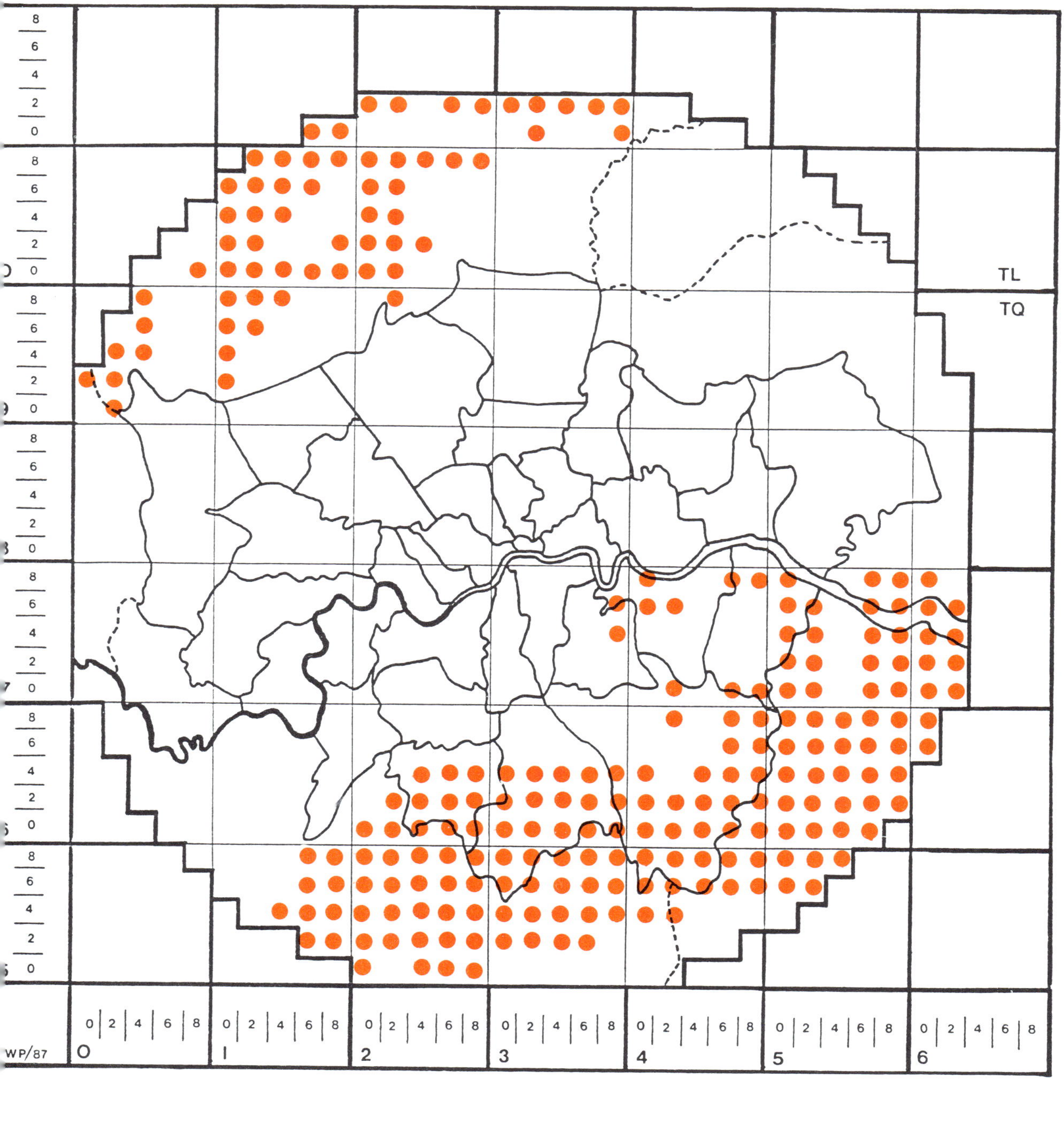

Essentially these consist of clays, sands and gravels laid down in the geologically recent past by ice, melt-waters and rivers, and as the products of the weathering of pre-existing rocks. The most important drift deposits in the London area are the extensive flood plain terraces of gravel laid down by the Thames and its tributaries: it is here that many of the gravel workings, as well as the reservoirs, are situated. On higher terrace gravel such as at Dartford Heath, the vegetation is frequently similar to that on the Lower Greensand, thus allowing for the development of a comparable fauna.

As far as the distributions of butterflies are concerned, it is principally the distribution of chalk which affects the ranges of certain of the chalk grassland species, and to aid interpretation of the maps, Fig. 4 shows those tetrads in the London area which contain at least some chalk *at the surface.*

BUTTERFLY HABITATS IN THE LONDON AREA

The sheer size of the London area as presently defined (3424 square kilometres) allows for a considerable diversity in the environment, and accordingly the number of habitats available for colonisation by butterflies is equally large. There can be little doubt that whilst a number of our butterflies, such as, for example, the Large White or the Small Tortoiseshell, are able to survive in any reasonable presence of the larval foodplant, there are others, such as the White Admiral or the Silver-spotted Skipper which demonstrate highly specific habitat requirements. It is therefore perhaps worth a look at the several different types of habitat which are available to butterflies, and for that matter other insects, in the London area and the butterfly faunas which they support.

WOODLAND COMMUNITIES

With the retreat of the ice sheet which covered much of Britain around about 10,000 years ago, there came a simultaneous amelioration of the climate which provided ideal conditions for colonisation by trees of various species, and it was not long, at least in geological terms, before much of the country was covered in a dense blanket of woodland. Such habitat was probably quite inhospitable as far as many butterflies were concerned, since the closeness of the trees would have restricted the sunlight and, as a result, there would have been little or no ground layer of plants to provide either nectar for adults or food for larvae. Even the true woodland species, such as the Purple Emperor and the White Admiral, prefer sunny glades to closed canopy, and these would have been restricted, along with other species, to river margins and other clearings in the wildwood. Around 5,000 years ago, man, according to popular theory, began to clear the landscape of trees (though recent evidence suggests that man's impact, though considerable, was aided by a major epidemic of dutch elm disease which essentially denuded the landscape). Whatever the cause, this clearance must have marked a considerable change in the butterfly fauna. It is interesting to speculate that many species such as the Large White, Small Heath and Common Blue would have been quite rare insects prior to this clearance, as too, of course, would have been species which are associated with open grasslands. Two particular types of woodland management pattern which began to emerge at this period however would have had a particular effect upon our traditionally *woodland* butterflies, since they resulted in two important but not dissimilar woodland types which persist today. These are:

Coppice and Wood Pasture

In the days when industry, even every day life, depended upon wood for building and burning, it was important that trees were grown as a crop. Clearly, there would be a long delay if trees were sown as seed and harvested in the traditional manner employed for other crops, so an alternative system was essential. There thus developed two basic systems of taming and harvesting the wildwood: coppicing, and the creation of wood pasture. In a coppice, whilst several trees were left to reach maturity to provide timber, the majority were regularly cut at ground level, forcing them to sprout new growth after each felling. Typically, the timber trees would be oak and ash, and would be harvested every seventy to eighty years, whilst the more frequently harvested crop was usually hazel, which, if cut every seven years or so, provided long straight poles for fencing, building houses and a host of other uses. Since the trees were cut at ground level, the new growth would be susceptible to grazing by deer, rabbits and other animals, and so most coppices were fenced or otherwise protected from such damage. Not so wood pasture, which developed earlier in our history. Here the crop was taken by regularly lopping, or pollarding the trees – that is cutting them at two or three metres above the ground so that the new growth was out of the reach of deer. The forest floor could then be used by foraging "swine" or other animals. Whatever the merits of each system from a human viewpoint, there were some important considerations for the butterflies. In both systems, sunlight was regularly allowed to reach the woodland floor as the canopy was removed by cutting. Thus there developed a rich and diverse ground flora which could be exploited by the insects. The fact that cutting was on a rotational basis meant that a woodland block contained a variety of stages from "just coppiced" to "ready for coppicing", providing a considerable diversity of plant species and light conditions. In wood pasture, however, the grazing by animals was a limiting factor, and such a system would have attracted fewer species of butterfly than coppicing. The Purple Emperor would certainly have been one such species, at least wherever sallows were allowed to remain, and the White Admiral too would have been common on the wild honeysuckle hanging down from the trees. Purple Hairstreaks would have been common in the canopy, and so too would have been White-letter Hairstreaks. In the London area, the most important area of former wood pasture is Epping Forest, together with Hainault Forest and many of the smaller woodland areas in the Essex sector. These woods were, of course, all joined as one not so many years ago. The lack of grazing in the coppice woodland, would have allowed for a different butterfly fauna to develop. The White Admiral would have been less common, as the forester would regularly have removed honeysuckle as a 'weed', but the violets on the woodland floor would doubtless have supported Pearl-bordered and Small Pearl-bordered Fritillaries, and other typical butterflies would have included the Wood White, Duke of Burgundy, Ringlet, Speckled Wood and Gatekeeper. The Heath Fritillary too was a butterfly of coppice woodlands.

During the last century however, the demand for wood of this type has almost vanished, and most wood pasture and coppice has been neglected. The butterflies in Epping Forest are now nothing compared to what the records show they once were, though recent changes to a management policy more in tune with nature conservation have included the reintroduction of pollarding in some areas. It will be very interesting to see which, if any, butterflies return, and how they go about doing so. It is in the former coppice woodlands, however, that the greatest interest lies. Many conservation bodies now recognise the reinstatement of coppicing as a means not only of maintaining populations of many species, but also of allowing the re-establishment of endangered species in a strictly controlled manner. Just outside our own part of Essex, for example, the Essex Naturalists' Trust have been coppicing a particular woodland for several years, and during 1984 introduced fifty adult Heath Fritillaries to a glade rich in cow-wheat. It survived, and it was estimated that over one thousand adults were successfully reared in the 1986 season!

Though coppice woodlands are undoubtedly the best woodland butterfly habitats, there are of course other types of woodland which support a variety of species.

Planted Woodlands

Within the London area Richmond Park probably contains the greatest area of planted woodland, some thirty acres having been planted in the last 150 or so years. Oak predominates, but there is also beech, birch, larch and sweet chestnut. Not surprisingly the Purple Hairstreak appears here in some quantity.

The greatest value of planted deciduous woodlands lies in their rides, and clearings, or around their edges. The Dark Green Fritillary is one butterfly which will thrive in such habitat, provided the foodplant is also present; the Duke of Burgundy is another, whilst more common species would include the Speckled Wood, Gatekeeper and Green Hairstreak. There are also a number of conifer plantations scattered across the area, although the area covered is small. In a 1984 habitat survey, ecologists from the Greater London Council noted only approximately 161 hectares of predominantly coniferised woodland within the thirty-three London boroughs, (*GLC Ecology Handbook Number 4:* 1985), though there is more in the London area as a whole, notably in the complex of woods around Broxbourne in Hertfordshire. Such woodland areas are of practically no value to butterflies except where the provision of rides as in planted deciduous woodland either provides sheltered breeding sites for non-woodland species, particularly Small and Essex Skippers, or where these rides are bordered with deciduous trees such as elms, which would support White-letter Hairstreaks. It is sad to note therefore that much of the 161 hectares reported lies on former ancient semi-natural woodland sites, or on sites which once were important grasslands.

Recent Secondary Woodland

Recent secondary woodlands in the London area tend to be more prevalent in the truly urban zone and although not lacking in academic interest they are of little or no value to butterflies in most cases. In some areas where the growth has developed uninterrupted for several years, however, something approaching a semi-mature woodland may result, usually dominated by sycamore. In such areas where brambles and other woody shrub layer plants are allowed to develop butterflies such as the Speckled Wood may colonise, although these often appear to stem from introductions rather than from natural colonisation.

Scrub Habitats

There are two types of scrub habitat important to butterflies in the London area. First there are the dense thickets of blackthorn which form in some areas. Such areas support colonies of Brown Hairstreak in three, or possibly four, localities around London. The habits of the butterfly make this a difficult species to record as an adult, and of all the "rare" London butterflies this is the one which is most likely to be found in any number at new sites over the next few years. The second type of "scrub" habitat is a variable one: areas of broom, gorse or occasionally other species may support colonies of Green Hairstreaks.

GRASSLAND COMMUNITIES

There are probably as many different types of grassland as there are of woodland, and much of the London area is covered by grassland of one type or another. From the point of view of butterflies there are two basic divisions, however, based upon geological considerations: calcareous grassland and neutral grassland, both of which may be "unimproved" (i.e. native) "semi-improved" (e.g., treated with selective herbicide) or "improved" (re-seeded, recently planted, etc). Not surprisingly, it is the unimproved grasslands which are the best for butterflies.

Calcareous Grassland

Calcareous grassland is a declining habitat in the London area, confined to the southern peripheral area in Kent and Surrey. Much has been taken for agricultural or other farming uses, more has been built on, including a considerable amount which disappeared under the M.25 motorway, and yet more has been planted with conifers. Further, like woodland, calcareous grassland is affected by various management methods. Traditionally, the North Downs, which is where the vast bulk of this habitat is to be found in our area, have been grazed, both naturally by rabbits, and artificially by sheep. This has provided the very short turf essential to such rare species as the Silver-spotted Skipper and the Adonis Blue. The arrival of the disease myxomatosis in the 1950s wiped out the bulk of the rabbit population, and thus caused a very great change in the grazing patterns of the Downs. Further, changes in farming methods favoured growing crops rather than rearing sheep, and between these two factors there remain today very few areas indeed where the short turf needed by these species remains. On the other hand, other butterflies of open calcareous grassland, such as Chalk Hill Blue and Marbled White are not so dependent upon grazing. The Marbled White in particular prefers lightly cropped or ungrazed swards, containing timothy, cock's-foot or tor-grass upon which the caterpillars feed. Indeed, it is not entirely confined to calcareous grassland, although it is far more abundant there than in neutral areas, at least in the London region. Chalk Hill Blue females will lay eggs on horseshoe vetch in a range of vegetation heights, although if the grass becomes so tall that it shades out the vetch the butterfly will clearly not stay.

Non-Calcareous Grassland

There are small areas of acid grassland in the London area, though the bulk of the non-calcareous grasslands are neutral, and indeed there seems to be little discernible difference between the butterflies found on each of the two types. Marbled Whites at least are absent from the more acidic areas, though they are sometimes quite common in neutral ones. Meadow Browns, Small Skippers and Essex Skippers are abundant in most years, alongside lesser numbers of Large Skippers and Small Heaths. In unimproved neutral grasslands species such as the Common Blue and Small Copper may prevail, and in certain areas the Silver-studded Blue may still perhaps be present in very small numbers.

OTHER COMMUNITIES

A number of other habitats are available to the butterflies of the London area. Many of these are linear, such as roadside verges, field margins or river banks, and so are difficult to define, as they may vary considerably along their length. The urban area too varies in character, containing parks, gardens (themselves extremely varied) "waste" sites and so on.

Hedgerows, Verges and Field Margins

In many parts of Essex in particular, the landscape has suffered from the loss of hedgerows. In many areas, the original field boundaries too have been lost under the plough to become yet a further small addition to the arable desert, presumably adding still further to the various food mountains which modern farming seems to generate. In some areas, however, often as a token (and sometimes well intentioned!) gesture to nature conservation, fields are separated from roads, or even from each other, by strips of rough grass a few feet wide. Surprisingly, butterflies often thrive here. The Wall is a common butterfly in this situation around the eastern end of Havering Borough and in the area north of Ockenden, South Essex, whilst many roadside strips contain numbers of Small and Essex Skippers. The total fauna is severely limited, however, and restricted to mobile, grass-feeding species, since the strips regularly receive doses of insecticide and selective herbicide sprays from the fields. Where hedgerows do remain, however, in parts of Kent, Surrey and Hertfordshire in particular, there is a far greater variety of butterflies to be found. Wall, Gatekeeper and Meadow Brown represent the Satyridae, with other species including White-letter Hairstreak at one Hertfordshire site, and Orange-tips almost everywhere. The Wood White too, if it were to recolonise the north-west of our area, would be likely to do so using suitable hedgerows as a line of entry. If it were not for the winter cutting (thrashing would be a more appropriate description of the operation) of blackthorn hedges there might be far more Brown Hairstreaks than at present. Older hedgerows, with a well-developed flora beneath the bushes, may well turn up the occasional Dark Green Fritillary in appropriate areas.

Railway Embankments

This type of habitat is very variable, both between sites and within a given stretch from year to year. Most are mown from time to time, though rarely regularly, and most have thriving populations of a number of butterflies, particularly the crucifer-feeders such as the three cabbage whites, as well as the Small Copper, Common Blue, Red Admiral, Painted Lady, Small Tortoiseshell, Peacock, Comma, Meadow Brown and Small Heath. Such habitats, because of their very purpose, penetrate deep into the metropolis, serving as corridors connecting the town centre with the surrounding countryside, and along which various butterflies and other animals can move. The use of these corridors by foxes is well documented and well known. Their importance to butterflies is no less significant, and accordingly they are an area to which the various conservation bodies in London might like to address themselves. The recent introduction of burning as a money-saving alternative to mowing does little to enhance the butterfly fauna, however.

Churchyards, Parks and Gardens

The vast bulk of the urban area is, of course, quite unsuitable for butterflies. Adaptable as some species may be, there is not yet an evolutionary tendency towards the utilisation of concrete as a larval food! However, this urban desert is punctuated by a number of small areas in the form of gardens of varying sizes, particularly in the outer London boroughs, and parks and churchyards which also occur further in towards the centre where gardens are smaller or, more often, absent. Such sites do not usually support any particularly rare species, but they are immensely valuable in bringing butterflies within range of the ordinary city-dwelling human, whose life may be considerably brightened as a result. Butterflies such as the Small and Large Skipper will thrive in the larger overgrown churchyards, whilst even in the smaller ones, the presence of ivy will usually ensure that the Holly Blue is present. There is not necessarily a need for holly to be present, though it helps: most Holly Blues will adapt to alternative spring foodplants in neighbouring gardens. In these gardens, as in churchyards and parks, a number of butterflies will thrive if a "wild" corner is left for them. A tangle of coarse grasses will often support Meadow Browns, whilst the inevitable nettles will allow Small Tortoiseshells and Red Admirals to breed, amongst others. There is much that can be done by local authorities to encourage this, thus enhancing the leisure facilities available to the residents in their area at the same time as saving money by not "tidying" certain areas of their parks.

"Wasteland" Sites

A number of sites in London fall into the category of "wasteland", the use of inverted commas indicating the author's dislike of this description of often quite valuable parcels of land. Vast tracts of "wasteland" still exist at the time of writing in February 1987, in the area administered by the London Docklands Development Corporation (LDDC). Much of this lies in Newham, where once thrived an active industry associated with the "Royal" Docks. Smaller sites exist throughout the Capital, though bombed sites from the Blitz of 1940 have largely been built upon, to be replaced by land cleared for redevelopment. Such derelict sites are to a large extent temporary, and thus have little time to develop a complex fauna and flora. However, opportunist and highly mobile species can, and do, move in quite quickly. The most frequent amongst these, and often the first to arrive, are the nettle feeders, such as the Small Tortoiseshell, Peacock and Comma, attracted in many cases by the nectar-bearing blooms of the *Buddleia* which seems to be an obligatory plant on any site left alone for a couple of years or more. These are often followed by the Common Blue, which breeds readily on either the traditional bird's-foot trefoil or an a variety of clovers. Small coppers too will often colonise, and, as the site gives way to tall grasses, and the Small Copper moves on, the Small Skipper, Essex Skipper and to a lesser degree the Large Skipper will take over. One assumes that if left alone, such sites would eventually develop a scrub community and ultimately, secondary woodland (doubtless sycamore!) which would again alter the butterfly fauna. Sadly for the serious entomologist, however, such sites are usually developed long before that stage is reached.

Abandoned Chalk Quarries

These are few in the London area, but good examples exist in parts of Kent and at Grays in Essex. Two species which affect the London area are typical of such habitats, namely the Small Blue and the Grayling.

BUTTERFLY CONSERVATION

The reasons for wanting to conserve butterflies are probably as varied as the people who want to conserve them. From a purely aesthetic point of view, they give pleasure to many thousands of people, adding colour and movement to what little remains of our countryside. Particularly because several species are able to thrive in the urban setting, they are often the first introduction, along with birds, that many city-dwelling humans have to the natural world. Butterflies also provide useful tools for elementary biology lessons: breeding through from caterpillar to adult can be marvellous fun, especially for children, and this is likely to stimulate a lasting interest, both in butterflies specifically and in wildlife and the environment in general. Further, because they are, in general, such obvious insects, they can act at a basic level as indicators of the overall state of the environment. The lack of all but a few of the coarse grass feeding butterflies from many roadside verges and field margins in Essex, for example, is an indication of the effect which modern farming is having on the landscape as a whole, particularly through the grubbing out of hedges, and the use of pesticides. In general terms, a lack of butterflies is bad news for the environment.

There is, however, much confusion over the use of the word "conservation" today. It implies an attempt to maintain an existing situation, and this in itself is unlikely to be wise in the majority of cases. The environment as a whole, together with the species in it, is naturally in a state of constant change. Open bodies of water for example, will, if left to nature, ultimately silt up and be colonised – first by emergent vegetation, then by a succcession of land plants until the one time lake has become mature woodland. New forms of plants and animals are ever so slowly evolving, and old forms are dying out – becoming extinct – where they have been unsuccessful. The world is full of such *natural* extinctions: species on the extreme northern edge of their geographical range in Britain for example, are likely to become extinct here through changes in climate. The White-letter Hairstreak declined sharply as a result of a disease of elm trees which occurs naturally. However, much of the modern landscape of Britain has in any case resulted from man's interference with these natural processes, and therefore there can be justification in many cases for maintaining this artificial *status quo* when not to do so may mean the loss of species. The alteration in land use on the North Downs for example has caused the sharp decline or loss of many butterflies, such as the Adonis Blue, whilst the deliberate introduction of the rabbit disease myxomatosis caused a drastic change in grazing patterns on the chalk grasslands in Surrey, leading to the near extinction of the Silver-spotted Skipper. At similar sites in Kent, many colonies of this butterfly were ploughed up for crop planting at the same period! The decline of coppicing as a woodland management technique was very largely responsible for the reduction in numbers and range of the Pearl-bordered Fritillary. These are all examples of man's activities causing species loss, where intervention in the form of "conservation" is clearly justified.

It is important to realise that the proper conservation of butterflies requires the safeguarding of the group as a whole, or at the very least a single species: this is distinct from the conservation of individual specimens which is more akin to what has been popularly termed "animal rights". There is really only one way to perform this task, and that is by the preservation of the the different habitats occupied by the different species. This will automatically involve the parallel conservation of a whole range of other organisms which are as much a part of the ecosystem as the objects of our conservation endeavours here. To achieve this objective is, however, an arduous task, and it is appropriate to record here our appreciation as naturalists of the efforts of the various County Trusts operating in the London area, as well as those of the London Branch of the British Butterfly Conservation Society. The addresses of all these organisations are given on page 41.

BUTTERFLY COLLECTING

This is a somewhat touchy item! Those people who have an opinion either way are as a rule rather firm in their attitude, and often quite unable to see the other point of view. For every argument in favour of collecting there is an argument against, whilst every fresh argument against can be countered by a reason for. We do tend, though quite illogically, to treat butterflies as a special case, probably on the basis of the overall aesthetic appeal of the group, which I have already said is, in my opinion, justification for their conservation. Yet the fact that butterflies are generally large and pretty does not make them any more vulnerable to collecting than, say, spiders, fleas or flies. They constitute only a miniscule part of Britain's rare, vulnerable and endangered invertebrates, and there can be no doubt that if they were all small and brown we would not get so worked up about individual examples being killed. In order to form a balanced opinion, let us look at some facts.

It is certainly not the case that butterflies in this country need to be killed and set to identify them, though many will require a close examination after capture, particularly the fritillaries. However, apart from very few rare species, the overall populations of butterflies are only very rarely affected by casual collecting (such as by children). The population dynamics of invertebrates are quite different from those of, say, birds or mammals. Large numbers of young are produced simply because of the extremely high death rate amongst the early stages. Consequently, collecting a dozen Small Tortoiseshells for example would have absolutely no effect whatsoever on either the local numbers of the species or the environment in general. The same cannot be said for shooting a dozen blackbirds! Populations may be seriously depleted at a local level, however, if collecting is carried out to excess. Popular opinion has it that this was an accepted pastime in the Victorian and Edwardian eras – cabinet drawers bulging with long "series" of rare species, but this was in fact only rarely true: most collectors of that period would not have dreamed of placing battered, wild-caught specimens in their nice neat cabinets! The fact is that most long series were bred from the eggs obtained from the capture of a single female. It is most unlikely that this would adversely affect butterfly populations, except in very few cases, and this is certainly borne out by the fact that the greatest decline in butterfly numbers in this country took place in the 1950s, largely as a result of environmental damage caused by pesticides and habitat loss, and not during the Victorian and Edwardian periods when "series collecting" was at its peak.

Of course, some butterflies are now protected by the law in this country. The Wildlife and Countryside Act of 1981 makes the collecting of Chequered Skippers, Swallowtails and Heath Fritillaries illegal. It stops short of protecting other species however, acknowledging that collecting is no threat to their survival. All in all, however, there seems to be little justification for amateur collecting of British butterflies today, though one acknowledges the need for scientific collecting in certain circumstances, and that many youngsters who develop their interest in wildlife through this relatively harmless pastime will move on to more laudable things. Photography seems a good alternative, and with the current cost of entomological cabinets I would suggest that it is quite a bit cheaper! It also allows the naturalist an opportunity to actually stalk and study his prey and so make new discoveries, rather than to simply catch it and kill it.

CODE OF CONDUCT FOR INSECT COLLECTING

A voluntary code for insect collecting has been drawn up by the Joint Committee for the Conservation of British Insects, and though it applies to all insects, butterfly collecting is covered by a number of the "rules". A copy of the Code can be obtained from the Committee at the address on page 41. Some of the points which are relevant to butterflies are as follows:

1. Take no more specimens than are needed for the specific purpose;
2. Do not take the same species year after year from the same locality;
3. When collecting caterpillars, never collect all that can be found: make sure some are left to allow the population to recover;
4. Consider photography as an alternative to collecting;
5. Specimens should not normally be taken for exchange or disposal to other collectors;
6. Butterflies should not be collected from the wild for commercial purposes, eg. jewellery;
7. Rare species should be collected with great restraint or not at all;
8. Collectors should work in new areas and contribute their records rather than continually working known localities;
9. Do as little damage to the environment as possible, particularly when "beating" for larvae.

It is worth remembering that what is common in one part of the country may be rare in another. There could be no justification for collecting even a single example of the Silver-studded Blue in the London area's only locality, though such an act may be permissible at Chobham Common a few miles away where the butterfly occurs in plenty. In recognition of the fact that butterfly collecting will continue regardless, however, I would make the following recommendations to collectors in the London area, based upon the results of the survey from 1980 to 1986, and with nothing more in mind than the preservation of the species as a whole in the London area:

THE FOLLOWING BUTTERFLIES SHOULD NOT BE COLLECTED AT ALL IN THE LONDON AREA AS THEIR POPULATIONS HERE ARE VULNERABLE

Silver-spotted Skipper
Dingy Skipper – north of the Thames only
Grizzled Skipper – north of the Thames only
Brown Hairstreak
Silver-studded Blue
Adonis Blue
all fritillaries except Silver Washed;
Grayling

GREAT RESTRAINT SHOULD BE SHOWN WHEN COLLECTING THE FOLLOWING SPECIES IN THE LONDON AREA AS THEIR POPULATIONS COULD BECOME VULNERABLE THROUGH OVER-COLLECTING.

Dingy Skipper
Grizzled Skipper
White-letter Hairstreak
Small Blue
Chalk Hill Blue
White Admiral
Purple Emperor
Silver Washed Fritillary;
Marbled White

There is one further contentious area of butterfly conservation – that of the artificial introductions to the wild of butterflies reared in captivity.

INTRODUCTIONS

One must be most careful over the use of words here. The Joint Committee for the Conservation of British Insects has prepared a *Code of Conservation Practice for Insect Re-establishment*, and define various terms as follows:

INTRODUCTIONS are attempts to establish butterflies in areas where they have not previously occurred;

REINTRODUCTION means an attempt to establish the species in an area where an introduction has failed;

RE-ESTABLISHMENT is a deliberate release of a species to an area where it formerly occurred but is now extinct;

REINFORCEMENT is an attempt to increase the size of an existing population by deliberate releases.

Introductions are, in general, frowned upon. They are seldom justified and in some cases, including the release of non-British stock, are also illegal. Re-establishments can, however, be of value to conservation in some cases, provided that they are carried out in a scientific manner. The code, which is available from the Committee, makes several recommendations, summarised as follows:

Consult widely before deciding to attempt any re-establishment;

Every re-establishment should have a clear objective;

The ecology of the species to be re-established should be known;

Permission should be obtained for the use of the receiving site, and for the removal from the source site;

The management of the receiving site should be appropriate;

Specific parasites should be introduced with the butterflies;

Numbers released should be large enough to ensure success;

Full details of the release should be meticulously (recorded, and reported;

The success of the re-establishment should be continually assessed and recorded;

All re-establishments, introductions, re-introductions and reinforcements should be reported to the JCCBI.

Reinforcing wild populations of butterflies is rarely a good idea: those who think it is may do better directing their energies towards discovering why the local population is declining at all! Fluctuations, often drastic ones, occur naturally in a butterfly population in a given area from year to year, often linked to the population levels of specific parasites, or to disease or foodplant availability. Sudden additions of large numbers of fresh, disease- and parasite-free individuals may cause untold damage to the finely balanced natural system, and have the exact opposite effect to the one desired. In cases where reinforcements are indicated, it is by far the best method to capture stock from the existing native population and breed from these for later release. Captive breeding, if done properly, allows for the survival of far greater numbers than is possible in the wild, but even so, reinforcment should be regarded as a rather long-term project.

Anyone considering an introduction, re-establishment or reinforcement of butterflies in the London area is invited to contact the author at the address on page 2. It is most important that such activities do not continue unrecorded, not least because this causes considerable confusion to those engaged in serious research into the causes of local declines.

ATTRACTING BUTTERFLIES TO THE GARDEN

No modern book on butterflies seems complete without a few words of wisdom on this subject! It is probably best to consider the topic in stages:

STAGE 1: What butterfly species am I likely to attract?
This will depend upon where your garden is situated. If it is adjacent to large areas of deciduous woodland in the south-west of our area, in Surrey, then White Admiral and Purple Emperor are possibilities; if it lies in the more urban area these species are very unlikely to put in even the briefest of appearances. Do not expect the impossible, and you will not be disappointed. Further, if the "impossible" does happen, you will be surprised and delighted! Most gardens can be tailored to suit the needs of common residents and regular immigrant species such as Red Admiral and Painted Lady. Less common immigrants, such as the Clouded Yellow also may pass through, but it will be none of your doing in most cases, unless you have a large crop of lucerne! If your garden already attracts good numbers of the common species in your area, therefore, there is probably little you can do to improve your total list, and you should consider providing breeding sites for the butterflies which you have. If however, this is not the case, then you can progress to

STAGE 2: Is my garden safe for the butterflies when they get here?
It is absolutely pointless your attracting dozens of butterflies if your next-door neighbour is in the habit of being less than careful about which way the wind is blowing when he sprays his roses. Similarly, you could be less than popular with him if he has an allotment full of cabbages and you start to attract Large Whites! Most of these problems can be sorted out quite easily, but do this first. Then you can ask

STAGE 3: How do I go about attracting the butterflies?
Consider the basic ecological function of the adult butterfly: it is merely to mate, then lay eggs successfully. After this its role is fulfilled and it will live on only as long as food is available. Thus, there are two basic requirements for the butterfly garden – the correct plants to enable the butterflies present to lay their eggs, and food, in the form of nectar, for the adults to eat. Most people remember the second but neglect the first, with the result that the butterflies are only rarely anything other than casual visitors. With a little thought and effort, though, they can be encouraged to breed and become permanent additions to the garden list. It may seem "old hat", but leaving a wild corner really does work. Nettles will provide for the greatest number of species, particularly Red Admiral, Peacock,

Comma and Small Tortoiseshell. Hops may be a useful substitute for some species. Nasturtiums may attract the "cabbage" whites. Larger gardens may be enhanced by the odd oak tree for Purple Hairstreaks, though these will rarely be seen at ground level. Thicken out your privet hedge with buckthorn for Brimstones, and include a little Dogwood or Holly and some ivy for the Holly Blue. A wide, permanently unmown strip along the edge of the lawn may eventually provide a breeding site for Meadow Browns: I have even seen the larvae of this butterfly on a neglected patch of grass only four yards square in front of a block of flats in the middle of a Dagenham council estate! Garlic mustard along the hedge will possibly attract Orange-tips, and if your lawn has a damp area, try planting cuckoo flower, alias lady's smock, an alternative larval food for this species. If the lawn is dry, obtain a wild seed mix which contains bird's-foot trefoil for the Common Blue, and either common sorrel or sheep's sorrel for the Small Copper.

Having provided the food for their caterpillars, one can probably do little more to physically attract, for example, Small Coppers and Common Blues except to simply sit back and await the hoped for arrival of the adult butterflies. However, many of the commoner "aristocrats" (Red Admiral, Small Tortoiseshell, Comma, Peacock and Painted Lady) and some of the satyrids (Meadow Brown, Gatekeeper, Small Heath and Ringlet) will visit nectar-bearing flowers if the correct type are provided. Ice plants *Sedum spectabile*, michaelmas daisies *Aster novi-belgii* and the butterfly bush *Buddleia davidii* are well-known favourites, and a *must* in the garden of any serious butterfly person, but there are others, and these will flower at different times of the year, attracting butterflies throughout the seasons. Garden plants such as *Polyanthus*, *Aubretia*, honesty, valerian, sweet william, catmint and golden rod are useful additions to the flower-bed or, if your garden is less formal, wild plants such as primrose, dandelion, thistles and knapweeds are usually successful attractants (but remember it is illegal, as well as rather senseless, to uproot plants from the wild). A number of good practical guides are available in many bookshops, and some examples are given on page 43.

SOME USEFUL ADDRESSES

NATURAL HISTORY SOCIETIES WITH BUTTERFLY INTERESTS

London Natural History Society

Membership Secretary, Flat 9, Pinewood Court, 23 Clarence Avenue, Clapham, London SW4 8LB.

British Butterfly Conservation Society

London Branch Membership Secretary, 42 Woodfield Close, Ashtead, Surrey, KT21 2RT.

Amateur Entomologists' Society

355 Hounslow Road, Hanworth, Feltham, Middlesex, TW13 5JH.

British Entomological and Natural History Society

c/o, The Alpine Club, 74 South Audley Street, London W1Y 5FF.

Royal Entomological Society of London,

41 Queen's Gate, London SW7 5HU

CONSERVATION BODIES

Joint Committee for the Conservation of British Insects

c/o 41 Queen's Gate, London SW7 5HU

Berks., Bucks. and Oxon Naturalists' Trust,

3 Church Cowley Road, Rose Hill, Oxford, OX4 3JR.

Essex Naturalists' Trust:

Fingringhoe Wick Nature Reserve, South Green Road, Fingringhoe, Colchester, Essex, CO5 7DN

Herts. and Middlesex Wildlife Trust

Grebe House, St. Michael's Street, St. Albans, Hertfordshire, AL3 4SN.

Kent Trust for Nature Conservation

The Annexe, 1a Bower Mount Road, Maidstone, Kent, ME16 8AX.

London Wildlife Trust

80 York Way, London N1 9AG.

Surrey Trust for Nature Conservation

c/o, Hatchlands, East Clandon, Guildford, GU4 7RT.

SUPPLIERS OF PLANTS AND SEEDS FOR ATTRACTING BUTTERFLIES

John Chambers – seeds
15 Westleigh Road, Barton Seagrave, Kettering, Northants NN15 5AJ.

Careby Manor Gardens – plants
Stamford, Lincolnshire PE9 4EA.

FIELD AND COLLECTING EQUIPMENT INCLUDING NETS

Marris House Nets,
54 Richmond Park Avenue, Bournemouth, BH8 9DR

Bioscience Supplies
4 Long Mill North, Wednesfield, Wolverhampton, WV11 1JD.

Watkins and Doncaster Ltd
Four Throws, Hawkhurst, Kent, TN18 5ED.

SUPPLIERS OF ENTOMOLOGICAL CABINETS

Stephenson Blake and Co. Ltd
Sheaf Works, Maltravers Street, Sheffield, S4 7YL.

RECOMMENDED FURTHER READING

There are a vast number of butterfly books on the market today, covering practically all aspects of the group. Most are quite good, and a few are excellent, whilst inevitably there are some which are simply not worth the money. Sorting out the best from this array is difficult, not to say impossible from the beginner's point of view, added to which different styles of presentation will suit different readers. The following is a suggested shopping list of books for beginners, though some of the general reading will be of continuing value as your interest in butterflies develops. The absence of a book from this list in no way indicates that it is one which should be avoided, however.

IDENTIFICATION OF SPECIES

The Butterflies of Britain and Europe, by Lionel Higgins and Brian Hargreaves. Published by Collins, London in 1983.

LIFE CYCLES

A Complete Guide to British Butterflies, by Margaret Brooks and Charles Knight. Published by Jonathan Cape, London, 1982 in hardback, but reprinted in softback 1985.

ATTRACTING BUTTERFLIES TO GARDENS

Garden Plants for Butterflies, by Matthew Oates. Published by Brian Masterton & Associates, Hampshire: 1985.

DISTRIBUTION

The Atlas of the Butterflies of Britain and Ireland, by J. Heath, E. Pollard and J. Thomas. Published by Viking, London in 1984.

GENERAL READING

The Natural History of Butterflies, by John Feltwell. Published by Croom Helm, Beckenham, Kent in 1986.

Butterfly Watching, by Paul Whalley. Published by Severn House Publishers, London, in 1980.

Butterflies, by E.B. Ford. Fontana New Naturalist: London in paperback, (originally as a Collins New Naturalist hardback in 1945).

South's British Butterflies, by T.G. Howarth. Published by Warne, London in 1973.

ACKNOWLEDGEMENTS

It would have been impossible to produce this book without the cooperation of a great many naturalists and others.

Several publications carried my various appeals for records and information, notably *The London Naturalist*, *The Entomologist's Record and Journal of Variation*, *The Entomologist's Monthly Magazine*, *The Entomologist's Gazette*, the London Branch Newsletter of the British Butterfly Conservation Society, *Habitat* and the magazines and journals of the London Wildlife Trust, Essex Naturalists' Trust, Kent Trust for Nature Conservation, Surrey Trust for Nature Conservation, Berks., Bucks. and Oxon. Naturalists' Trust, Herts. and Middlesex Trust for Nature Conservation, Essex Field Club, and the Hertfordshire Natural History Society. A number of local natural history societies and London local newspapers also carried my appeals, and I am grateful to them all for the publicity given. I would also like to thank BBC Radio London, LBC Radio, and Capital Radio for their great help in interviewing me "on the air" about the project: This resulted in many valuable records being submitted. Ian Robertson, Curator of the Passmore Edwards Museum kindly allowed me to use the Museum's address for the submission of records by members of the public, and as a publication address for the London Natural History Society on this occasion, and I am grateful to him for this service. I am particularly grateful to the staff, past and present, in the Administration Section of the Museum, namely Barbara Ellis, Annette Hall, Charlotte Lang, Julia Montague, Fiona Poulter, Lesley Richardson, Gursharan Kaur Sian and Keith Wilkinson, for their efficient handling of a great volume of mail, particularly following radio or newspaper announcements, as well as for dealing with a number of telephone callers.

Gerard Harris provided me with excellent (and most essential!) technical backup for the computer and word processor. Paul Sokoloff and Keith Hyatt both read early drafts of various parts of the text, and offered helpful advice in many areas. Maitland Emmet most kindly read through the "final" draft, and made a large number of extremely useful comments on the content and presentation, all of which I have incorporated. Col Emmet also drew my attention to a number of seventeenth century and other early records in literature to which I had no easy access, and I am most grateful to him for the consequential enrichment of the species accounts. My thanks also to the London Natural History Society members who responded to my appeal for colour photographs to illustrate the book. It has been difficult to decide which slides to use, and inevitably some excellent material has had to be rejected. I have however, tried to include at least one picture from each amateur photographer where possible, and the name of the supplier of the original appears under each photograph. As far as records are concerned I have to thank Eric Philp at the Kent Biological Archives and Records Centre, and also Phil Collins, Trevor James and Brian Sawford at the two Hertfordshire Records Centres. Russell Bretherton and David Agassiz have earlier scrutinised and commented on the records of the immigrant butterflies. Beyond that, it would be most unfair to single out any small group of people as having supplied important records. ALL the records are as important as each other, be they of cabbage whites on an allotment in the suburbs or of High Brown Fritillaries on the North Downs. Accordingly, I offer my profound gratitude to the following observers:

Adams, J., Adams, K.J., Adams, P., Agassiz, D.J.L., Albertini, M., Aldridge, M., Alexander, K., Allan, J., Allday, P.S.A., Allen, A.A., Allen, B., Ambrose Flemming School, Anderson, J.E., Anderson, E.F., Andrews, J.N., Archway School, Armstrong, W.M., Ashby, C.B., Ashby, J., Atkinson, L.J., Bacon, S., Baker, H., Baker, J., Baker, R.F., Baker, P.J., Baldwin, M., Balfour, C., Bantock, C., Baxter, A., Baxter, R.N., Beard, P.E., Bearham, S., Bennett, J., Benton, E., Berks. Bucks. and Oxon Naturalists Trust Ltd., Betton, K.F., Bevan, D., Bishops Stortford Natural History Society, Blatchley, Mrs F., Booth, D.J., Bovis, A., Bowden, S.R., Bowdrey, J.P., Bowes, R., Bowman, N., Boxter, A., Boyd, D., Boyle, C.L., Boyle, V., Boyt, A., Bradford, E.S., Bradley, J.D., Bratton, J., Bretherton, R.F., Brewitt, L.C., Briggs (the family), Brightman, C.J., Bristow, C.R., Bristow, R., British Butterfly Conservation Society, (including London Branch), Brooks, A., Brooks, G.M., Brooks, S., Brown, B.A., Brown, M.R., Brown, N., Brown, S., Browning, F., Brydon, I., Buisson, R.S.K., Burchfield, D.S., Burge, J., Burley, R., Burnaby, R., Burton, J.F., Burton, R.M., Campbell, A., Carr, D.G., Carter, D.J., Cassidy, A., Castle, B.W. Castle, D.W., Catt, M., Chacksfield, E.M., Chalk, M., Chalmers-Hunt, J.M., Chance, K., Chandler, E., Chandler, P.J., Chandler, R.J., Chatelain, R.G., Chipperfield, H.E., Clement, D., Coleman, D.A., Colla, B.A., Collecott, G., Collins, G.A., Collins, G.S., Collins, P., Collins, P.F., Colmans, D., Conway, A., Conway, K., Conway (the family), Cooke, C., Coombes, J., Copley, G., Corbett, J, Cotton, J., Couzens, D., Crawford, L., Cresswell, J., Cribb, P.W., Crossland, D.P., Croydon Natural History and Scientific Society, Currie, M., Dacie, J.V., Dale, C., David, R., Davies, D.C., Davis, R.W., Dawe, P., Dawkins, M., Day, R., Dell, D., Dennis, M.K., Dews, J., Dickerson, G., Dinkel, M., Dougherty, G.E., Drakeford, D.R., Drew, R., Dring, K.A., Dudley, L., Dunn, R., Dupuis, T., Dyke, R., Earle F., Earningshaw, T., Earp, M., Eaves, S.L., Edwards, A.B., Edwards, P., Edwards, P.J., Element, D., Eltham and Kentish Times, Emmet, A.M., Enfield, M., English, P., Epping District Council, Epping Forest Conservation Centre, Essex County Council, Essex Field Club, Essex Naturalists Trust Ltd., Evans, H.W., Evans, K.G.W., Evans, S.L., Eve, G., Eversham, B., Fentiman, C., Ferguson, I.D., Ferris, P.R., Findon, R., Fisher, D., Fitter, R.S.R., Fitzpatrick, J., Flanagan, J., Flanagan, J.P., Flint, E., Flynn, G.E., Foster, A.H., Foster, C., Foster, M.C., Franklin, T., Franklin, V., Frazer, A., Freed, T., Freeman, D., Freeman, G., Freeman, R., Frost, F.A., Gale, S.W., Gandy, M., Gange, A., Gardiner, C.J., Garrad, L.S., Gasson, P., Geen, G., George, A.M., George Orwell School, Gibson, A., Gill, M., Gittings, T., Gladwin, T., Goad, J., Goater, B., Goff, R., Golder, G.M., Goldsmith, P., Goodey, C.A., Gosling, A.P., Goulding, R.V., Graham, B., Gray, G., Gray, M., Greater London Ecology Unit, Green, G., Green, T.W.V., Greenwood, P.R., Griffin, C., Griffith, D., Griffiths, D., Griffiths, J., Groves, E., Gudgion, A., Hadley, M., Haggis, M.J., Hale, M., Hall, A.C., Hall, Cdr., Hall, O., Hall, P.R., Hammerson, M.J., Hancock, V., Hannay, N., Hanson, R., Hanson, M.J., Hardy, I., Hardy, J., Hare, A., Haringey Wildlife Group, Harlow Wildlife Group, Harper, D., Harris, A., Harris, G.J., Hartley, B.C., Harvey, P., Harvey, M.S., Harvey, J.E., Hastings, R.B., Hastings, R., Hatward, R., Haynes, P.G., Hayward, R.A., Headon, G.W., Heaton, A., Hendy, J.D., Herbert, C., Herts. and Middlesex Trust for Nature Conservation Ltd., Hewitt, J.P.A., Hicklenton, D., Hickman, D.R., Hicks, L.P., Highgate Junior School, Hill, P.A., Hilliard, R.D., Hillman, E.M., Hinchliff, R., Hoare, A.M.V., Hobbs, R.N., Holland, P.C., Hollingdale, J., Holloway, G., Holyday, L., Honey, M.R., Hook, J., Hooker, D.,Hooper, J., Hornsey School for Girls, Hough, M.J., Hughes

Anna, Hughes, Anne, Hughes, T.E., Humble, A., Hyatt, K.H., Hyman, P.S., Islington Wildlife Group, Jack, J., Jacobs, S.N.A., Jacobs, R., James, T., Jefferies, J., Jeffery, P., Jeffery Harrison Memorial Trust, Jenkins, A., Jennings, M., Jennings, P., Johnson, I.G., Jones, P., Jones, R.A., Jupp, P., Keesing, J.L.S., Kennedy, M.E., Kenrick, D., Kent Field Club, Kent Trust for Nature Conservation Ltd., Kettle, R., Khan, A., Kierman, N.S., Kiernan, R.S., King, J., King, P., Kirby, P., Kitching, I., Kite, D., Knill-Jones, S.A., Knill-Jones, R.P., Lambert, S.J.J., Langham, S., Langley, R.R., Latham, J.B., Leader, G., Leanan, A., Le Corney, R., Lever, R.A., Levy, J., Lines, J., Lloyd, T.P., Loan, A., Lock, M., Lockwood, F.R., Lockwood, F.W., London Wildlife Trust, Lorimer, I., Lowe, R.T., Lucas, D., Lyall, A.W., Lyle, T., Mackworth-Praed, H.W., Madden, J., Magee, J.D., Mallett, N., Martin, P.M., Maskray, J., Mason, R., Matthews, G., Maxwell, R., Mayes, S., McCord, A., McCormick, R.F., McGrath, T., McIntyre, E., McRitchie, B., Merritt, A., Messenbird, G., Mickleburgh, S., Milner, J.E.D., Minnion, W.E., Mist, B., Mitchell, J.W., Moohan, D., Moohan, V., Moon, A.V., Morris, H., Morris, R.K.A., Moxey, P.A., Moxey, T., Munns, G.F.A., Murdoch, D., Murphy, F., Murray, D., Mussellwhite, A.F., Mussellwhite, B.S., Nash, N., Nature Conservancy Council, Naylor, A., Naylor, P., Netherwood, M., Newton, J., Newton, R., Norris, M.L., Oakman, R.F., Odipu, Z.J., Ongar Wildlife Group, Ormerod, E.C., Osborne, K., Ovenden, D., Owen, D., Owen, D.F., Oxford, E., O'Brien, I., O'Donnell, D., Paine, A., Palmer, A.C., Palmer, R.A., Parker, R., Parliament Hill School, Parndon Wood Nature Reserve, Parry, J., Parsons, D. Passmore Edwards Museum, Pater, C., Patterson, R.M., Paxon, R., Peck, C., Pendlebury, J.B., Penney, C., Penrose, R., Pepper, Peters, T.C., Peters, R.W., Peters, R., Petrie, A.B., Philp, E., Pittaway, T., Plant, L.C., Plant, A.R., Plant, W.S., Power, M.W., Prance, D., Price, J., Prior, G., Proctor, K.H., Pryer, I.F., Pyman, G.A., Railton, P., Rayment, S.M., Reed, J., Reidy, J., Robbins, R., Robertson, D., Robertson, D.H., Robertson, T.S., Robinson, G., Rogers, I.H., Rooum, D., Ruislip and District Natural History Society, Samuels, K., Sand, J., Sankey, J., Sankey, J.H.P., Sawford, B., Sayers, J.A., Seage, M.P., Sellar, P.J., Sempkins, A., Seth-Smith, D., Shanks, Shoenberg, R., Shoenbery, R.J., Skinner, B., Skinner, J., Skinner, P., Smart, C., Smith, C., Smith, D., Smith, D.A., Smith, R., Smith, R.E., Softly, R.A., Sokoloff, P.A., Soreasen, C., South Herts. Biological Records Centre, Spall, T., Sparrow, W., Spinks, J.A., Stacey, A., Stevens, A., Strangeman, P., Stubbs, D., Surrey Trust for Nature Conservation Ltd., Sutton, R.D., Symes, M.J., Tagg, D., Teagle, J.F., Teagle, W.G., Thompson, I., Thompson, P., Thompson, R.T., Todd, J.M., Tomlins, A.D., Tonothy, R., Tout, P., Trelease, B., Trewin, D., Trumpshaw, G.O., Tuck, K., Tyler, J., Tyson, N., Unsworth, B.M.E., Urban Spaces Scheme, Vaughan, A., Veal, V., Wallace, G., Walton, P., Ward, I., Warren, A., Warren, D. Washer, P., Wason, R., Waterton, P., Watling, P.R., Watson, A., Watson, A.N., Watson, B., Webber, C., Wells, M.J., Welsh , A., West, B.K., Whalley, P., Wheatcroft, P., Wheeler, A.S., Wheeler-Holohan, B., White, G.J., Whitehouse, S., Widgery , J.P., Wild, E.H., Wild, R., Wild, T., Wildridge, B., Wildridge, T., Williams, L., Williams, L.B., Williams, L.R., Willmott, K.J., Wills, M., Wilsdon, A., Wilsdon, H.M.V., Wilsdon, M., Wilson, M., Withrington, D., Wood, B., Wood, C.W., Wood Green School, Woods, D., Wren Conservation Group, Wright, D., Wright, J.R., Wright, R., Wright, R.A., Wurzell, B.

My thanks are due also to a large number of landowners and agents, who kindly allowed me access to otherwise private land for the purpose of recording butterflies. Finally, I must thank my wife Lesley, and my two children Rosemary and Edward, for putting up with my self-imposed exile to my study during the evenings and weekends whilst the text was being written, and for keeping me supplied with refreshments whilst I was attempting to reconcile several very large, very untidy piles of paper with modern microcomputer technology!

THE BUTTERFLIES

SMALL SKIPPER

Thymelicus sylvestris (Poda)

The Small Skipper is a widespread and fairly common insect over much of England and Wales, though it is absent from north-west England and has been reported only from two localities in Scotland, neither of them recently. It is absent from Ireland. There is much confusion, however, between this and the next species, the Essex Skipper *Thymelicus lineola*, and unless the insect settles in an observable position it is necessary to capture adult insects in the field for closer examination than is possible on the wing. Both sexes of the Small Skipper have orangey-brown to dark brown tips to the *undersides* of their antennae: in the Essex Skipper these tips are black. Some confusingly intermediate examples can be found, particularly on Hampstead Heath, and these would all seem to be rather darkened examples of Small Skippers. In both species, the males can be distinguished by the presence of a dark line of scales, visible on the upper side of each front wing. This is called the "sex brand" and is absent from females.

The Small Skipper is a widespread and often extremely common butterfly in the London area, equally at home on the calcareous grasslands in the south as on the neutral grasslands and acid heaths elsewhere. Historically, it was recorded for London on Hampstead Heath by Petiver in 1704. Cockerell (1891) lists only Old Oak Common and Isleworth in his *Preliminary List of the Insect Fauna of Middlesex*, and later Buckell and Prout added Hale End, Croydon, Highgate and Wimbledon Common. De Worms (1950) notes it as widespread in the London area and lists several non-urban localities. Except that it seems to no longer occur in much of the northern part of Lewisham it seems to have always been a common butterfly in the London area. In more urban zones it appears to thrive on railway embankments, on the grassed areas around reservoirs and in overgrown cemeteries and churchyards. It is single-brooded and can be seen on the wing in London from the end of June to the end of August (reported between 20 June and 3 September) though the peak period is from the start of July to about 10 August in most years. As in other areas of southern Britain, it appears on the wing about ten days before the Essex Skipper, though after this period both species often seem to fly together making it necessary to capture a representative sample for examination to ascertain whether both or only one species are present. It appears to be genuinely absent from the bulk of the officially designated "Inner London" area, as well as from a large part of the truly urban areas around here, particularly south of the River Thames where the amount of available habitat is miniscule. In the east, it penetrates to Tower Hamlets, whilst north of the City it seems widespread but probably not common in the Stoke Newington and Hackney districts.

It appears that this butterfly forms discrete and often quite small colonies, particularly on derelict sites where small temporary colonies may build to twenty or so individuals after two or three years, only to die out as the site is developed. This is not the norm, however, and a total of twenty individuals is a very small colony indeed. On the other hand, large colonies have been reported, such as at the Lonsdale Road Reservoir, Staines Reservoir, Wimbledon Common and Hampstead Heath. With such large numbers, however, it is often difficult to tell whether one has a single colony or more than one overlapping with each other.

The eggs are laid inside the sheaths of grass stems, usually in rows of four or five. Hatching takes about 50 to 60 days. The larva, upon hatching, eats its eggshell then spins a silk cocoon inside the sheath of the grass stem, in which it immediately becomes dormant. After hibernation it usually commences feeding in April after the danger of frost has passed, spinning together several blades of grass to form a shelter. A succession of such shelters are made until the final instar which feeds exposed. Pupation takes place in a coarse open cocoon attached to a grass stem, and the adult emerges after about three weeks.

Reported larval foodplants are *Phleum pratense*, *P. bertolonii*, *Holcus mollis*, *Holcus lanatus*, and *Brachypodium pinnatum* and *B. sylvaticum*. All grow in the London area, though *H. mollis* is less evenly distributed, and *B. pinnatum* is decidedly local, occurring principally in the south (Burton 1983). In this area, larvae have only been found feeding on *H. mollis*, *H. lanatus* and *P. pratense*, though this may be because proper searching has not been undertaken.

ESSEX SKIPPER

Thymelicus lineola (Ochsenheimer)

Though by no means now confined to the County of Essex, it was indeed here that the butterfly was added to the British list in July 1988 (Hawes 1890). It is however, a butterfly of the south-east in this country, seemingly not venturing beyond a line drawn from the Wash to the Severn Estuary. The similarity of the adult butterfly to the Small Skipper has already been mentioned, and many reports have had to be treated with caution in view of the difficulties encountered by many non-specialists. The most commonly rejected record has been when the observer has assumed Small Skipper without checking, because they believe the Essex Skipper to be confined to a small part of that county. An examination of the map, however, reveals that this is not the case, and the Essex

Skipper is well distributed across the London area. Within this broad general statement, however, there is room for interpretation, for it is clear from the map that although the word "widespread" does indeed apply, the distribution is a patchy one, with fair-sized portions of Kent, Surrey and Middlesex lacking in records. Although like the former species it is largely absent from the Inner London area, the Essex Skipper seems far more ready to colonise small patches of temporarily available land in the urban zone. This is perhaps in part due to the ability of the larvae to feed upon the cock's-foot grass *Dactylis glomerata*, a species unrecorded from only three of the tetrads of the London area, and one which is very common and well able to tolerate the droughty conditions of urban waste sites (Burton 1983). Indeed, in the London area the cocksfoot grass together with *Holcus mollis* and *Brachypodium sylvaticum* are the only recorded foodplants, though Frowhawk (1934) also lists *Phleum pratense* whilst Allan (1949), Brooks and Knight (1982), and Garland (1981) also list common couch grass *Agropyron repens* – a common weed in London but apparently not utilised here.

Historical records include Hale End, Forest Gate, Croydon, Brockley, Dulwich, Fulham, Wimbledon Common, Southall, Kilburn and Highgate (Buckell and Prout 1899), though there is no mention of the species in the earlier work by Cockerell (1891). The butterfly appeared to be restricted to the coast of Essex and the Thames estuary area in the nineteenth century but was noted to be more widespread during the period 1900 to 1935. The first recorded occurrence in our part of north-west Kent was not until 1911, at Eltham, and since then it has expanded its range considerably here, with many colonies throughout the Kent sector by the late 1940s. The 1950 work by de Worms states a presence in a number of localities in Kent and Essex only. As de Worms himself lived at Woking in Surrey, and since he would certainly have recognised the insect had it been in his area at the time, we may assume that it had not then spread to our part of that county, and thus has done so in the last thirty years. For Middlesex, Cribb (1962) records the butterfly from the south-west region in 1960, and comments "*I have not been able to trace any previous record of this species in Middlesex*"; presumably he overlooked Buckell and Prout's records just given. There is certainly no doubt that the Essex Skipper has spread in recent years, northwards through Suffolk (Mendel and Piotrowski 1986) and westwards into Berkshire, Buckinghamshire and Oxfordshire (Steel and Steel 1985). It may, however, have been in some of these areas undetected and ignored for many years, thus making a proper analysis of its spread difficult. The use of roadside verges as a habitat has been put forward as a popular theory for its spread in recent times. Peak counts in the London area have all been on reservoir embankments (eg in excess of 140 at Lonsdale Road Reservoir on 24 July 1979, and over 100 at Barn Elms and Staines Reservoirs in 1978) the one exception being Perry Oaks Sewage Farm, where over 100 were noted at the western end of the site on 16 July 1984, when Small Skippers were apparently absent.

The eggs are deposited in sheaths of grass stems in a similar manner to the Small Skipper, but unlike that species the larva does not hatch until the following April. It then feeds slowly to pupate during the second or third week of June. The cocoon is made at the base of the grass stems. In the London area adults are on the wing from 29 June to 11 September, though the peak seems to be from the end of the first week of July until the end of August. Certainly 11 September is an extreme date.

SILVER-SPOTTED SKIPPER

Hesperia comma (Linnaeus)

That the Silver-spotted Skipper is now a nationally rare, and still declining, species is in very large part due to alterations in the management regimes of the calcareous grasslands of south-east England to which the butterfly is strictly limited in this country. The cessation of grazing, together with the resultant encroachment of scrub onto the grassland has all but eliminated the very precise habitat required by the insect. The larva feeds, largely by night, on *Festuca ovina*, a grass itself confined to a calcareous substrate. Several works (eg Allan 1949) state that other grasses are probably utilised, though the source of

Silver-spotted Skipper — *Photographer: Ian G. Johnson*

this less than precise information is not clear. It is certain that all the colonies in the London area are dependent upon *F.ovina* ssp.*ovina*, growing in a grazed short turf on the North Downs in Surrey. Recent agricultural "improvements" have eliminated the *Festuca* from many formerly suitable areas, although in the London area major declines may have resulted from the loss of rabbits due to myxomatosis. Chalmers-Hunt (1979) states that in Kent the loss of this butterfly from many of its localities was directly caused by the ploughing up of its breeding grounds. So rare was the butterfly considered in 1982 that the Joint Committee for the Conservation of British Insects undertook a major survey to discover all current colonies. The results showed that a mere 33 localities, (holding 53 colonies) represented the entire British population at that date: seven of these localities are within the London area, representing exactly twenty-five per cent of the total Surrey population.

Adult Silver-spotted Skippers are frequent visitors to knapweed and thistle flowers, from which they take nectar, although they are more regularly noted resting on the ground. They fly only on the hottest days during August, and consequently can be missed by the inexperienced observer. Historically, Cockerell (1891) lists Old Oak Common, Middlesex, whilst the later work by Buckell and Prout (1899) lists only "*Croydon – rare*". The Woolwich Survey of 1909 listed Shoreham and Eynsford in Kent. In 1950, de Worms listed Box Hill, Surrey, "*and in that vicinity along the Downs*", and from Kent at Magpie Bottom, Shoreham. Surprisingly, he seems to have missed a record from Haileybury, Hertfordshire in 1898 given in Foster's 1937 list of Hertfordshire Lepidoptera. Chalmers-Hunt (1961) again mentions Magpie Bottom, where it was plentiful in 1947 but not since, and lists a number of records in the Eynsford area, where it seems to have been fairly common in the late 1930s to mid 1940s. Heath, Pollard and Thomas (1984) summarised the national situation in the form of ten-kilometre dot maps, and for our area gave the Squares TQ 18, 28, 45,46 and 67 and TL 31(presumably the Haileybury record missed by de Worms) for records made prior to 1940. For the period 1940 to 1969, TQ 26, 36 and 56 were listed alongside TQ 15 and 25 for 1970 to 1982. The present maps, for 1980 to 1986 agree with the post 1970 maps in that work.

The seven localities in the London area affect only five tetrads in two ten-kilometre squares. All are on south-facing slopes on a chalk substrate. Three of the colonies are under current threat from scrub invasion; two more are situated near to a scrub habitat but do not appear to be in any imminent danger. One colony is said to be under no threat at the present , whilst the final site is actively managed specifically for the butterflies.

The eggs are laid singly low down on the plant, the adult female often proving exceedingly fussy about her choice of plant. Optimum conditions appear to be on young plants growing in practically bare earth, with those growing in dense swards being ignored. Plants in very sunny situations, particularly in depressions are favoured. The egg remains attached to the plant throughout the winter, and is easily spotted by the experienced eye. The larva hatches rather early, in late February or early March, and one is forced to wonder how it manages to survive the late frosts typical of this country. It is largely nocturnal, spinning a shelter from blades of grass at the base of the plant, where it remains until the middle of July, pupating in a quite strong cocoon. The adult emerges in August, and in the London area it has been noted between 30 July and 30 August. On the latter date (obtained during 1985) it was said to be abundant at the site in question, indicating that the true "last date" would have been much later.

LARGE SKIPPER

Ochlodes venata (Bremer & Grey) ssp. *faunus* (Turati)

A widespread and plentiful butterfly over almost all of England and Wales, barring the tops of the Welsh mountains and a few quite unsuitable parts of arable East Anglia, the Large Skipper is as common now in the London area as it has ever been, having neither increased nor declined save in a few areas where urbanisation has forced it away. The distribution map shows a marked absence from the central eastern area of the recording circle, though this is probably, at least in part, a result of under-recording. However, Chalmers-Hunt, in the Supplement to his *magnum opus* on the butterflies and moths of Kent states that whilst in that county there has been no change in status over the past two decades (he was writing in 1979) "*it continues to be much restricted in the extreme north-west*". The present maps agree well with his statement.

The larval foodplant in our area, where noted, has always been, with one exception, the cock's-foot grass *Dactylis glomerata*, though elsewhere *Brachypodium sylvaticum* has been recorded (Heath Pollard and Thomas 1984) as well as *Phleum pratense*, *Holcus lanatus*, *H. mollis*, and *Agropyron repens* (Allan 1949). The one exception referred to relates to a larva found spun up in the leaves of wheat *Triticum* at Sidcup on 5 May 1927, from which the finder bred the adult (Chalmers-Hunt 1979). Its preference for this particular foodplant ought to allow it to adapt to life in temporary urban sites as does the Essex Skipper, and whilst this is true to a certain extent, it nevertheless seems unable to thrive on many of the smaller sites: this, in spite of the fact that on the larger sites where it occurs, breeding colonies may be confined to a few square metres of what, to human eyes, appears to be a bigger area of reasonably suitable habitat. Generally speaking it is absent from most roadside verges, although there are some healthy colonies on the larger embankments of motorways, such as the M.11 in Essex, and parts of the M.25. During July 1947, one was noted at a bombed site at Cripplegate (de Worms 1950): the present-day Inner London records hale principally from Regent's and Battersea Parks, though in the east

Large Skipper *Photographer: Neil Bowman*

there are some small but healthy colonies in the Rotherhithe area. In 1946 it was reported as "*common on every grassy patch in the Lewisham area*", a statement which does not appear to hold true today. The earliest London area record available seems to be the one given by Petiver in 1704 for Hampstead Heath.

Unlike the Small and Essex Skipper females, this butterfly deposits its eggs singly on the undersurface of a blade of the grass, rather than within a sheath, and the larva emerges after about 18 days. Having eaten its eggshell, it feeds until the fifth instar in September, whereupon it constructs a tent of grass blades pulled together with silk and hibernates until March. Following this, it feeds again until the final instar, when it pupates in a similar grass tent to emerge after about three weeks. In London, the flight period ranges from the extremes of 3 June to 21 August, though the peak period seems to be from about 12 June to 30 July, depending upon the earliness or lateness of the season.

DINGY SKIPPER

Erynnis tages (Linnaeus) ssp. *tages* (Linnaeus)

The Dingy Skipper was first recorded from the London area by Handley, and was reported by Petiver in 1704. Sadly, however, this butterfly has declined drastically in the London area in recent years. De Worms (1950) in his list of the "Butterflies of London and Its Surroundings" records it as being common in the London area making the particular comments that it was "*plentiful in 1944 at Box Hill, and at Esher in 1945; very numerous at Caterham in 1946; common at Northwood in 1945; seen at Broxbourne; common all over north-west Kent especially around Lewisham, Elmstead, Joyden's Wood, Shooter's Hill, and Pett's Wood*". None of these statements hold true today, a mere thirty-six years later, with the butterfly being confined principally to the south of the area, and scattered colonies in Hertfordshire together with an isolated sighting in Grays Chalk Quarry, Essex, during 1980, and two in the west at Black Park Country Park, Buckinghamshire and Ruislip Common, Middlesex.

Dingy Skipper *Photographer: Ian G. Johnson*

It is a butterfly of grassland areas, including woodland rides and railway cuttings and its drab colouration from which the vernacular name derives sometimes renders it difficult to detect. Although the map almost certainly presents a true summary of the butterfly's overall London area distribution, and is unlikely to alter its overall appearance,there will doubtless be one or two dots to add as small colonies of this species which have yet to be located are discovered. The caterpillars feed on common bird's-foot trefoil *Lotus corniculatus*, greater bird's-foot trefoil *L. uliginosus* or on horseshoe vetch *Hippocrepis comosa*: it is particularly interesting to discover that, in spite of the presence of all three foodplants in the southern half of the map, the butterflies in Kent and Surrey appear to be confined to the *Hippocrepis*, apparently scorning the available *Lotus* plants, whereas in the north *Hippocrepis* is absent and *Lotus corniculatus* is the favoured pabulum. Quite why there should be this distinction is unclear at present, but it is perhaps equally noteworthy that the butterfly is far more plentiful in the southern colonies where open grassland is preferred than it is in the northern ones, where woodland rides (such as in the Broxbourne Woods complex) and railway cuttings are the favoured habitat).

Although many text books would indicate that the reasons for the decline of this less than striking insect are not clear, it is probably a combination of a number of differing factors, all of which in one way or another have caused a decline in the availability of the correct type of grassland habitat. In the London area at least, two major causes are evident: urbanisation has accounted for the loss of the butterfly from many of the areas closer to the centre of town to the south of the River Thames, whilst elsewhere the decline of grasslands has resulted from the cessation of rabbit grazing following myxomatosis. The alteration in the management of woodlands too will have had its effect on the rides.

The adult insect is on the wing from 29 April to 29 June in our area, with most being seen from the end of the second week of May until about 10 June. It is possible that its early appearance has been responsible for some under-recording. The eggs are laid singly on the shoots of the foodplant and hatch after about 14 days. Like the other species in this family, the larva constructs a tent of leaves spun together with silk, from which it ventures forth to feed at night. It hibernates fully fed in a similar structure, becoming dormant towards the beginning of August, and does not pupate until the following late March or early April. The butterflies emerge after about four weeks as a chrysalis. Just occasionally, the full grown-larva pupates in the autumn, rather than after hibernation, and this gives rise to a partial second brood in some areas. In London, however, second broods have not been recorded in the study period from 1980 to 1986.

GRIZZLED SKIPPER

Pyrgus malvae (Linnaeus)

On a national level, the Grizzled Skipper seems to be declining in the north of its range (Heath, Pollard and Thomas 1984) as well as in the east (Mendel and Piotrowski 1986). In the London area, although it has disappeared from all of its known former Middlesex localities as a result of habitat loss through urbanisation, it generally appears to be holding its own, being particularly prevalent in Kent and Surrey as well as in Hertfordshire. The isolated record

Grizzled Skipper *Photographer: Ian G. Johnson*

from Thamesmead in square 48 (a single example in 1982) probably relates to a release or introduction, although the nearby Abbey Wood was listed by de Worms as a site where the butterfly was plentiful in the 1940s. It has apparently not survived in this locality. The single records for Middlesex and Buckinghamshire are from Kempton Park and Black Park respectively. The actual number of butterflies at each colony site seems to be lower now than it was fifty years ago, and indeed the number of discrete colonies within a given tetrad may too have declined. The earliest London area record to hand is of one taken on 30 April 1696 in a boggy area of Hampstead Heath by Petiver (Petiver 1699). This date, of course, relates to the old calendar: conversion to the present day system gives the capture date as 11 May.

For a butterfly with such a choice of larval foodplants, a wider distribution would be expected. Recorded plants include barren strawberry *Potentilla sterilis*, wild strawberry *Fragaria vesca*, creeping cinquefoil *Potentilla reptans*, silverweed *Potentilla anserina*, tormentil *Potentilla erecta*, agrimony *Agrimonia eupatoria*, bramble *Rubus fruticosus* and raspberry *Rubus idaeus*.

In our area, the wild strawberry seems to be the plant of choice where information is available, and it is useful to compare the distribution of the insect with the map of the plant on page 66 of the *Flora of the London Area* (Burton 1983): although the wild strawberry is recorded over a much greater area the ranges of plant and animal are compatible.

The Grizzled Skipper is amongst the few British butterflies which normally over-winter as a chrysalis. The adults are on the wing from the end of April in a good year to the middle of June (in the London area most are seen from the middle of May onwards). In years when spring comes early, the adults may emerge slightly sooner giving rise to caterpillars which are able to pupate sooner than usual. This may give rise to a small second brood of butterflies in July and August, and if weather conditions remain favourable, the progeny will feed successfully and pupate to give an enhanced peak of adults the following year. In London, such a second brood was noted in 1983 in some areas.

[OBERTHÜR'S GRIZZLED SKIPPER

Pyrgus armoricanus Oberthür

Dr Arthur Foster in his *List of the Lepidoptera of Hertfordshire* published in 1937, records under the heading "*Hesperia alveus*, Hubn. (?*H. armoricanus* Oberth.)", that "*one specimen was taken near Haileybury on 20 May 1897 and was identified at the Natural History Museum*". The record is credited to H.M. Edelsten.

This specimen is still in the British butterfly collection at South Kensington, bearing the label "*Presented by Miss G. Edelsten (ex. coll. H.M. Edelsten) BM 1959-304*", but it is considered that the date would have been too early for it to have been captured by this collector. Whatever the arguments, however, the origin of the specimen remains highly suspect, and it is most unlikely, even if genuinely captured in Britain, that it was anything other than an escape or release.]

THE APOLLO

Parnassius apollo (Linnaeus)

This is a rare butterfly of the alpine regions of continental Europe, though there are in excess of twenty records, most of them authentic, for the British Isles in the last hundred years or so. There are rumours that it once bred in the Highlands of Scotland, though this is not the right place to discuss the validity of such a claim. As far as London is concerned, there are just two valid records amongst several summarised by Morley and Chalmers-Hunt (1959): one was taken "*by the son of G.B. Holmes at Epping, about 1847 or 1848*", originally reported in the journal *Entomologist* during 1889, whilst a very battered specimen was found on the pavement at Tavistock Square, in our Inner London zone, on 26 September 1957 (Ransom 1957). The possibility of these being deliberate releases or escapes cannot be ruled out.

Apollo *Photographer: Bryan Ceney*

SWALLOWTAIL

Papilio machaon Linnaeus

The earliest record from the London area reads as follows: "*The Royal William. The only one I have seen about London was caught by my ingenious friend Mr Tilliman Bobart in the Royal Garden at St James*" (Petiver 1699). St James' Palace was then the royal residence, and it is likely that Bobart showed the King the butterfly caught in his garden and named it in his honour. Bobart was a good entomologist: his brother was Professor of the Physic Garden at Oxford. Petiver's 1699 list was completed on 31 August, so the capture could have been that year, but was more probably a year or two earlier. In his work *Papilionum Britanniae* published in 1717, Petiver further commented on this insect, still under the then common name "Royal William", that "*This has been caught about London and divers countries in England, yet rarely*". In 1747, however, it was rare in London (if indeed it was ever common) and to find it entomologists had to travel south where it was said that the butterfly "*may be taken in the meadows and clover fields about Cookham, near Westram, in Kent*" (Wilkes 1747).

Before we progress with the records for this most attractive of insects it is necessary to bear in mind that there are two quite distinct subspecies of the Swallowtail. The resident British subspecies *britannicus* Seitz is today a rather local insect, though often common where it occurs, and as a strictly fenland species is confined to Norfolk on the Broads. It is a brighter insect than the continental subspecies *bigeneratus* Verity, is relatively sedentary and has only one brood per year, the larvae being restricted to milk parsley *Peucedanum palustre*. By contrast, the continental form, which reaches Britain solely as an immigrant or as an introduction or escape from breeding stock, often has two broods a year and has a range of pabula which include *P. palustre*. It is to this latter subspecies that all available London area records relate, with the single possible exception of several larvae found on Tottenham Marshes in the 1820s (Newman 1869).

In addition to the references by Petiver and Wilkes above, the Swallowtail used to be found at Epping Forest and at Stepney (Stephens 1830), whilst in 1828 Stephens gave "*near Peckham*" – presumably the Surrey locality? Cockerell (1891) lists Whitton Park, Isleworth as a locality, ("*one seen by E.O. Meyers*").

During the present century, records of subspecies *bigeneratus*, all of which are thought to relate to primary immigrants, are as follows:

> Enfield, Middlesex – 17 August 1911; Oxted, Surrey – 1934; Richmond 29 June 1935; Pinden (near Dartford), Kent – 1 May 1945; Orpington, Kent – 1945; Shooters Hill, Kent – 6 June 1946; Orpington, Kent – 2 September 1947; Hayes, Middlesex – 31 May 1949; Bexleyheath, Kent – 28 August 1962.

Records of individuals of unspecified race are from the Surrey Docks on 2 July 1982, Wood Street, Walthamstow in the first half of July 1984 and Harrow on 1 July 1985. These may all relate to escapes or releases. In addition to the Tottenham Marshes record above, caterpillars have been noted on one occasion only: three were found on garden carrot at Farnborough, near Orpington, Kent, on 17 July 1900. It is most likely that these were the progeny of an immigrant female.

CHINESE PEACOCK

[*Papilio bianor* Linnaeus

There is a single record of this far-eastern butterfly in our area, at Welling, Kent, given in *Proceedings of the South London Entomological and Natural History Society* for 1918/1919. This is now known for certain to have originated as a deliberate release.]

SCARCE SWALLOWTAIL

Iphiclides podalirius (Scopoli)

Robson (*Young Nat.* **29**) states that on the authority of his friend Mr Walker of Chester, Captain Russell is alleged to have taken one *P. podalirius* at Sevenoaks, and that this was exhibited at a meeting of the Entomological Society on 3 February 1862. However, it is stated in the *Proceedings of the Entomological Society of London* for 1861, that a number of specimens had been released at Sevenoaks by a woman who had bred them from imported pupae (Chalmers-Hunt 1980). If nothing else, this will serve as a reminder to butterfly breeders of the great importance they should attach to ensuring that if they must release these exotic insects to the wild (which is now illegal in any case) they should always inform the appropriate recorder. The only other record seems to be the one given in Morris (1895) where it is stated that "*Mr Standish was also certain that he saw this species on or about September 20th, 1829, near Richmond Park*". It seems highly unlikely that this relates to an immigrant.]

Scarce Swallowtail *Photographer: Bryan Ceney*

WOOD WHITE

Leptidea sinapis (Linnaeus) ssp. *sinapis* (Linnaeus)

This is essentially a species of rides and clearings in open woodlands, and must have been a common butterfly in many areas when coppicing was in vogue. The decline in this management method however, has resulted in a loss of the butterfly from many areas. In the London area, Petiver (1699) notes it from Hampstead, and it was formerly taken at Darenth Wood, Kent by Stephens (*Haustellata* 1 : 25) and this locality is also mentioned by Newman in 1860. Swanscombe Wood and Birch Wood were also Kentish localities at that period. In 1852 however, Newman was asking, in the preface to that year's volume of the journal *Zoologist*, what had happened to *sinapis* at Darenth, and it is thought that the species had become extinct in north-west Kent after the last record from West Wickham in 1856. In Essex it is said to have been common near Epping in 1839 and up to the 1850s, and was taken at Ongar Park Wood, TL 50T02 (which is not the same as Park Wood, Ongar, TL 50T40, marked on current OS maps) up to 1888 (Fitch 1891). It was taken at Warlingham in Surrey in 1900, and a dozen specimens were collected there from 1926 to 1929 (de Worms 1959). In the Cockayne - Kettlewell collection at the Natural History Museum there is a mixed gynandromorph from the Reigate area, which lacks a date (label "BM. 1947-114"). A "pre-1950" record submitted to Monks Wood from TQ 07 lacks locality data, and is possibly an error. Foster (1937) lists a record from Haileybury Heath [= Hertford Heath], Hertfordshire, published in *List of Macrolepidoptera of Haileybury School* (Bower, 1888). Heath, Pollard and Thomas (1984) list TL 40 and 50, TQ 49, 08, 37,47,57,67, and 36 as the ten-kilometre squares of our area having records made prior to 1940, whilst there are 1940 to 1969 period records from Princes Coverts, near Oxshott, Surrey (TQ 16) in 1969, and Richings Park, Iver, Buckinghamshire (TQ 07) for "post-1960".

As to more recent reports, one was seen at Balls Wood, Hertfordshire on 28 June 1976, and a probable at Bricketwood Common in the same county during 1983. The species is normally fairly sedentary, and is not prone to wandering about setting up new colonies. On the other hand if it does spread in our direction, the source is most likely to be the population centred upon the Northamptonshire - Oxfordshire area. Suitable woodlands in Hertfordshire, which contain the principal foodplants of meadow vetchling *Lathyrus pratensis*, bitter vetch *L.montanus* or bird's-foot trefoil *Lotus corniculatus* should be worth watching in future years.

PALE CLOUDED YELLOW
Colias hyale (Linnaeus) and
BERGER'S CLOUDED YELLOW
Colias australis Verity

These two yellow butterflies are impossible to separate in flight, and very nearly equally so when neatly pinned and set in a cabinet! Indeed, several specimens so preserved in various of our museums are still to be critically reviewed. Berger's Clouded Yellow was for a long time considered a minor variety of the other species, until, in 1947, the Belgian entomologist L.A. Berger made the discovery that the two were separate. Indeed, the caterpillars are strikingly dissimilar! Both species are extremely rare in Britain, only reaching our southern counties as immigrants from Europe during exceptionally good years. Example of such years are 1900, 1933, 1934, 1945, 1947 and 1948. Influxes do not necessarily coincide with the arrivals here of the more frequent Clouded Yellow *Colias croceus*, of which the pale form *helice* Hubner of the female is often confused with this species pair. London area records are so few that it is perhaps worth listing here those which have been traced. It is likely that the following refer to *hyale* rather than *australis*, as the latter is considered to be rare. This, however, is a less than scientific statement! All relate to single examples unless stated:

Lee, Kent – July 1868; Dartford, Kent – March 1902; Epsom, Surrey – 27 August 1945; Harrow, Middlesex – 4 October 1945; Surbiton, Surrey – a female on 11 July 1946; Box Hill, Surrey – three on 10 July 1946; Walton, Surrey – a female on 4 October 1947; Joyden's Wood, Kent – 1947; Eynsford/Shoreham area, Kent – 53 in 1947; Worcester Park, Surrey – a male on marigold blossom on 6 October 1947; Eynsford, Kent – a freshly emerged example on 23 May 1948, and male here on 30 May 1948; Lewisham, Kent – 27 August 1948; Dartford Marshes, Kent – September 1948; Walton, Surrey – a male on 27 August 1949; Bookham, Surrey – 9 July 1956; Upminster, Essex – three on 2 September 1964 and one on 5 September of the same year.

There is only one confirmed record of Berger's Clouded Yellow – a single specimen was taken at Shoreham, West Kent in 1950 (Bretherton 1987).

CLOUDED YELLOW
Colias croceus (Geoffroy)

This is one of the more regular of what can be termed the scarcer immigrants to

Britain, and it is certainly the commonest amongst the three *Colias* species. A few reach this country in most years in the spring (though not in all) and may lay eggs to produce a scattering of butterflies in the autumn. In some years however, large numbers arrive in the spring and give rise to a proportionately larger number of offspring in the autumn. Notably good years have been 1877 (known as "the year of the *edusa*" amongst collectors of the day, after the old name *Colias edusa* for the butterfly) 1947(when colossal numbers were reported between May and September) 1967 and then 1983. It seems that all the butterflies are killed off by the combination of cold and damp which is the British winter since, as the species maintains a succession of broods on the continent, there is no hibernating stage. It therefore depends entirely upon immigration to maintain its claim to a position on the British list. The earliest London area records are given by Petiver (1699) who lists Deptford and Peckham.

The most recent immigration, during 1983, produced sightings of just under three hundred individual butterflies in the London area, between the first at Battersea Park (a male) on 8 June, and the last on 4 November at Sewardstone, near Chingford in Essex (also a male). During the 1980 to 1986 period, very few records were made outside 1983, and these are now listed

1981: Headley Warren, Surrey – one on 15 August; Rye Meads, Hertfordshire – two in August;

1984: Lea Bridge, Essex/Middlesex border – one on 2 September;

The pale, almost white form *helice* Hubner of the female is said to occur in about ten per cent of the population, but this does not seem to apply to our area, where the only record from 1983 was of a singleton at Salt Box Hill, near Biggin Hill, Kent on 7 July.

The larvae are said to feed principally on lucerne *Medicago sativa*, but are also noted on clovers *Trifolium* spp. and other leguminous plants, but there is no evidence to either confirm or deny this statement for the London area.

BRIMSTONE

Gonepteryx rhamni (Linnaeus) ssp. *rhamni* (Linnaeus)

The Brimstone is the only British butterfly not a member of the family Nymphalidae which hibernates as an adult, and as a result it is often amongst the first butterflies seen in the year, appearing during the mild spells at the beginning of March, or, sometimes, as early as the end of February. The eggs are laid in May on leaves of buckthorn *Rhamnus catharticus* or alder buckthorn *Frangula alnus* where they are very easy to find. The green caterpillar feeds voraciously and pupates in July to give rise to the adult insect in late July to August.

Brimstone *Photographer: Neil Bowman*

Brimstones breed principally in the wooded areas of the southern part of London, where there is a readily available supply of buckthorn bushes. Here they are frequently a common sight in woodland glades and clearings, as well as in more open areas. They avoid the urban area completely, however, at least as a breeding species, although occasional sightings of wandering males are sometimes made, and more rarely females, such as one which appeared at the Apollo Theatre in Shaftesbury Avenue on 20 July 1977. In the north of the area they penetrate the town at Hampstead Heath and Highgate Woods, along the western side of Epping Forest, and in a rather peculiar fashion into north-west Middlesex in the region of Pinner, Northolt, Rayners Lane and on Horsenden Hill, from where they are almost joined to a north-westerly intrusion across Richmond Park, Kew Gardens and Wimbledon and Putney Commons. This distribution is not reflected in the availability of what we mere humans would regard as ideal habitat for Brimstones, nor in the distribution of either of the two foodplants. This latter factor is also somewhat of a mystery as regards the clear abundance of the species in the north of the London area where, according to the maps in Burton (1984), neither of the buckthorns is widely available. A similar situation exists in Suffolk, where the butterfly is strongest in the western-vice county where the food plant is quite widespread, but also occurs in much of East Suffolk where both foodplants are uncommon, and absent from many areas (Mendel *pers. comm.*). Whether there is an as yet undiscovered alternative foodplant, or whether the large number of sightings of both sexes in unsuitable areas represents wanderers is not clear, although larvae have twice been found on dock plants *Rumex* sp. in Hertfordshire (James 1987). There is some evidence that Brimstones hibernate away from their breeding sites in some parts of the country.

Historically, the 1899 list by Buckell and Prout gives Isleworth, Southall, Finchley, Hammersmith and Hackney as localities, though the earliest reference to the insect in our area may be the one given in Chalmers-Hunt's *Butterflies and Moths of Kent*, for the Gravesend district in 1811: Gravesend straddles the border of the London area in the eastern half. The later list by de Worms (1950) indicates that the butterfly occurred then in most of the places that it does today, except that he also included the statement that it was widely distributed round Lewisham – a fact which no longer holds true. In general terms therefore, it seems that the Brimstone has undergone little change in its status in the London area, with its distribution being limited only by the advance of the urban zone.

BLACK-VEINED WHITE

Aporia crataegi (Linnaeus)

This butterfly, which from time to time was locally common, was first mentioned as English in 1666 by Christopher Merrett, and colonies were present in most counties south of Yorkshire up until the beginning of the nineteenth century. At one stage it was considered to be a pest of orchards, as indeed it is today in parts of continental Europe. During the 1800s however, there was a severe decline: in Dorset there is no reliable record since 1815 (Thomas and Webb 1984) and it had gone from Hampshire by 1883 in spite of being present "*in thousands*" in the New Forest from 1860 to 1870 (Goater 1974). It finally petered out in this country some time during the 1920s, when it disappeared from its last known locality in East Kent, and has been officially extinct in Britain since. As far as London records are concerned, there are a few scattered in the literature. Petiver saw it only once "*in a garden", (no locality, but probably London),* and Cockerell's 1891 list for Middlesex simply states "*Isleworth, reported to Mr Fenn by Mr E.O. Myers. I know nothing further about the record*". There is no mention of the species in Buckell's and Prout's 1899 list, whilst de Worms (1950) states that "*Stephens reports it from Epping Forest in the 1850s*". Richard South, in his *The Butterflies of the British Isles* (1906) tells us that "*Authors from Haworth (1803) to Stephens (1827) mention Chelsea, ... and Muswell Hill in Middlesex, among other localities for the butterfly*". I have been unable to trace any other records.

THE "CABBAGE" WHITES

LARGE WHITE *Pieris brassicae* (Linnaeus)
SMALL WHITE *Pieris rapae* (Linnaeus)
GREEN-VEINED WHITE *Pieris napi* (Linnaeus)

These three species together are often called the "cabbage whites", though strictly speaking the Green-veined White has done little to earn this title, since only rarely are the caterpillars found on commercially grown cabbage or similar crops. Identification of the trio is a relatively easy task, though separation in flight is best left to the experienced and even then is subject to error. In spite of this however, many people do have difficulties in separating them from each other, and many reports of "cabbage white" have therefore had to be disregarded.

LARGE WHITE

Pieris brassicae (Linnaeus)

This is the largest of the white-coloured butterflies in this country, and, together with the Small White is often regarded as a serious pest of commercially grown cabbages and related plants. It is generally the more destructive of the two however, since the caterpillars feed gregariously, sometimes defoliating entire fields of crops. Apart from cultivated cabbage, other foods recorded include rape *Brassica napus*, turnip *B. rapa*, radish *Raphanus sativus*, honesty *Lunularia annua*, the garden nasturtium *Tropaeolum majus*, wild mignonette *Reseda lutea* and weld *R. luteola*. The garden nasturtium in particular, is a favourite foodplant in London, and it may be this plant, often grown in window boxes in London, together with cabbages, cauliflowers and brussels sprouts grown on allotments which allows the butterfly to penetrate into the urban zone of the London area. Whilst many of the gaps on the distribution map will doubtless be filled in due course, it is true to say that the Large White is the least common of the trio in the urban area, presumably because its feeding habits make it more likely to be sprayed with insecticide than the other pair, and that its patchy distribution here may reflect an approximation to the true situation.

There are two broods of adults each year, in April to June and then from June to October, with the two generations overlapping in most years so that the butterfly is on the wing continuously from April to October. In exceptional years there is a partial third brood. Winter is passed as a chrysalis. Records from the Butterfly Monitoring Scheme suggest that in recent years migration has played

Large White *Photographer: Michael Hammerson*

Small White *Photographer: Bryan Ceney*

little part in annual fluctuations. The seasonal appearance of the two generations of adults is very regular, and this is inconsistent with major migratory movements. It is likely that "migration years" are simply years of great abundance over large areas, when insects may disperse and fly across the English Channel from the continent to Britain and *vice versa* (Heath, Pollard and Thomas 1984). This may, however, be inconsistent with the report of over 4000 within an eight mile radius of Oxshott in 1947, in which year over 6000 Small Whites and over 3000 Green-veined Whites were seen in the same area. The year 1947 was, of course, an exceptional year for immigrant Clouded Yellows (de Worms 1950). It is a pity that this author did not give any dates in his report.

SMALL WHITE

Pieris rapae (Linnaeus)

There seems to be no part of the Capital where this butterfly is not to be found, a success which is due very largely to three factors: first, it has a much wider range of foodplants than the Large White; second it generally has solitary larvae, which allows it to feed in areas where there are only one or two plants, whereas the Large White,being gregarious would need a much greater supply of food; and third the caterpillars are well camouflaged, which presumably makes them less visible to predators than the very obvious groups of *brassicae* larvae. It is only a matter of time before the present gaps on the map in the Boroughs of Ealing, Hounslow and Richmond and around the Thames in Kent and Essex are filled: the butterflies are certainly there, and doubtless commonly so, as elsewhere in the area. A peak count of 6000 in the Oxshott area of Surrey during 1947 has already been mentioned in the discussion under Large White; more recently there were in excess of 1000 at Pett's Wood Kent on 29 July 1978.

Like the Large White, winter is spent in the pupal stage, although Small Whites tend on average to emerge about a month before the larger species, usually towards the beginning of April in London, though occasionally earlier. There are two generations per year again, but the partial third brood is also of regular occurrence in London, whereas in the Large White this is only an occasional happening. Small Whites therefore tend to be the last of the trio to be seen on the wing in a given year, with the latest record on file for London being of two at Rainham Marsh, Essex on 10 November 1984. Numbers of the second generation, in keeping with the rest of southern Britain, are generally larger than those of the first brood, which may perhaps indicate an influx of continental immigrants. On the other hand, the fact that the numbers are consistently higher, including during years when there is little other migration activity, may simply indicate that a greater survival rate to the adult stage is achieved by the offspring of the spring generation than by the overwintering summer and autumn generations.

GREEN-VEINED WHITE

Pieris napi ssp. *sabellicae* (Stephens)

Though this distinctive insect is widely distributed in the London area, and frequently quite common where it occurs, there are several initially quite surprising gaps on the distribution map. In addition there are areas where, although the butterfly is widespread, it is less than common. It would appear genuinely less able to adapt to life in the city, although it is present throughout Haringey, and in the northern parts of both Camden and Islington. There are some striking differences in the ecology of this butterfly, which seem to separate it from the Small and Large Whites. First, it tends to avoid commercially grown crops, the principal foodplants being cuckoo-flower *Cardamine pratense*, garlic mustard *Alliaria petiolata*, hedge mustard *Sisymbrium officinale* and water cress *Rorippa nasturtium-aquaticum*. All four have been reported as larval foods in our area during the survey period. Elsewhere in Britain it is reported occasionally from commercially grown crops, particularly rape *Brassica napus*. This is a plant grown extensively in the desert which is Essex, but here there are such high concentrations of pesticides in use that the butterfly is never seen in good number. Secondly, whilst it can thrive in a range of habitats, the optimum conditions in the south of England appear to be represented by damp woodland rides and wood margins, hedgerows and country lanes. There are precious few such habitats remaining in our somewhat urbanised area, but the preferences above are clearly reflected in the relative abundance of the species in the different parts of its London area range – the woodlands of Kent, Surrey and Hertfordshire provide by far the greatest populations, followed by the more "well-to-do" suburbs with their slightly larger gardens, and by various river valley systems where there remains some damp habitat containing *Cardamine pratense*. The less "well-to-do" areas with smaller gardens fare far worse, whilst in the urban zone itself the butterfly is severely restricted and, in some areas, genuinely absent. The Butterfly Monitoring Project recorded a sharp decline in numbers after the drought in 1976, and in view of the insect's predilection for damp habitats this is hardly surprising.

As with the other two "cabbage whites" the Green-veined passes the winter as a chrysalis, and emerges early in the year during March or April, depending upon the prevailing weather conditions, vying with the Small White for the earliest appearance. In most years there are two broods, with a second generation of adults from July to August. The first brood is usually over by the end of June and so, like the Small White, this insect differs from the Large White in that it cannot normally be seen continuously throughout the summer. In practice however, the gap between broods is rarely more than a fortnight, and with the variation in brood dates between years it is often difficult to relate casual sightings to a specific emergence. Normally, several of the pupae from

Green-veined White *Photographer: Neil Bowman*

the first brood of adults will lie over in this state from June until the following March/April, so in reality the second brood is only partial. In some parts of the country third broods have apparently been recorded, but there is no evidence to suggest this is the case in the London Natural History Society area, with the butterflies being finished by the end of the first week of September in most years.

BATH WHITE

Pontia daplidice (Linnaeus)

The Bath White is an extremely rare immigrant to Britain. Prior to 1945, only about sixty examples had been reported in Britain, but in that year some 650 individual sightings were made, of which thirteen affected the London area. Outside this year, there are only four records including one at Feltham on 21 April 1946. In view of the very early date of this record, and of the fact that the previous year was the one in which the insect arrived in quantity, there is just a possibility that this represented a hibernated individual. The records are as follows:

1894: One at Addington, Surrey
1918: A male at Watford;
1921: One at St Albans, Hertfordshire;
1945: Epsom Downs, Surrey – a female on 15 July and another on 17 July; Tattenham Corner, Surrey – one each on 20 and 23 July; Hounslow, Middlesex – one on 8 August; North Downs between Wrotham and Eynsford, Kent – seven at the end of July;
1946: Feltham, Middlesex – one on 21 April.

A summary of the 1945 immigration can be found in Danreuther (1946).

Superficially, the Bath White resembles the female Orange-tip, and inexperienced observers sometimes make this mistake. A close examination of the Bath White however, will reveal that the black tips to the fore wing contain a patch of white, a feature quite unknown in the female Orange-tip. There are other differences, less easy to see, including the presence of white in the discal spot on the upper forewings, and a far denser green mottling on the underside of the hindwings (though this last feature is variable and of value only to the experienced).

ORANGE-TIP

Anthocharis cardamines ssp. *britannica* Verity

This is perhaps the most attractive of all our smaller British butterflies, particularly the male, with its bright orange patches at the tips of the forewings, a feature which is quite lacking in the female. It is a common sight in open woodland and along hedges and lanes over much of the British Isles (Heath, Pollard and Thomas 1984). It has a variety of food plants, in which are included thirty-three species of Cruciferae and two of the closely related Resedaceae (Courtney 1982), but of these two, cuckoo-flower *Cardamine pratense* and garlic mustard *Alliaria petiolata* are reportedly used by most individuals. In the London area, larvae have been found on both these plants and on hedge mustard *Sisymbrium officinale*, but not on other species in a truly wild situation, although it is most likely that other plants are used in this area. In suburban gardens there are several reported colonies of Orange-tips on sweet rocket *Hesperis matronalis*, the favoured and often reported foodplant for captive

Orange-tip *Photographer: Neil Bowman*

breeding. It would appear, however, that many of these colonies stem from introductions, and generally speaking the butterfly is not able to arrive and thrive naturally in most gardens.

Adult Orange-tips are on the wing from the end of April in a good year in the London area, with the earliest recorded date here being 26 April, though the first ten days of May are more normal. This early emergence, combined with their almost complete invisibility when sitting wings folded on the flowering heads of garlic mustard or similar plants, means that there are doubtless areas from which the butterfly has still to be recorded, particularly in the south. This apart, the distribution map presented here reflects the general situation, with the insect quite clearly avoiding the urban zone. The eggs are generally laid on a flower-head of the foodplant during May, and rapidly assume a bright orange colour which is very easy to spot. They hatch after about a week, and after eating the eggshell, the caterpillar feeds on the seed-pods. They are actively cannibalistic, as many a disappointed child has discovered to his cost, and there is seldom more than one survivor per flower head! After about four weeks the chrysalis, which may be either brown or green, is formed on the stem of an adjacent plant, and in this stage the butterfly passes the winter before emerging in the spring. The chrysalis bears a striking resemblance to the withered seed pods of the foodplant, yet despite this apparent camouflage it generally pupates on a more substantial stem of a different species of plant a short distance away.

This makes good sense, particularly if it is feeding on *Cardamine pratense* which tends to grow in damp situations: it would be a disaster if, half way through the winter, the stem supporting the pupa was to wither and descend into the water! The adult butterfly is normally finished by the end of June, exceptionally July, and is single-brooded only.

Old records in our area include Old Oak Common, Mill Hill, Stamford Hill, Tottenham, Isleworth and Bedford Park, all in Middlesex (Cockerell 1891) and in the 1899 list by Buckell and Prout from Tottenham, Lee Valley, Hackney Marshes, Chingford, Muswell Hill, Finchley, Highgate and Hampstead. De Worms (1950) records it as having been seen in all parts of the London district including Lewisham and Greenwich Park from which areas it seems to be absent today. The first British record was made by Petiver (1699) who gave the sexes different names, the white marbled male butterfly and the white marbled female butterfly. It is likely that his specimens were collected from the London area but I have not yet been able to check the labels to confirm this. Specimens at the British Museum (Natural History) taken by Leonard Plunkenet, the Queen's Botanist, between May 1696 and May 1697, were almost certainly from the Palace garden.The first written record of the Orange-tip from our area, however, did not appear until 1795, when Lewin, in his *Insects of Great Britain* stated that "*I have bred these elegant little butterflies from caterpillars taken off the green iole in my garden*". His garden was at Darenth. It is likely that earlier authors thought the species too common to warrant locality data!

The Orange-tip is particularly sensitive to the spring-time "tidying" of road-side verges which local authorities seem to have been so keen on in recent years. This over-zealous activity destroys the eggs and caterpillars in one of their favoured habitats. Another threat to the future of this butterfly is the drainage of damp areas for "development", which destroys the habitat of the cuckoo flower.

GREEN HAIRSTREAK

Callophrys rubi (Linnaeus)

Although this is reportedly the commonest and most widely spread of our British hairstreaks, in the London area the Green Hairstreak is far from either of these descriptions. An examination of the map will, at a glance, show that it is restricted principally to the Surrey region, with odd records at Mitcham Common in Merton and at Beddington in Sutton, with fewer records in the Kent sector. North of the Thames there are scattered colonies in Hertfordshire, at Hainault Forest in South Essex, and isolated spots in Ealing. At none of these sites is it a particularly numerous butterfly, though there are, of course, variations in colony sizes from year to year. The spot in tetrad 27T68 relates to a most unexpected sighting of an adult which alighted on a pedestrian waiting to cross Exhibition Road, SW7 at its junction with Thurloe Place, on 6 May 1987. Luckily for us, the event was witnessed by a member of the entomological staff at the British Museum (Natural History) who gave chase and was subsequently able to examine the insect closely (M. Honey *pers. comm.*). Marking experiments conducted by other workers away from the London area seem to indicate that typical Green Hairstreak colonies are very localised, and contain in the order of ten to twenty males, and an equal number of females (Heath, Pollard and Thomas 1984). The males are very territorial, rising to challenge any passing butterfly from a suitable high vantage point on a bush, to which they will then return, if not usurped in the meantime by another male.

Green Hairstreak *Photographer: Ian G. Johnson*

The past distribution of this species is relatively easy to trace and not without interest. Cockerell (1891) gave only one record of one individual for the County of Middlesex – at Acton Lane, on the Acton side of Old Oak Common. This could be in either 28T02 or 18T82, but either way ties in very nicely with the present pair of colonies in Ealing, indicating that there has probably been a population here for at least a century. Later, the 1899 list by Buckell and Prout has this species as "*very scarce: Croydon?*". It must be remembered however that their area was a smaller circle of ten miles radius, not twenty, and based upon

Charing Cross as the centre. This effectively excludes most of the presently recorded colonies in any case, and it is not the only instance where records published by Cockerell only eight years earlier have been either missed or disregarded by these two authors.

Amongst the localities mentioned by de Worms in his 1950 list, are Ealing in Middlesex, Joyden's Wood and the Shoreham/Eynsford area of Kent, Broxbourne in Hertfordshire and in Surrey at Box Hill and Epsom. The butterfly still persists at these localities. A number of other sites given by de Worms however, have not yielded the butterfly during the present survey. These are Northolt in Middlesex, Pett's Wood, Greenwich Park and "*the Lewisham area*" in the Kent sector, Purfleet in Essex, and Richmond Park, Ham Common and Surbiton Golf Course in Surrey. With the possible exception of Lewisham and Greenwich Park, there seems no reason to suppose that Green Hairstreaks could not still persist at these sites, and diligent searching at the appropriate season may well prove fruitfiul.

On a national scale, typical sites for this butterfly vary from unimproved calcareous grassland, to acid heaths, moors and bogs. One constant feature, however, seems to be that "shrubs" are always present (Heath, Pollard and Thomas 1984). In the London area all known colonies are associated with a woodland-edge habitat, although the quality and type of the woodland seems to be of little importance. The principal foodplant on calcareous grassland is said to be the common rockrose *Helianthemum chamaecistus*, which is distributed as a solid band across the south and south-east of the London area (Burton 1983). Not withstanding this, the available information from our area indicates that gorse *Ulex europaeus* and broom *Sarothamnus scoparius* are the two plants used by most colonies. Elsewhere, other foodplants include dwarf gorse *Ulex galii*, bird's-foot trefoil *Lotus corniculatus*, dyer's greenweed *Genista tinctoria*, whortleberry *Vaccinium myrtillus*, berries of buckthorn *Rhamnus catharticus*, buds of dogwood *Cornus sanguinea* and of bramble *Rubus fruticosus*. It is worth noting that whichever pabulum a given colony utilises, it will be unlikely to transfer to an alternative should the first be removed, and this makes the small, very isolated colonies extremely susceptible to threats posed by various human activities.

The green eggs are laid singly during June, and hatch after about a week. The caterpillars are solitary, and feed very quickly; they are cannibalistic after the first moult. Once fully fed, they descend to the ground and generally pupate unprotected amongst litter, quite unattached to any support. They are almost always then taken underground by ants, as are many other lycaenid butterfly pupae, although the reasons for this are unclear in this species. It is likely, however, that a pupa remaining on the surface would either succumb to frost or else be eaten by a predator, in spite of its renowned ability to "squeak". Following the winter, there is a protracted emergence from mid-May to the end of June, with 26 June being the latest date recorded in our area.

Brown Hairstreak *Photographer: Michael Hammerson*

BROWN HAIRSTREAK

Thecla betulae (Linnaeus)

The Brown Hairstreak is a very rare butterfly in the London area, and according to the available information has always been so. The national situation was discussed by Heath, Pollard and Thomas (1984) and the butterfly was said by them to have a wide southerly distribution, but to be none the less scarce, and mainly confined to localities which have heavy soils and high densities of woodland and hedgerows. The caterpillars appear to be totally restricted to blackthorn *Prunus spinosa*, particularly where this forms dense patches.

Benjamin Harris took a specimen at Croydon on 31 August 1702 (which becomes 11 September on conversion of the calendar) this being recorded by Petiver in 1703. Petiver named the sexes the brown double streak and the golden double streak, which he altered to the brown hairstreak and the golden hairstreak in 1717. He got the sexes the wrong way round having assumed that the male would be the more brightly coloured! The 1891 list by Cockerell makes no mention of the Brown Hairstreak for Middlesex, and the work by Buckell and Prout eight years later is similarly lacking. For Kent, Curtis (1824) and Newman

(1869) both list "*Birch Wood*", whilst Stephens (1828) gives Darenth Wood (no date) and Dartford in 1852. Chalmers-Hunt (1961) gives Farnborough in 1946 and Cudham in 1953, and in his 1979 *Supplement* to this work states that "*The Brown Hairstreak has been assiduously searched for since it was last seen in 1971, and may be presumed now to be no longer present in the county*". He continues to say that destruction of its foodplant was undoubtedly a contributory factor, but a natural contraction of range was perhaps the main cause of the decrease. There is no London area record in Foster's *Lepidoptera of Hertfordshire* (1937) and indeed he gives only three localities for the entire county – none of them recent. De Worms' 1950 list states only that it was recorded from the latter end of the last century from Epping Forest. It is here that one of the present-day colonies can be found. There are one or two present-day colonies outside our area in Buckinghamshire (Steel and Steel 1985) whilst in Essex there is only one other locality outside the Epping Forest site listed in the present work (Emmet, Pyman and Corke 1985).

The four dots on the distribution map represent two confirmed breeding colonies, and one positive sighting. A further unconfirmed sighting is not mapped. To deal with these in reverse order, there was a reported sighting of an adult on a flower of *Angelica* at Ickenham (08T64) adjacent to the A.40 road just north of Uxbridge Common, during July 1983. This seems a little early for a butterfly which generally does not appear until August, though 1983 was an excellent year from the point of view of weather, and the date is not impossible. I was unable to visit the site until April 1986, when in the company of Dr A.M. George I searched for the normally obvious white eggs on the blackthorn twigs. No such signs were found, and although under normal circumstances April would have been too late for such a search, the spring of 1986 was so late in arriving in that particular year that any Brown Hairstreak eggs would almost certainly not yet have hatched. It is not impossible, however, that the sighting may still be verified.

The positive sighting was made at Wimbledon Common on 31 August 1986 when one or possibly two were seen. Quite independently, another Brown Hairstreak was reported by a different observer also during July of 1986, and this may therefore indicate that there is a colony on the blackthorn bushes here.

The two confirmed colonies exist at Epping Forest in Essex (spread thinly over two tetrads) and at Bricketwood Common in Hertfordshire. It is sad to note that since the Epping Forest colony was first reported it has apparently been visited by a number of entomologists who have taken away twigs bearing the eggs, presumably to breed adults for the cabinet. This has resulted in a severe depletion of the colony to the point where it is now in a most precarious state, and collectors are urged to visit more established sites such as those in the Oxford area where the butterfly is numerous, rather than risking the extinction of a butterfly so rare in this region. The Bricketwood Common colony, first noted in 1954, and rediscovered in 1984, is equally precarious.

Adult butterflies are normally on the wing during August, and lay eggs singly in the forks of twigs on small blackthorn bushes. The eggs do not hatch until April or May. The caterpillar, which resembles a green woodlouse, rests on the underside of a blackthorn leaf and is difficult to spot. It pupates after about ten weeks and the adult emerges from the pupal case about three weeks later. One of the greatest threats to the continued survival of the Brown Hairstreak in general is the winter pruning of hedges, which removes the overwintering eggs, particularly when coupled with the burning of the trimmings. In the London sites, however, this is not a real problem, since the colonies are not in hedgerow situations. The Ickenham site, however, is scheduled to vanish under a road-widening scheme, and indeed may have already disappeared by the time this work is published.

PURPLE HAIRSTREAK

Quercusia quercus (Linnaeus)

Although on a national level the Green Hairstreak is the more widely spread of the five British hairstreaks, in the London area it is the Purple Hairstreak which occurs in the greater number of localities, and it is frequently in abundance. It is an attractive species, occurring in a number of woodland areas, although a prerequisite is the presence of oak trees. This requirement usually manifests itself in the presence of a number of trees together, although in some places a single large oak tree can support an isolated colony of this butterfly, as is the case in Battersea Park. Mill Hill and Croydon are the localities given by Cockerell and Buckell and Prout respectively: the former apparently indicating another example of a single tree supporting a colony ("*one larva beaten from an oak in the garden*"). The earliest London record however, appears to be that of Moses Harris, who, writing in 1766 stated that Purple Hairstreaks "*... are commonly taken in plenty on Oak-of-Honour Wood, near Peckham, in Surry*". Foster's 1937 Hertfordshire list indicates a healthy abundance in the woods of the South Hertfordshire Plateau, whilst de Worms (1950) indicated a situation much the same as the one we have today, with a widespread distribution in the woodlands containing oak around the more rural parts of the London area, and with a penetration into that zone wherever the presence of oak trees permits. It is missing on the present maps from Darenth Wood and Joyden's Wood, both of which were listed as localities by de Worms, and from Lewisham. At the latter locality it is almost certainly genuinely absent, there being little in the way of suitable habitat(?) whilst the extensive coniferisation of Joyden's Wood may have had the same effect here. At Darenth Wood, its omission from the current list must surely be due to inadequate searching. Adult butterflies can indeed be most difficult to spot, unless the observer is tuned in to the fact that their flight area is the very tops of tall oak trees, and not at human eye level! On a suitably sunny day during July or August, when the wind is at a minimum, they often can be seen in quite large "swarms" in this situation, well beyond the reach of the average butterfly net. If this seems too difficult, then the winter months can be equally productive, as the whitish eggs are generally extremely obvious, being laid singly either on the buds of the oak tree, or else in a fork of a smaller twig of the tree, in the manner adopted by the Brown Hairstreak on blackthorn bushes.

The timing of the hatching of Purple Hairstreak eggs is something of a mystery, since they coincide this event with the bursting of the oak buds on the tree on which they are laid. Presumably some form of chemical stimulus is involved. This event generally occurs during the month of April. The first instar is spent inside the leaf-bud of the oak tree, feeding on the immature leaves within, but after the first skin is shed, it feeds externally, resting on the bud, and looking to all intent and purpose like one of the bud scales. As such they are exceedingly well camouflaged amongst the debris which collects in the beating-tray, and if one is employing this method of searching it is wise to dwell a little longer than usual after each examination and look for the scales which start to crawl away after several minutes have elapsed.

The loss of woodland through coniferisation and felling is a major threat to the survival of the Purple Hairstreak. In the London area, however, apart from the loss of woodland altogether in the name of "development", there is a more insidious danger in the form of the sycamore tree *Acer pseudoplatanus*, whose highly competitive growth and colossal fecundity effectively prevents regeneration of oaks in a woodland system. This will, without a shadow of doubt, ultimately lead to the loss of oaks, as well as other native species, from the woodland system as mature trees eventually die, and in its turn this would involve the loss of this particular species of butterfly.

WHITE-LETTER HAIRSTREAK

Strymonidia w-album (Knoch)

The Latin name of this little butterfly derives from the fact that the underside of the hind wings are marked with a white letter "W". From above it is essentially "a little brown job", and frankly rather uninteresting in appearance. Its principal food has been said by most authors to be the wych elm *Ulmus glabra*, and whilst this may or may not have been the case elsewhere, it certainly does not apply to the London area, where almost invariably the English elm *Ulmus procera* is chosen. Not surprisingly, the butterfly declined drastically during the 1970's as

White-letter Hairstreak *Photographer: Paul Thompson*

a direct result of the loss of elm trees from the English landscape through Dutch elm disease.

It would appear, however, that the White-letter Hairstreak has always been an uncommon butterfly in the London area. It gains no mention at all in either of the two early lists by Cockerell or Buckell and Prout, and de Worms' 1950 list gives only eight localities, at Box Hill in Surrey, Brentwood in South Essex, Watford and Broxbourne in Hertfordshire, and Shoreham, Eynsford, Darenth Wood and Holwood Park in Kent. The present distribution map shows it to be currently absent from all those localities apart form Watford, although there are records at 46T20 and 46T42, which surround Holwood Park in 46T22/24, and may in fact represent the survivors from that colony. Some additional former localities are given in the 1937 list by Foster, who notes Cheshunt, Haileybury, Watford (again), Symond's Hyde, Bushey Heath, Broxbourne Woods and Waltham Cross. Watford has already been mentioned, but apart from a record in Balls Wood during 1980 (in the same tetrad as Haileybury at 31T40) there are no current records from any of these sites either. A number of records are also given for Kent by Chalmers-Hunt (1961). The pattern which emerges, therefore, is one of a butterfly which has always been very local in its occurrence in the London area, and which has apparently became extinct in many of its traditional sites.

What is more interesting, however, is the reappearance of this butterfly in sites other than those already reported above, from which it vanished during the height of the Dutch elm disease episode. At the High Elms SSSI in Orpington, for example, it apparently virtually vanished from 1968 to 1981, when it suddenly appeared again, and where it now continues to maintain a slow but steady comeback. This pattern is repeated at many of the other current localities. Indeed, it is questionable whether or not the old colonies did in fact die out, and that we are now seeing a recolonisation by outsider hairsteaks, or whether the population crashed to such an extremely low level that it simply remained undetected by human animals until its level had started to rebuild. Some evidence to support the latter theory, which, in view of the extremely wide scale of the butterfly's demise seems the most likely, comes in the form of a small but nevertheless continuing colony in Battersea Park (27T86) where the insects have thrived for at least forty years on three mature specimens of Exeter Elm, a cultivar of the wych elm known as *exoniensis.* It seems highly probable that the small colony on Wimbledon Common is also a survivor, and likewise another at Trent Country Park in Hertfordshire.

Not all of the dots on the map represent breeding colonies however. Indeed, apart from the sites already mentioned, there are breeding records only from Park Street (10T44) Balls Wood (31T40) and in the Ruislip area at 08T68, 08T48 and 09T40, the other dots relating largely to casual sightings of adult butterflies.

The adult butterflies are on the wing from July to August, and are particularly attracted to creeping thistle *Cirsium arvense* and bramble flowers, where they often seem to be so engrossed in sipping nectar that photography is a relatively simple exercise. The eggs are laid singly on the elm twigs, usually at the junction of the present year's growth with the previous year's . Each egg remains there until the following March or April, when the caterpillar hatches and typically starts to feed inside the flower buds. As the season wears on, it converts to feeding on the ripening seeds, and only in its later instars does it eat the leaves of the tree. On elm suckers in the London area, which do not usually flower, it has been beaten from the leaves in its early stages, which suggests that in such instances it must begin feeding on the leaves straight away, presumably on the tender newly formed ones. Pupation usually takes place during June, with the chrysalis attaching itself to the elm tree, and the butterfly emerges after about twenty-eight days.

SMALL COPPER

Lycaena phlaeas (Linnaeus) ssp. *eleus* (Fabricius)

The Small Copper is a quite surprising butterfly. Several years can elapse in some parts of the London area with very few, or even none, being seen, then all of a sudden there is a tremendous population explosion and the butterfly is seen

Small Copper — *Photographer: Frank W. Lockwood*

here, there and everywhere. In a good year the adult can appear as early as mid-April, with 14 April the earliest recorded during our survey, in 1983. It is not unusual for it to attain three broods of adults in a single year (though the third brood is usually a partial one with many larvae lying over to pupate in March of the next year) with adults appearing in May/June, again from late June to early September and then from mid-August to early October. With all three broods overlapping it is difficult to separate the adults out in the field. In truly exceptional years there may be a fourth brood, giving rise to adults from October to, rarely, as late as the first week of November. This is presumably the source of the single adult noted near Hainault Forest, South Essex, on 7 December 1984, since the winter is passed as a caterpillar, and not as an hibernating adult (though Moses Harris (1766) was misled into supposing that the adult *did* hibernate). The caterpillars will feed on either sheep's sorrel *Rumex acetosella* or common sorrel *R. acetosa*, and both have been recorded in use by the insects in the London area.

A study of the distribution map, presented here for the period from 1980 to 1986, indicates that the Small Copper is a widespread butterfly throughout much of the London area. It is one of a select band of butterflies that is equally at home in a largely urban environment as it is in more pastoral settings, and much of this success is due to its liking for sheep's sorrel, which is far more adaptable at growing on urban "waste" sites than the common sorrel, which much prefers more of a grassland habitat. Haringey, Islington, Hackney and Tower Hamlets are all fairly "built-up" boroughs that are well blessed with Small Coppers, and it is even present in the northern end of Southwark, as well as central Lewisham. Not withstanding this it remains unrecorded from a number of similar areas. There are few records, for example, from Wandsworth, only one from Hammersmith and Fulham, whilst there are none at all from Lambeth, Westminster and Kensington and Chelsea. These five boroughs, together with the north-western portion of Southwark, seem to form a block from which the butterfly may possibly be genuinely absent. In other areas where gaps are apparent it is more likely that under-recording has been responsible. The gap in Croydon is most surprising.

[LARGE COPPER

Lycaena dispar (Haworth) ssp. *dispar* (Haworth)

Evidence for the existence of the Large Copper as a former insect of the North Kent Marshes is slender. According to Chalmers-Hunt (1961) the diary of C. & J. Fenn for 13 February 1862 has the entry "*We noticed a specimen of* C. hippothoe *said to have been taken at Eltham*". This refers to an examination of the Laing collection. It is considered by the present author that *hippothoe* sensu Lewin was intended (a name synonymous with *dispar* of Haworth) rather than *hippothoe* of Linnaeus. It has been suggested to me (Emmet *pers. comm.*) that the name *hippothoe* was not generally used for the large copper after Haworth's application of *dispar* in 1803. Whilst this is undoubtedly correct, Coleman (1890) considered the British Large copper to be nothing more than a local variety of the Continental species *hippothoe*. This seems to me to be adequate evidence that the Large Copper was intended. Later, in 1893, C. Fenn reported to a meeting of the South London Entomological Society that he had heard of specimens of *Lycaena dispar* from Shooters Hill Wood, near Woolwich. There is no real reason why the Large Copper should not once have been a feature of the Thames marshes, but it is strange that these are the only records for an area so close to London and all its famous entomologists. Accordingly, this species must remain in square brackets for the time being.]

LONG-TAILED BLUE

Lampides boeticus (Linnaeus)

The Long-tailed Blue is a resident of much of the "Old World", including all of Europe south of about latitude 47 degrees north. North of this line it is a regular migrant, but there are surprisingly few records for Britain. The best year was

1945, when thirty-one were reported, although only five of these related to the London area. In all there are sixteen London area records, of which two can be regarded as introductions, the rest as primary immigrants. The probable importations are from Sutton, Surrey on 15 September 1979, and at the cargo area of Heathrow Airport on 16 September 1980. This latter individual was a gravid female which, upon being released at Portland Bill Bird Observatory a few days later, promptly laid eggs. The immigrant records are as follows:

> Dartford, Kent – 17 September 1893; Woolwich, Kent – 29 September 1898: Greenford, Kent – 24 July 1945; Epsom Station, Surrey – four on 27 August 1945; Streatham, Surrey – 7 September 1949; Wimbledon Common, Surrey – 3 October 1950; Finchley, Middlesex – 18 October 1967; Wisley, Surrey – 4 September 1971; Eltham, Kent – 15 September 1974; Surbiton, Surrey – 29 July 1977; Surrey Docks, Surrey – 26 August 1980;

All records are of single adult butterflies unless stated otherwise.

Long-tailed Blue *Photographer: Ray Softly*

[BROWN PLAYBOY

Hypokopelates antalus (Hopffer)

There is a single record of this African "blue" butterfly: a female was spotted on flowers of *Sedum spectabile* in Twickenham on 17 September 1974 and passed to the Natural History Museum where it was identified. Here it was kept alive, but died without producing any eggs. There would, however, appear to be no question of this being a primary immigrant, and it is much more likely that a chrysalis was imported with some produce of southern or tropical Africa which is the insect's true home. It is quite similar in appearance to the Long-tailed Blue.]

SMALL BLUE

Cupido minimus (Fuessly)

At first glance, the Small Blue, our smallest British butterfly, may not be regarded as a "blue" at all, since neither sex is of that colouration. The males are a dark brown, almost black colour, with a sprinkling of metallic blue scales which may be sparse in insects that have been on the wing for some time, whilst the females are a fairly uniform dull brown without any such adornments. Their undersides, on the other hand, readily give the game away, displaying their own particular variation on the typical "blue" pattern. They are insects of the chalk or limestone in this country, and are totally dependent upon the kidney vetch *Anthyllis vulneraria* on whose flowers they lay their distinctive pale blue eggs. They are usually single-brooded, though in good years there is a partial second brood, such as during 1984 on Banstead Downs when two were seen on 11 August.

In the London area they are confined, as a breeding species, to a few areas along the North Downs in Surrey, both in grassland sites and disused quarries, and we have located a total of eighteen known colonies for the study period from 1980 to 1986. These are all in the south of the area, and all in the Surrey vice-county. It is perhaps directly advantageous to the butterflies that they invariably occur in extremely confined areas, forming discrete, and often totally isolated colonies, which persist at the same small spot for many years. Thus, whilst the downs as a whole are becoming generally less and less suitable for the butterflies which depend upon them, as long as the particular pocket in which the colony persists is not affected, either directly or indirectly, the species will continue to survive. Sadly, this applies to few other species! The two tetrad records away from here relate to single individuals reliably reported from the canal bank to the west of Harefield Village (09T40) on 2 June 1984, and near Cole Green, Hertfordshire (31T00) during the same year. The nearest known colony to this last record is some ten kilometres away to the north, whilst to the west of the Harefield area, Steel and Steel (1985) record a presence in the adjacent centad SU 99.

Small Blue *Photographer: Bryan Ceney*

Of the breeding colonies, however, most are on south-facing slopes of the North Downs, or in depressions or excavations which act as "sun-traps". As expected, kidney vetch grows in reasonable quantity, though its presence seems to have been missed by Burton (1983) in 25T48, 16T80, 35T08, and 36T20. Colony sizes vary, and at most there has been no specific effort to make total counts. Three distinct colonies in the vicinity of Epsom Downs Station produced about twenty, about one hundred and around thirty individuals when counted in June 1984. There were about fifty at Banstead Downs on 18 June 1984, whilst during the same year, larvae were reported as "*abundant*" at Epsom Common. At Hutchinson's Bank, there were at least twenty when counted in July 1985. At Headley Warren numbers attain fifty in some years. Riddlesdown Quarry yielded some twenty to thirty adults in June 1984, although numbers may have temporarily declined in the two years since: this is the largest colony known within the area covered by the London boroughs.

There is an old record for Croydon given in Buckell and Prout's 1899 list, though not surprisingly, the earlier list for Middlesex by Cockerell makes no mention of this species. Foster (1937) gives Hertford as a former locality, and credits the record to J.F. Stephens' *Illustrations of British Entomology* produced between 1828 and 1834. Baron de Worms' list in 1950 makes mention of the downs at Epsom, Mickleham and Banstead, also recorded in the present survey, and also at Chipstead Downs and in the area around Eynsford and Shoreham, Kent, which localities have not displayed this species during the present work. There was a colony near Kenley in the mid 1960s, and Chalmers-Hunt (1979) lists Downe Golf Course (46T20) where three were seen in May 1979, Cudham (45T48) where a small colony of the butterfly was flourished but has not been seen since 1977, and between Shoreham and Otford (56T00 and/or 55T08) where there were two on 2 July 1977. In view of the habits of this butterfly it is likely that a few more colonies will be discovered along the line of the North Downs in the southern part of our area, though probably not many.

SILVER-STUDDED BLUE

Plebejus argus (Linnaeus)

This is one of our more variable butterflies, though the status of some of the various forms is a debatable point. Three extreme forms have been elevated to subspecific status in this country, with ssp. *masseyi* Tutt formerly in Lancashire and Westmorland, ssp. *caernensis* Thompson in North Wales, and ssp. *argus* Linnaeus elsewhere, including the south-east. Those colonies of ssp. *argus* which occur on the chalk grasslands of southern England are usually referable to a *race* known as *cretaceus* Tutt, though this form is elevated to the rank of subspecies by Kloet and Hincks (1972), an action clearly also acceptable to many other workers. The butterfly is absent from Scotland and Ireland.

Both the subspecies *argus* and *cretaceus* have occurred in the London area. In Surrey, the dominant form appears to have been *argus*, to which de Worms (1950) alludes as "*the smaller heathland race*". It was reported as "*occurring freely on the large tract of heathland around Oxshott, where a strong colony flourishes and was numerous in 1948*". De Worms also records it as being locally plentiful at that period on Wisley Common, and notes one seen on Surbiton Golf Course in 1943. During 1969, a few were seen at St George's Hill Weybridge (de Worms 1970). In the Middlesex area, Tutt (1909) recorded subspecies *argus* from Scratch Wood, Edgeware, Harrow and Ruislip, though they had long since vanished from here even at the time when de Worms was writing in 1950. From the Essex sector, there was a colony at Brentwood in 1949, and the butterfly was

Silver-Studded Blue *Photographer: Andrew Merritt*

certainly present in the Epping area of Epping Forest in the 1830s. In 1953, a colony of ssp. *cretaceus* was located in Grays Chalk Quarry, now a Site of Special Scientific Interest (SSSI). This is particularly interesting, since it represents the only record of the chalk subspecies north of The Thames (Emmet, Pyman and Corke 1985). Sadly this colony died out in about 1960.

De Worms reported the subspecies *cretaceus* as common in 1947 on the Downs at Eynsford, Otford, Magpie Bottom and round Wrotham, whilst many former localities are given by Chalmers-Hunt (1961). The demise of *cretaceus* in Kent, where this was the dominant form, has been chronicled by Chalmers-Hunt (1979). Up until about 1950, there were many colonies in both of the Kent vice-counties. Soon after, the insect went into decline, probably indirectly from the effects of myxomatosis, and in most colonies it became extinct, and in a number of others was completely annihilated owing to the destruction of the habitat, as at Badgers Mount, where it was plentiful in 1962, and where the site was planted with conifers and is now partly buried under the M.25 motorway, and at Biggin Hill where the ground was cleared for grazing horses. It was last reported in Kent in 1966. It seems likely that the subspecies *cretaceus* is now in fact extinct in the whole of Britain, though there are some less extreme forms in Dorset (R.N. Hobbs, *pers. comm.*).

There are no confirmed record of the heathland race *argus* in Kent for nearly fifty years. The record of a Silver-studded Blue at Downe, reported by de Worms (*London Naturalist* **57**:83), is an error, based on a misidentification.

Against this depressing background picture of a rapidly declining butterfly, only two localities were detected during the present survey – at Epsom Downs (25T08) and at Fairmile Common (16T00).

At Epsom Downs, the butterfly was reported in 1982 – "*On a sandy stretch of Epsom Downs,* Plebejus argus *may be found in some profusion in June, July and August.*" R.N. Hobbs visited the site in 1984, and found no sign of this butterfly (though larvae of the Small Blue were abundant) and subsequent searches made by a number of other entomologists have also failed to locate any signs of a colony. Sadly, therefore, we must presume it extinct at this locality. The "sandy" habitat would indicate that the heathland form *argus* was involved.

At Fairmile Common, a small area of heathland trapped between the A.3 trunk road and the A.307 Esher to Cobham road supported two fair-sized colonies of the heathland form of the Silver-studded Blue during 1986. A variety of foodplants are present, including gorse, dwarf gorse, broom and bird's-foot trefoil, though it is not known which are being used. The area is used for a variety of human leisure activities, including the flying of model aircraft, although this itself may pose little threat provided the vegetation is not cleared. On the other hand, the site is likely to undergo substantial development in the near future, which could involve construction of a roadway to give access to a newly completed bridge across the A.3 road. Approximate counts of the butterflies made on 27 July 1986 yielded twenty to thirty males and ten to twenty females in one colony, and a slightly greater number of males in company with an equal number of females in the other. In view of the fact that all the known former localities have been thoroughly searched to no avail, it seems likely that the Fairmile colony is the only remaining colony of Silver-studded Blue in the London area. It further seems likely, that unless very urgent action is taken to safeguard this site, the butterfly will shortly become extinct within the London area.

BROWN ARGUS

Aricia agestis (Denis & Schiffermüller)

The Brown Argus is commonest in Britain on calcareous soils, particularly on chalk and limestone downs. Other colonies breed on sand-dunes and heaths, often in quite acid environmental conditions. A very few colonies breed on heavy clay soils. It is commonest in open grassland, but is usually very localised, and often in low numbers where it occurs. Because of this split in habitats, two separate larval food-plants are involved, with those colonies on calcareous grassland usually utilising common rockrose *Helianthemum chamaecistus*, and those in non-calcareous areas feeding on stork's-bill *Erodium cicutarium*.

Brown Argus *Photographer: Neil Bowman*

In the London area, the Brown Argus has undergone a major decline in recent years. Cockerell listed it from Mill Hill, Middlesex in 1875, and from Isleworth. The 1899 list by Buckell and Prout gives Lee in Kent (Lewisham) and Croydon and Dulwich in Surrey. For Hertfordshire, Foster's 1937 list contributes Bricket Wood, Hertford, Watford, Haileybury, Symond's Hyde, Chorley Wood and Broxbourne in our area, whilst in 1950 de Worms listed Northwood and Chorley Wood under Middlesex, Epping Forest in Essex, Banstead, Epsom, Box Hill, Caterham and Surbiton Golf Course in Surrey, and near West Wickham, Sundridge Park, Joyden's Wood, Shoreham, Eynsford, and Darenth Wood in Kent, adding a sighting at Wimbledon Common during 1950 in his 1959 Supplement. Apart from isolated colonies at Banstead, Box Hill, Shoreham, Eynsford and "near" West Wickham, all of these reported colonies appear to have become extinct. There were also several colonies in the Purfleet area of Essex during the 1940s, where the M.25 motorway now runs down to the Dartford Tunnel, the larvae feeding on stork's-bill, but it certainly no longer exists there.

With one exception the present-day colonies of Brown Argus in the London area are confined to the Kent and Surrey vice-counties. The single exception relates to an apparently isolated colony at Stanstead Abbots Gravel Pit, where over twenty were seen during 1985. Whether or not this colony is truly isolated remains to be seen. It is possible that the butterfly has been misidentified in some areas as females of the Common Blue, which are, of course, largely brown, though this mistake is only likely if the insects were not captured. It seems quite possible that further colonies, though probably widely scattered and extremely localised, may be discovered in due course both in this part of Hertfordshire and in South Essex. In the south of the area, however, it is far more likely that additional colonies will be found, particularly on the chalk downs. It is of note perhaps, that in two of the tetrads where the butterfly occurs (46T04 and 46T26) the common rockrose is apparently not recorded, and one must assume that stork's-bill, which is present, is being used by the larvae. Barring major alterations to the habitat, the Brown Argus does not appear to be under any threat in the southern part of the London area, though it is seldom numerous. It is reported that dove's-foot crane's-bill *Geranium molle* may be a substitute foodplant in areas where the other two are absent, though there is no evidence from the present survey to support this.

The Brown Argus is generally a double-brooded insect. The overwintering larvae awaken in April and feed again, pupating in late April or May,to give rise to the first generation of adults in May to June. These lay their eggs singly on the underside of a leaf, and they hatch within a week. The larva feeds at first underneath the foliage, but later eating entire leaves. It is constantly attended by ants, who "milk" it of its "honey", and it is thought that such attention by ants is essential to the caterpillar's survival. After four moults, the caterpillar pupates during July, attached to the base of the foodplant, and the second generation of adults emerges in late July or August, and remain in evidence until early September. The progeny of these adults hibernate in their third instar, usually remaining on the foodplant, to feed again the following spring.

COMMON BLUE

Polyommatus icarus (Rottemburg) ssp. *icarus* (Rottemburg)

The Common Blue is one of the most widely distributed butterflies in the London area, occurring in every vice-county area, as well as in each of the London Boroughs and even in the City of London itself! However, it is a long way away from being numerically abundant, and in some areas the population level is apparently extremely low. Many people seem to have difficulties in separating Common Blues from Adonis Blues, at least in the males, and several reports of the latter species, which is an extreme rarity in our area, proved upon investigation to be males of this species. There should be no confusion between females, and if captured, the male Common Blue is instantly recognised by the clear white, albeit very narrow, fringes to all of its wings. In the male Adonis Blue this white border is crossed by dark lines giving a chequered appearance. This character is also found in the male Chalk Hill Blue, which is a quite different shade of blue and should not cause any difficulty.

The preferred foodplant in London, as elsewhere, is certainly the bird's-foot trefoil *Lotus corniculatus*, though in urban areas the common white clover *Trifolium repens* is regularly used, and quite possibly other species as well. It may be this plant, the first to be recorded in every tetrad of the London area during the field-work for the *Flora of the London Area* (Burton 1983) that accounts for the clear success demonstrated by the Common Blue in colonising new areas in the built-up parts of the Capital. This activity by the butterfly was particularly evident at smaller, derelict sites, an example being at Stratford (38T84) where a small area of land adjacent to a major through-road and busy shopping-centre was used on a temporary basis as a "butterfly garden" by local enthusiasts, prior to the site being developed for office accommodation.

Marking experiments have shown in some areas that the Common Blue forms discrete colonies which the adults rarely leave (Frazer 1961). Males are especially sedentary, sometimes sticking to a particular small bank where they also roost communally on tall grasses (Frazer 1981). Whilst this may be generally true, there is evidence from the urban parts of the London area to suggest that the species may be considerably more mobile than Frazer indicates. Many new colonies which have suddenly appeared one year, in isolated sites where there were certainly none before, are first noticed when there has apparently been a massed emergence of adults from pupae in August, which seems to be suggestive that a gravid female from the spring brood must have slipped on to the site unnoticed to lay its eggs on the *Trifolium* or other plants. As far as I am aware, no new colonies have appeared in the May/June period, nor in the early part of July, suggesting that colonisation, at least in London, may be the preserve of the spring brood only. Further evidence in support of this very slender theory is available, in that males have been observed flying in the most unlikely of places, particularly during June, such as in 1983 when two were seen flitting around the southern end of Vauxhall Bridge. No records of such "stray" males are available beyond 22 July.

Typically, adults from the first generation lay eggs on the upper surface of a leaf of the foodplant during May or early June. Those laid earliest will normally hatch inside a fortnight to produce larvae which rapidly feed and pupate in July, to give a second brood of adults in August and September. Those which are laid later hatch in an equivalent period but feed more slowly, and thus fail to pupate in time to prolong the second brood. Instead, they hibernate as partly fed caterpillars, and are joined, of course, by the progeny of the second brood. Both sets of larvae then continue feeding in the spring before pupating in May to produce the first generation of the following year. Unlike several of the other butterflies in this family, it does not appear that ants are required for the survival of the early stages, a fact which may possibly account for its relative abundance.

Common Blue *Photographer: Peter Gasson*

Chalk Hill Blue *Photographer: Andrew Merritt*

CHALK HILL BLUE

Lysandra coridon (Poda)

The Chalk Hill Blue is a butterfly restricted to old limestone or chalk grasslands in this country, and for this reason it has always been largely confined to the region of the North Downs of Surrey and Kent in the London area, though there were once temporary colonies in Epping Forest, Essex during the middle part of the last century, and at Broxbourne, Hertfordshire around the same period, with occasional sightings elsewhere. The earliest London record was made by Petiver who, in 1704, reported it from Banstead Downs, Surrey and Purfleet, Essex. Whilst males may stray away from breeding sites for some distance (Heath, Pollard and Thomas 1984) the butterfly seems reluctant to cross discontinuities such as valleys, so that opposing hillsides may house quite distinct, self-contained colonies (Frazer 1961, Frazer 1977). It was presumably a stray male which accounts for the record of one individual at Old Oak Common, Middlesex in July 1869, given by Cockerell (1891).

The present-day distribution in the London area reflects the distribution of those few secluded areas of original downland which have yet to be be destroyed by one or other of man's multitudinous activities. Indeed, several colonies have been wiped out in recent years, particularly in level areas where the land can be of use for grazing, farming or building. Former colonies at Riddlesdown and Sanderstead were built upon, for example (de Worms 1950) and other localities given by that author and no longer extant include Mickleham and Epsom Downs, as well as the vicinity of Pett's Wood. In spite of this, it remains present at a number of localities given by de Worms, though most of the present colonies seem to contain low numbers of individuals. Unlike several other downland butterflies, it can tolerate areas where grazing has ceased, and the grass has become too long for the rarer Adonis Blue. However, once the grass becomes so long that the horseshoe vetch upon which it is dependent is shaded out, the butterfly will no longer thrive. The map shows its distribution to follow the line of the chalk quite closely, but to be discontinuous within that band, so that most colonies are now totally isolated from their nearest neighbours by areas of human settlements. This clearly does not bode well for the future well-being of the butterfly, and whilst there may be one or two further colonies as yet undetected, it seems unlikely that the butterfly will spread across more tetrads to any appreciable degree. For this reason alone, the Chalk Hill Blue is to be regarded as vulnerable in the London area.

The Chalk Hill Blue is a single-brooded insect, on the wing during July and August in the London area. The eggs are usually deposited in apparently the most random of fashions, with the female marching around on the ground, scattering eggs amongst the bases of the various plants growing there. This agrees well with the views of Goodden (1978) but is at variance with the observations of Brooks and Knight (1982) who report that the female crawls down to the base of the herbage and deposits her eggs singly on the stems of plants, not necessarily the foodplant. The present author has watched Chalk Hill Blue females ovipositing only on two occasions, both in the London area, and at each event, the female walked rapidly amongst vegetation, stopping to lay a single egg every few inches. On these two occasions, the eggs were simply deposited on the ground, and not attached to any plants. It is possible that both methods may be employed by different females. The caterpillar, though fully developed inside the egg, does not emerge until the following April, when it feeds mainly by night on either the leaves or the flowers of horseshoe vetch *Hippocrepis comosa*. No other foodplants have been recorded in this area, though Goodden (1978) also records bird's-foot trefoil *Lotus corniculatus*, kidney vetch *Anthyllis vulneraria* and birdsfoot *Ornithopus perpusillus*. Pupation occurs during June, with the adult butterflies emerging about four weeks later.

ADONIS BLUE

Lysandra bellargus (Rottemburg)

The Adonis Blue, like the previous species, is a common butterfly over much of Europe, which reaches the northern limit of its geographical range in Britain, a range which has been steadily contracting in recent years. It was not recorded in Britain until 1775, nearly a century after active collecting began, so it must have been exceedingly rare or altogether absent before that date. It is restricted to horseshoe vetch, as is the Chalk Hill Blue, but for climatological reasons does not extend north to the limit of the range of this plant, and, not surprisingly, is more abundant in the southern part of its range than it is further north. It is far more precise than the Chalk Hill Blue in its habitat requirements, preferring warmer situations, which effectively confines it to south-facing chalk slopes in this country. Such slopes must be very closely grazed by rabbits or sheep, as the butterfly requires a turf somewhat reminiscent of a snooker table! Not surprisingly, therefore, the butterfly declined drastically in the aftermath of myxomatosis in the 1950s, and this, coupled with the later development of the North Downs, and the various alternative uses to which the formerly suitable chalk slopes were put, has resulted in a steady decline of the Adonis Blue in our area. In Surrey, it was common on the northern side of Box Hill, and at Epsom Downs from 1943 to 1946, but is certainly no longer in either of these localities, although there was an unconfirmed sighting of a pair of adults at the latter locality on 14 August 1978. De Worms also records Oxshott. The 1899 list gives

Croydon, from where it is also most certainly absent today. In Kent, it was fairly numerous at Otford on 2 September 1962, but has apparently not been seen here since. In 1948 it was apparently common on the downs around Shoreham and at Magpie Bottom. There is no confirmed record from the London area outside the Kent/Surrey portion.

The two tetrad dots presented in the present work for 1980 to 1986 represent sightings at Headley Warren (15T82) on 15 June 1980 and 16 August 1981, and a probable sighting at Happy Valley, Coulsdon (35T06) during 1986. The record in de Worms (1978) for "near Downe", Kent is based upon a misidentification, as is the later record from 46T00 in 1978 given in Plant (1981).

Given that Adonis Blue populations are noted for their enormous fluctuations, it is not beyond the bounds of possibility that we may see a return of this striking insect to one or two suitable localities on the North Downs, always assuming that these localities remain suitable. In view of the overall national decline of the butterfly however, this seems unlikely, and it must be regarded as potentially extinct in the London area.

It is a double-brooded insect, with adults in May/June, producing larvae which pupate in July to give more adults in August/September. The progeny of this generation overwinter as caterpillars, spun to a leaf or a stem of the horseshoe vetch on a mat of silk. They recommence feeding the following spring to pupate in late April, or early May in a "late" year.

Adonis Blue *Photographer: Peter Gasson*

[TURQUOISE BLUE

Plebicula dorylas (Denis & Schiffermüller)

A record of this European butterfly appears in Lewin's 1795 work *Insects of Great Britain* under the name *hyacinthus*, and reads "*I met with this new species of butterfly in the middle of July, flying on the side of a chalk hill, near Dartford in Kent, and have no doubt that there was a constant brood at this place, as I have found them there for two successive years on the wing, in the middle of the same month*". Kloet and Hincks (1972) give *hyacinthinus* (*sic*) Lewin as a synonym of *Lysandra bellargus*, the Adonis Blue. Lewin's illustration of the Dartford specimen, which is not in colour, appears to resemble the Adonis Blue, or, possibly, the Common Blue, but is clearly not the Turquoise Blue.]

MAZARINE BLUE

Cyaniris semiargus (Rottemburg)

The Mazarine Blue was first recorded in the literature for Britain in 1710, in John Ray's *Historia Insectorum*, published posthumously. Ray died in 1705, and the specimen captured by Dale and shown to him must have been taken before that. It is now an extinct species in Britain: the last known colony, as distinct from a record of an isolated individual, bred in Glamorgan, until it died out in 1877. It was certainly resident in Dorset, where about 300 were captured near Wooton Glanville between 1811 and 1841! There are two open circles on the national maps in Heath, Pollard and Thomas (1984) which affect the London area. These lie in TQ 25 and TQ 36. The former relates to sightings on *Ryegate Hill* and *near Headley*, Surrey, reported by Brewer in the *Victoria County History of Surrey*. These records were later accepted by Tutt (1902). The record from TQ 36 appears to relate to a sighting on Riddlesdown, Surrey on 5 September 1877 by a Mr Standish (Bretherton 1951). Abroad, its range extends over much of Europe.

HOLLY BLUE

Celastrina argiolus (Linnaeus) ssp. *britanna* Verity

The Holly Blue is unique amongst British butterflies in that its two separate broods within a single year are dependent upon differing foodplants for the

Holly Blue *Photographer: Frank W. Lockwood*

caterpillars. Hibernated chrysalids from the previous year produce the first generation of adults in April (earliest recorded in London 2 April, in 1983). These lay their eggs mainly on holly *Ilex aquifolium*, and the caterpillar feeds on the developing berries. According to the observations of K.J. Willmott (in Heath, Pollard and Thomas 1984) females lay freely on male or female flowers (which are on different trees in the holly) and inevitably, in the lack of developing berries, caterpillars on male trees will die! Other foodplants recorded for the larvae of the first generation are dogwood *Cornus sanguinea*, spindle *Euonymus* spp., alder buckthorn *Frangula alnus* and snowberry *Symphoricarpos rivularis*. Although we have not recorded positively any other pabulum than holly in this survey, the ability to utilise these other plants, particularly snowberry may well account for the butterfly's capacity to thrive in areas where, despite searching, holly could not be found. These larvae pupate in early July, and by the end of the month a second generation is on the wing. This generation is only partial however, with several pupae "lying over" until the following spring. The second generation are apparently restricted to ivy *Hedera helix* as an egg-laying site, and here the larvae are often attended by ants. Second generation larvae pupate in September and emerge with those from earlier in the year the following April. Apparently, in the West Country, gorse *Ulex europaeus* supports both generations in some colonies.

The butterfly's somewhat unusual life style means that it is not confined, as are many lycaenids, to open grassland or heathland areas. Instead it is found along country lanes, woodland edges, and in parks and gardens. In most rural villages surrounding London there is a colony in the local churchyard. As a London butterfly, the Holly Blue is extremely widespread, occurring in every London borough. Its existence in many of these areas seems to depend to a large extent on the many overgrown cemeteries and churchyards in London, where both holly and ivy are usually present. Indeed, the best way to record this species in tetrads where it has not yet been found is probably to visit the local churchyard in April or August. There is no doubt that many of the currently blank tetrads will be filled over the next few years.

In spite of its wide distribution, however, the Holly Blue is not a numerous insect, usually occurring at very low density indeed. At the St Mary's Churchyard Nature Reserve, East Ham (48T22) two large holly trees and a mass of ivy set in nine acres of overgrown graves, support a colony of Holly Blues which has not exceeded twenty adults in either brood during the study period. This is the general pattern over the whole of the Capital, with most records referring to sightings of individual butterflies. It further seems that over several years populations naturally rise and fall in dramatic proportions: the trough at the end of the last decline, which followed the 1976 drought, was reached during the second year of our survey – during 1981. Numbers appear to be rebuilding slowly, with 1986 being the year providing the greatest number of records to date. Certainly the Holly Blue is in no immediate danger in the London area. In the more rural periphery, numbers are slightly higher in most colonies.

LARGE BLUE

Maculinea arion (Linnaeus) ssp. *eutyphron* (Fruhstorfer)

The Large Blue has been presumed extinct in Britain since the last known colony died out in 1979. On the continent it is exceedingly abundant in some southern areas, and able to exist in very small isolated colonies of only a handful of individuals. Accordingly, there is always the possibility that amongst the very many hoaxes a genuine survivor colony may still be found, though as the years wear on the likelihood diminishes. In any event it would be most unwise to unleash any foreign subspecies into its former haunts whilst this possibility remains, particularly since in spite of all the efforts of some of our best entomologists we still do not fully understand why it became extinct! The caterpillar feeds on wild thyme *Thymus drucei* at first then wanders away from the food plant to be carried underground by ants of the genus *Myrmica*, particularly *Myrmica sabuleti*. Here it feeds on ant larvae until pupating still within the nest. The single brood of adults flies from the last week of June, through July and into the first fortnight of August.

From the London area, the only records are from Haileybury, in Hertfordshire (31T40) where there was apparently one in 1886, and three in 1898 (Foster 1937). It has not proved possible to check the reliability of these records, though there is no real reason to discount them.

DUKE OF BURGUNDY FRITILLARY

Hamearis lucina (Linnaeus)

The Duke of Burgundy is not one of the "true" fritillaries, but is in fact our only British representative of the largely exotic family of "metalmark" butterflies. Formerly widespread in woodlands in southern England (Frohawk 1934) it is now much reduced in its range and occurs in often quite isolated colonies – seldom in any great numbers. Essentially, it is a butterfly of woodland clearings and sunlit glades where the principal foodplants of primrose *Primula vulgaris* and cowslip *Primula veris* grow. The older woodlands on the southern chalk support the bulk of the British population. Here the female lays her eggs singly,

Duke of Burgundy *Photographer: Bryan Ceney*

or in small groups, on the underside of the biggest leaves of the biggest plants available during late May or June. The caterpillar hatches after about a fortnight and lives until fully fed in July on the underside of the leaves. Pupation then follows and the pupa hibernates until the following May when the adult emerges.

The butterfly's *penchant* for older deciduous woodlands on chalk, where one or other of the foodplants grow, is a severely limiting factor in its distribution in the London area. During 1924 it occurred "*in plenty*" at Chorley Wood Hertfordshire (Foster 1937), and de Worms (1950) reported this as being "*a flourishing colony*". Foster also makes mention of Bricket Wood in 1921, but gives no details. It would appear to be quite absent from south Hertfordshire today. It has also gone from a number of localities where it once flourished in the Kent and Surrey parts of our area. Petiver (1704) gives Hornsey Wood as a locality, and later (1717) says that it occurred "*in several woods around London*". Ray (1710) gives Boxhill and Dulwich, both in Surrey. It was still at the latter locality in the 1830s, and at that time had also once occurred in Darenth Wood, Joyden's Wood, around Chislehurst and at West Wickham, and doubtless in several of the other old woodlands present in the south-east sector at that time. In the first half of the present century it occurred in the Eynsford area of Kent, and was seen at Mickleham Downs, whilst Wheeler (1955) reports "*a few observed*" on Bookham Common. Chalmers-Hunt (1979) indicates there is no record in the Kent portion of the London area since 1960.

As far as the present situation is concerned, the butterfly now seems to be confined to the extreme south-west corner of the London area, with small colonies in four tetrads. At 15T62 the insect was reported common on 17 May 1980, and at 15T44 ova were found on 29 May 1981. At an old, established colony in 15T84, there were twenty-five to thirty adults seen in 1980, though the butterfly was reported less numerous there at that time than it was twenty years previously. As far as is known the butterfly is still present in each of the four tetrads shown on the map. Its small size and early appearance may perhaps suggest that it has been missed at some sites, though it is thought unlikely that the overall situation presented by the map will alter significantly.

WHITE ADMIRAL

Ladoga camilla (Linnaeus)

This most attractive of butterflies is strictly a woodland dweller where it depends upon wild honeysuckle *Lonicera periclymenum* in lightly shaded situations to sustain its caterpillars. The spread of the White Admiral in Britain

White Admiral *Photographer: Neil Bowman*

has been well documented in the entomological literature, since prior to the late 1930s it was a quite rare insect. In the early part of the present century it was confined to Hampshire and a few other neighbouring counties, but it then began to spread rapidly outwards. This expansion probably continued until the early 1950s, when the butterfly again went into a decline, reducing to a low level, or even to zero, in some areas. During the last few years, however, there seems to have been another increase, and this expansion is still apparently continuing. For Kent, Chalmers-Hunt (1960) comments "*during the past thirty years* camilla *has spread from the west over most of Kent, reaching its widest distribution about 1945 ... but has been seemingly less plentiful since 1954*". This spread was however, essentially a reoccupation of areas in which it had previously occurred during the early part of the nineteenth century, and it is possible that the butterfly may expand and contract its range on a cyclical basis. Interestingly enough, it may well be that the decline in coppicing as a woodland management technique, the cause of so many losses amongst the insects as a whole, is in fact the reason for the present spread of the White Admiral, since in the increased shade of neglected coppices, honeysuckle can grow in profusion. In an open coppice the plant is both restricted by the light, and controlled as a weed by the forester.

In the London area, there are two principal centres for this black and white butterfly, in the woodlands of Surrey to the south-west, and in the complex of woodlands around Broxbourne in Hertfordshire. At both of these major centres it is sometimes quite a numerous butterfly. In Hertfordshire it has recently spread from the Broxbourne Woods area to colonise parts of Essex in Epping Forest, particularly the Galleyhill Wood area near Waltham Abbey, where eight were seen during 1986. In Surrey, many of the suitable woods now contain this striking insect, and it will doubtless be discovered in others as it continues its current range expansion. An all black variety, known as ab. *nigrina* Weymer, was recorded on Bookham Common on 4 July 1974. A number of sightings at the western extremity of our area, in Buckinghamshire, seems to indicate that there is a healthy population in that area, and indeed that county as a whole seems to have White Admirals in most areas (although both the squares 07 and 08 lack records in the recent work covering Berkshire, Buckinghamshire and Oxfordshire [Steel and Steel 1985]). It is doubtless from here that the insect has spread to Whippendell and Bricket Woods in Hertfordshire. In Kent, on the other hand, the White Admiral seems to have contracted its range away from the London area in recent years, but is now making a comeback. During 1983 it reappeared in the Shoreham area at Meenfield Wood, after an absence of thirty years, and during 1986 appeared at Sparrow Wood in Orpington. No doubt it will return to many of the other quite suitable woodlands in that quarter over the next few years. There are only very few records available for Middlesex. The earliest appears to be that from Mill Hill in 1874, given in Cockerell (1891) whilst James (1940) states that "*it is established ... in a private wood at Mill Hill ...*", and places on record a singleton in Finsbury Square on 19 July 1940. The earliest record for our area seems to be from the Kent sector: Petiver (1703) named this species the white leghorn admiral, having received his first specimen from Italy, but added "*since which it was caught in London by Dr Bonavert*". He later gave the London locality as Dulwich, and later still, in 1717, recorded the butterfly from "*Wickham, near Croydon*" [=West Wickham], at the same time changing the name to White Admiral.

There are also a number of quite reliable yet rather surprising records of White Admirals in the most unlikely of places in London. A number of these can be positively attributed to well intentioned but rather senseless releases by butterfly breeders, notably a large number of records from the New Addington area. The record of a rather battered specimen which flew into a garden at Connaught Gardens (28T88), adjacent to Queens Wood, is more interesting, as it almost certainly represented a genuine wanderer, as does the specimen seen flying along hedges at Westmoreland Road, Bromley (46T08) during 1982. The former example was photographed and subsequently released.

July and August are the best times to see White Admirals, when they fly along woodland rides or edges in bright sunshine. The eggs are laid on the leaves of long, mature strands of honeysuckle hanging down from trees. After about one week the caterpillar hatches and feeds until after the second moult in August. Each caterpillar then selects a suitable leaf and eats across it at right angles to the mid-rib, and then spins the two edges of the resultant triangle of leaf together. It also spins a silk harness connecting the leaf petiole to the main stem to prevent it from falling from the plant during the autumn. Here it hibernates until the following April when, awakened by warmer weather, it recommences feeding until pupation in June. Adults emerge after about two weeks.

PURPLE EMPEROR

Apatura iris (Linnaeus)

The Purple Emperor is our largest resident butterfly, and one of most striking appearance. It inhabits only the "best" woodlands, where mature oaks and ashes are available in proximity with sallows, on which it lays its eggs. It is a butterfly of hot days in July and August, being mostly on the wing during the morning, and far less commonly seen after midday. Both sexes are normally to be found at the very tops of tall oak or ash trees, where they can be watched from woodland rides flying well beyond the reach of the average entomologist! The males will frequently engage in an aerial combat with each other, leaping from high perches and chasing round in circling flight. In this manner they also pursue females, and mating takes place in the tree tops. From here the females descend to lay their eggs on the leaves of sallow bushes *Salix caprea*, though *Salix cinerea* is apparently used in the Weald. Male Purple Emperors are most often seen on hot summer mornings when they periodically descend to the ground to feed on the liquids of decaying organic matter such as animal droppings or carrion. In the London area, dog faeces seem particularly popular. The extremely distinctive "horned" larva goes into hibernation during October, in its third instar, and awakens to feed again in March. Pupation occurs in June and the adults emerge after about a fortnight.

Because of its particular life style, the Purple Emperor may well be under-recorded in the London area, though it seems unlikely that the general pattern of distribution shown on the map here will be significantly altered during the next few years. Certainly the butterfly has drastically declined from Kent, and has not been seen in the county as a whole since a female was spotted in 1967 (outside the London area). It is now presumed extinct in that county. Foster's 1937 Hertfordshire list gives a record for Oxhey Wood, with "*six specimens flying over tree tops during two days in 1878, 1879 or 1880*", whilst more recently there is a record from Northaw Great Wood in 1965. Newman (1869) had earlier noted a record of the butterfly made by Stephens at Caen Wood (=Ken Wood) Middlesex, in the 1850s. In the same vice-county area, one was also seen at Enfield in 1909, and another, a male, at Northwood in July 1966 (de Worms 1969). Essex provides us with the earliest record for the area: Harris (1766) writes "*On 26th of May, in the year 1758, Mr Drury, an ingenious Aurelian, in searching for caterpillars beat four off the sallow, near Brentwood, in Essex*". It is of some interest that Drury gave one of these larvae to Harris who reared it successfully, thus discovering the previously unknown life history. Two adults were apparently also seen in this locality in 1882. Elsewhere in Essex, Doubleday (1836) recorded a single confirmed record in Epping Forest, adding that it also occurred in Ongar Great Wood, and it was reported at Woodford in the 1899 list by Buckell and Prout. A further example was seen in Epping Forest in about 1890, but there have been no further reports from this locality until one was seen in the car park of the "Volunteer" public house during 1983. Sadly, there are no records since for Epping Forest.

It seems therefore, that the Surrey sector is the last stronghold of this magnificent butterfly in our area.There was one seen in Prince's Coverts, Oxshott during August 1943, and two were captured at Ashtead Woods during 1945. A small number have been reported at Bookham Common in most years from the early forties to the present. Today, it remains restricted to that same small corner of Surrey in our area, where it appears to be under no immediate threat.

[ALBIN'S HAMPSTEAD EYE

Junonia villida (Fabricius)

Jacobus Petiver (1717) in his pre-Linnaean work *Papilionum Britanniae*, described and illustrated a specimen of this Indo-Australasian species said to have been taken at Hampstead by Aleazar Albin. Later, Laetitia Jermyn (1824) called this specimen *Papilio hampstediensis*, though in 1827 she changed her opinion and placed it in the genus *Hipparchia* of the Satyridae. Indeed, it was thought by many to be a variety of the Speckled Wood. The specimen was acquired by Petiver, and after his death in 1718 it passed into the collections of Sir Hans Sloane, thus to become, ultimately, a part of the National Collection at the Natural History Museum in South Kensington. It remains in that institution today. There is no doubt about the identity of the insect, and it seems very unlikely indeed that a small butterfly such as this could fly all the way from the far east. Further, it is quite impossible in the days when travel by sea was under sail, that it could have been imported (there would have had to have been a succession of generations on board the ship for the time it took to travel so far in those days!). These facts, together with other evidence lead to the inevitable conclusion that Albin muddled his labels, placing a Hampstead label of this butterfly by accident.]

[BLUE PANSY

Junonia oenone (Linnaeus)

A specimen of this African butterfly was captured "*in an exhausted condition*" in Clarence Avenue, Roehampton, on 5 June 1950, and is now in the National Collection at South Kensington. It was doubtless an escape or release from captivity.]

[SMALL BROWN SHOEMAKER

Hypanartia lethe (Fabricius)

A specimen of this species, which occurs in Central and South America from Mexico to the Argentine, was taken alive in Covent Garden Market on 17 October 1935, and presented to the Natural History Museum. It was certainly imported with produce].

RED ADMIRAL

Vanessa atalanta (Linnaeus)

Whilst most people will be aware that the Red Admiral is an immigrant butterfly to Britain, many will not realise that, apart from isolated incidents in the West Country, it is thought to be quite unable to survive the British winters, and so depends entirely upon fresh immigration each year to maintain its place on the British list. It is true that many people report finding hibernating Red Admirals in their sheds and elsewhere, and one was reliably seen on the wing in Park Wood, Ruislip in early February during the 1950s. Of those examples which do not eventually prove to be either Peacocks or Small Tortoiseshells, the reader is invited to consider that the winter is not over in January or February when most of these are found. There remain no confirmed records of Red Admirals truly surviving the winter in the London area.

Migrants arriving in the spring (usually late May but sometimes earlier) readily mate and lay eggs on stinging nettle *Urtica dioica*, and on hops *Humulus lupulus* in the London area, though elsewhere they are reported to lay also on pellitory of the wall *Parietaria judaica*. This gives rise to a larger number of

Red Admiral *Photographer: Neil Bowman*

Painted Lady *Photographer: Frank W. Lockwood*

adults in August/September which are invariably boosted by fresh immigrants from the continent of Europe. Then, they are a familiar sight in good years on the *Buddleia* bushes and on michaelmas daisies *Aster novi-belgii* or ice plants *Sedum spectabile*, as well as other garden blooms.

Because they are migrants, they are apt to occur in almost all parts of the Capital, including the very centre, and their particular attachment to the stinging nettle means that there is normally a ready supply of food available for their caterpillars. A point of minor interest here is that British-bred specimens seem to have slightly longer wings than southern European examples. The latest recorded date for the butterfly actively flying in the London area is 10 November (in 1984) when there were three at Rainham Marsh, Essex.

PAINTED LADY

Cynthia cardui (Linnaeus)

The Painted Lady is probably the greatest of all migrants in the entire Palearctic Region, and has been found in almost all parts of the world. Unlike the Red Admiral, which can survive at temperatures around 0°C, the Painted Lady is reported to die at anything less than 5°C, and there is no doubt that it is entirely an immigrant to Britain. The number of individuals reaching our shores varies however, from year to year, with some years having none at all, or at least very few, and others having a super-abundance. Almost invariably, the number of Painted Ladies corresponds well with the number of Red Admirals, at least in the London area, the principal exception being in 1973, when the Red Admiral was abundant in the autumn but the Painted Lady was scarce. Whether this was a reflection of immigration, or of breeding success for the two species is uncertain. Poor years in the London area have included 1961, 1967, 1970 and 1984. Years of abundance have included 1943, 1945, 1947, 1952, 1966, 1968, 1969, 1973, 1976, 1980, 1982 and 1983. Of interest was the observation of several at rest on Hounslow Heath on 31 August 1977, at around 07.00 hours. These had all gone by the afternoon, and were no doubt a part of a larger movement.

Early immigrants usually breed, and eggs are laid on creeping thistle *Cirsium arvense* at least in the London area, and doubtless on most, if not all other species of thistle, as well as burdock *Arctium* spp., mallows *Malva* spp. and stinging nettle *Urtica dioica*. A resultant generation of adults in September is often added to by fresh immigration. The arrival of cold weather kills off all the butterflies, however, in all of the stages of their life cycle, and it is rare to see a Painted Lady in the London area beyond the end of the first week of October, though this will depend on the season.

SMALL TORTOISESHELL

Aglais urticae (Linnaeus)

Beyond all shadow of doubt, the Small Tortoiseshell is the most widespread and common of all of our butterflies, occurring, as the map shows, in every tetrad of our area during the survey period from 1980 to 1986. It is particularly evident in the autumn when our resident population may in some years be boosted by immigrants from across the Channel. At this time they are usually to be found feeding on the flowering spikes of *Buddleia* or on other nectar-bearing blossoms, particularly ice-plants *Sedum spectabile* and michaelmas daisies *Aster novi-belgii*. Results of the Butterfly Monitoring Scheme, carried out across the whole of Britain, and summarised in Heath, Pollard and Thomas (1984) indicate that there is a considerable fluctuation in the numbers of Small Tortoiseshells from year to year, with there being good numbers in some years and low numbers at other times . This seems to be borne out in London, where there were very few records, for example, during 1981 or 1986, but a superabundance in, for example, 1983 and 1984. These years of abundance seem to be quite unrelated to levels of immigration: 1983 was a good year for Red Admiral and Painted Lady numbers, but the following year was exceptionally poor.

The caterpillar feeds principally on stinging nettle *Urtica dioica*, but annual nettle *Urtica urens* is also used less commonly. At East Ham (48T22) larvae were found on hops *Humulus lupulus* during 1983, apparently a new natural foodplant record in Britain, although the caterpillars will often accept hops in captivity, usually producing under-sized adults (Allan 1949). The butterfly usually occurs in two broods in the London area, the first in June, and the second in August. Adults from both generations will usually survive to hibernate from about late October until late February or early March, dependent upon the season. It is not unusual, during spells of temporarily mild weather, to see Small Tortoiseshells on the wing at the most unlikely of times: two were at Rainham, Marshes in Essex on 10 November 1984, whilst others have been seen in December and even January in more urban areas. Garden sheds, garages or outhouses are popular sites for hibernating adults: it is not entirely clear whether the individuals which awaken during these mild winter spells are able to resume hibernation afterwards, or whether, deluded by the warmth of the daytime sun, they succumb to the next overnight frost. Goodden (1978) suggests that the butterflies may use the same patch of nettles year after year for breeding, provided that the habitat remains suitable. Whilst this may well be the case it is likely that quite different groups of individuals are involved. Recent work by Baker (1972) seems to indicate that Small Tortoiseshells do not form distinct colonies, but have a more dispersive habit, using any suitable nettles they encounter for egg-laying or flowers for feeding. This would go some way to explaining their presence in places such as the City of London or the Euston Road, a considerable distance from the nearest patch of nettles.

The rare aberration *seminigra* Frohawk was noted on the Platform of Bookham Station, Surrey during 1982. Aberrant forms of this species normally seem to be quite rare, in spite of the large number of individuals present.

Clearly the Small Tortoiseshell is under no threat in the London area at present. However, the larvae live gregariously for the most part of their lives, spinning the tips of nettle shoots with silk to make "tents" in which they reside: In their efforts to control the spread of the Brown-tailed Moth *Euproctis chrysorrhoea* (Linnaeus), a number of local authorities have mistaken these larval spinnings for the tents of this pest species and have either sprayed or burned them. It would be a mistake to become too complacent about a very common butterfly: the Passenger Pigeon once occurred in an even greater abundance in America!

Small Tortoiseshell *Photographer: Neil Bowman*

LARGE TORTOISESHELL

Nymphalis polychloros (Linnaeus)

The Large Tortoiseshell is now an extreme rarity in the London area, in spite of the frequency with which many people claim to have seen it. Many would argue that it was probably only ever a temporary resident in this country, though others would disagree (e.g. Mendel and Piotrowski 1986). In the London area, evidence suggests that it was indeed a permanent resident: it was included by Mouffet (1634), and Petiver, describing it in 1699, said it was "*not common*". Almost every subsequent author included it as a well known breeding species, some referring to it as the Elm Tortoiseshell. Cockerell (1891) for example, stated under the entry for this butterfly "*Mill Hill – common in 1876, pupae under branches of fruit trees*". There is no doubt that the number of butterflies fluctuated considerably, but there does not seem to have been a serious decline until about 1902. After this date, most records relate to either primary immigrants or, occasionally, deliberate releases by breeders. There have been thirty-eight individuals reliably recorded this century in the London area, details of most of which were given in Plant (1986). During the 1980 to 1986 study period, there have been six sightings only as follows:

> Hayes, Kent – 15 July 1982; Beckenham, Kent – 29 July 1982, and another, perhaps the same one, on the next day; Radlett, Hertfordshire – 29 May 1983; Wanstead, Essex – 14 July 1985; and Rickmansworth, Hertfordshire - 21 July 1985.

It will be evident from the above that July is the optimum month for this species, though records from earlier years also occur in April, and occasionally in March or August.

[SCARCE TORTOISESHELL

Nymphalis xanthomelas (Denis & Schiffermüller)

Also known as the Yellow-legged Tortoiseshell, this eastern European species has been recorded once only in Britain, at Borough Green, Kent, where a female was found on 2 July 1953. The insect was erroneously included in a list of immigrants in the London area in Plant (1986): Borough Green is in fact outside the London boundary, lying just to the north-east of Sevenoaks.]

Camberwell Beauty *Photographer: Michael Hammerson*

CAMBERWELL BEAUTY

Nymphalis antiopa (Linnaeus)

The first recorded capture (Wilkes 1749) of this magnificent insect in Britain was in August 1748 at Camberwell, Surrey, giving rise to the common English name of the butterfly. Certain later workers have incorrectly stated that Harris (1766) was responsible for adding it to the British list referring to the statement in *The Aurelian* that "*This is one of the scarcest flies known in England... the first two were taken about the middle of August 1748, in Cool Arbour Lane, near Camberwell; the last in St. George's Fields, near Newington Butts, the beginning of that month*". Amongst collectors, the Camberwell Beauty is on a par with the Deaths'-head Hawk-moth, in being one of the most sought after trophies. Quite why this should be, for either species, is somewhat illogical, for there are certainly both rarer and more attractive insects available to those so inclined.

The Camberwell Beauty is a common butterfly in many areas of Europe, though in this country it is known only as an immigrant. In the London area it is a regular, but quite infrequent visitor, and the available evidence suggests that it reaches us from Scandinavia during most invasions, and perhaps also from Germany. There have been at least fifty-seven reported in our area during the present century, and of these, no fewer than twenty-one were noted during the marvellous summer of 1976, when many of our resident species were having a hard time of it through the withering of their foodplants during the drought. During the present study period, there have been but eight records as follows:

> 1981: South Croydon, Surrey – 15 August; Kew Gardens, Surrey – 25 August;
>
> 1983: Epping, Essex – 14 August; Loughton, Essex – late July; Euston Road, Middlesex – 27 October;
>
> 1984: Grange Park, Middlesex – 25 September; Hailey Lane, Hertfordshire - 29 September; Isle of Dogs, Middlesex – one during that year.

A single butterfly seen in a car park by the River Mole in Surrey on the early date of 22 May 1977 (the year following the big invasion of 1976) may have over wintered, although it could just as easily have been an early immigrant. There is no other record, confirmed or otherwise, of Camberwell Beauties successfully hibernating in the London area.

PEACOCK

Inachis io (Linnaeus)

The Peacock is a large and attractive butterfly which is quite widespread, and usually fairly common over all of England and Wales, as well as much of Ireland, though becoming progressively rarer in Scotland, being absent from the north and east of that country. It is one of the commonest butterflies to visit town gardens, particularly during the late summer when it often can be seen on the flowers of *Buddleia* and other nectar-bearing plants. Although it can in fact be seen in most habitats, it is primarily a woodland insect. In spring time, after emerging from hibernation, the males will rapidly establish territories along hedgerows, or in woodland clearings, and will actively discourage other males by flying at them. Passing females will also be intercepted in this way for mating (Baker 1972). The eggs are laid on the under surface of the leaves of stinging nettles *Urtica dioica*, and it would seem that this is the only natural foodplant, though hops *Humulus lupulus* will be accepted in captivity, usually resulting in undersized adults. After about two weeks, the eggs will hatch, and the caterpillars will move *en masse* to the nearest growing shoot of the nettle where they will spin a protective silk web in which they feed communally. When one nettle shoot has been eaten, the "army" will march on to another, spinning a new shelter each time, and making it possible to "track" their movements by following the line of abandoned shelters. After their final moult however, the larvae disperse, each completing its feeding alone, before pupating, usually during July, about one month after hatching from the egg. About a fortnight later the adult butterfly emerges. Hibernation begins any time from late August to the end of October, and it seems that only rarely does mating occur in the autumn, most taking place the following spring. Very rarely, there is a partial second brood, but this has never been reported for the London area. During mild spells in the winter period, Peacocks sometimes awaken, one particular example being at a locality near Rickmansworth, Hertfordshire when one flew into a house through an open window on 9 December 1985.

The present-day distribution map shows an interesting pattern, which seems to bear out the statement above that the Peacock is essentially a woodland butterfly. It is essentially absent from the highly urbanised south bank of the River Thames in Wandsworth, Lambeth, Southwark, Lewisham and Greenwich, as well as from the central area of the City of London, and the inner reaches of Camden, Islington, Hackney and Tower Hamlets. There is a surprising gap in the distribution in Croydon, which can probably be put down to under-recording in that area. In general it is far more widely distributed and common in the rural areas, than it is in the urban zone, though it is likely to occur in low numbers in most parts of the Capital. There are occasional records of adult Peacocks being seen travelling on the London Underground: most of these observations arise during August or September, and it is presumed that the butterflies initially entered the underground system in search of hibernation sites.

Peacock *Photographer: Neil Bowman*

COMMA

Polygonia c-album (Linnaeus)

The Latin name of *"c-album"* literally means "white letter C", and derives from a letter "C"-shaped mark on the underside of each hindwing. To the bestower of the English vernacular name, which was used by both Petiver and Ray, this presumably looked more like the "comma" punctuation mark. In any event the white markings serve an extremely useful purpose for the survival of the butterfly. As an adult, it hibernates on tree-trunks, in hedges or amongst vegetation generally where its colouration and naturally ragged wing margins ensure that it closely resembles a dead leaf. The addition of a brilliant white "C" or "comma" adds a touch of authenticity to the deception, looking to all intent and purpose like a tear in the leaf through which the light is penetrating.

There are two forms of the Comma butterfly, differing in the intensity of colouration and the degree of "raggedness" of the wings. Both types are produced as the progeny of overwintering adults, which lay eggs in April to produce more adults in late June or July. A proportion of these summer offspring go into "hibernation" more or less immediately after emergence in that month, whilst the remainder lay eggs to produce a second brood. Those which do lay

Comma *Photographer: Neil Bowman*

eggs are brighter and less "ragged" than those which become dormant straight away, and are referred to as form *hutchinsoni* Frohawk. Petiver had noted this form and, according to Ray (1710) had thought it to be a distinct species. The progeny of the *hutchinsoni* brood are all of the duller more ragged over-wintering form. The larvae of both generations are to be found principally on the stinging nettle *Urtica dioica*, but have also been noted on hops *Humulus lupulus* in the London area, and it is possible that this may once have been the principal foodplant in parts of London in the days when hops were widely grown, and before the advent of nitrate fertilisers which have encouraged the spread of nettles around field edges. Elsewhere they are reported to take a variety of foodplants including elm *Ulmus* and sallow *Salix*. The caterpillar is extremely distinctive, being essentially black with a pure white back and spines: its resemblance to a bird dropping is almost perfect.

The distribution of the Comma has probably always been one of drastic expansions and declines. During the last fifty years of the last century, it was in a decline, and by the turn of the century was extremely rare. Richard South, writing in 1906, stated *"the butterfly seems to have dissappeared from many localities in England where it formerly flourished"* and went on to state that *"seventy or eighty years ago* [about 1820 to 1830] *it was plentiful in Epping Forest, in Herts and in Dorset . . . .Probably it is now entirely confined to favoured districts embraced within the area represented by the counties of Hereford, Worcestershire and Monmouthshire"*. Since then it has spread, and an examination of the 1984 maps by Heath, Pollard and Thomas show it to be widespread in the southern third of Great Britain.

In the London area, with which we are mainly concerned here, tracing the spread of the butterfly during its current range expansion is difficult. The 1899 list of Buckell and Prout gives a record for Clapton, but does not accompany this with a date. Cockerell (1891) gives "Isleworth" and "near Edgeware" in his Middlesex list. By the time de Worms reviewed London's butterflies in 1950 the Comma had been *"recently recorded from all over the London area"*, and the absence of any details indicates that de Worms had not been able to properly chronicle its spread. Foster (1937) lists Symond's Hyde in 1919, one seen at St Albans on 26 August 1923, one at Haileybury on 30 May 1924, and one at Welwyn in 1936. For Kent, Edward Newman, writing in 1857 stated that it was formerly frequent at Penge Common, but had not been seen there, or elsewhere near London to his knowledge for over twenty years. In Middlesex, one individual was seen by the Brent Bridge Hotel at Hendon, on the North Circular Road during 1930. By 1934 it was "common at Broxbourne Woods" in Hertfordshire, and by the end of the second world war it appears to have spread right across the London area. It would appear therefore, that the steady eastwards spread reached London around the early 1930s, and within ten years the Comma had become a common London butterfly. The present-day map shows a wide distribution across the London area, albeit rather patchy in some parts.

SMALL PEARL-BORDERED FRITILLARY

Boloria selene (Denis & Schiffermüller) ssp. *selene* (D. & S).

The Small Pearl-bordered Fritillary is almost certainly now extinct in the London area, the single dot on the map relating to two adults at Kew Gardens during 1981, which are attributable to released individuals. There is an unconfirmed sighting from 06T68 on 26 September 1984, which, if true, would relate to the usually uncommon partial second brood.

A number of woodlands around the London area formerly used to support this butterfly, which generally emerges a couple of weeks later than the Pearl-bordered Fritillary. Cockerell (1891) lists Isleworth for Middlesex, and there is a further record for this vice-county in Newman (1869). From Hertfordshire there are old records from Bricket Wood and Broxbourne Woods, and possibly from Hadley Woods, near Barnet. In Essex it was reported to be plentiful near Brentwood, but has not been seen there since 1952. In Kent it was recorded from Shooters Hill in the 1870s, and from the woods around Chislehurst and West Wickham from 1932 to 1946, but has certainly not been seen anywhere in our small part of that county since prior to 1960. Prince's Coverts, near Oxshott was a former locality in Surrey, and during August 1945 one was seen in Hinchley Wood. Doubtless other earlier records will have been missed, but it is highly unlikely that the butterfly has occurred naturally in the London area for at least thirty-five years. The caterpillars, which are solitary, are dependent upon common dog violet *Viola riviniana*, and possibly other species of violets, whilst adults are on the wing during June and the first half of July, with a partial second brood in some years in the August/September period.

PEARL-BORDERED FRITILLARY

Boloria euphrosyne (Linnaeus)

The Pearl-bordered Fritillary is very easily confused with the Small Pearl-bordered Fritillary, particularly as in some parts of the country the two species fly together. To separate them it is necessary to examine the undersides of the hindwings of a settled specimen. Experience shows that much patience is often required for this exercise, and it is often more expedient to capture the butterfly and examine it in the hand, when the task becomes very simple. The Pearl-bordered is, as the other species' name implies, the slightly larger of the pair under normal circumstances, and generally is the first fritillary on the wing in this country, appearing during the last fortnight of May. Like the Small Pearl-bordered, there is a partial second brood in some years, the adults again

Small Pearl-bordered Fritillary — *Photographer: Peter Gasson*

Pearl-boardered Fritillary — *Photographer: Michael Hammerson*

appearing about two weeks in advance of the smaller species. The dog violet *Viola riviniana* is the preferred foodplant, though most related species of *Viola* will apparently suffice.

The Pearl-bordered Fritillary had formerly been the more common of this pair in the London area. There was a single sighting on Bookham Common (15T42) during 1981, but it has apparently not been seen here since. One was also seen at Banstead Downs (26T40) by the same observer during 1983, but is thought to relate to a release from captivity. It is feared that this attractive butterfly is likely now to be extinct in the London area. In the mid 1940s it was apparently widely distributed in several of the suitable woodlands in the Kent and Surrey portion of the area, with Epsom, Ashtead, Oxshott, Caterham and Surbiton Golf Course being amongst the Surrey localities given by de Worms in 1950, and West Wickham, Chislehurst, Bickley, Shoreham, Elmstead Wood, Joyden's Wood, Darenth Wood and Pett's Wood in Kent. In 1947 it was reported as the commonest butterfly on Hayes Common! Former Middlesex localities traced are few: Copse Wood, near Northwood, is the only one mentioned by de Worms, whilst Petiver (1699) stated that it was common at Cain Wood (=Ken Wood) and that it occured on Hampstead Heath. In Hertfordshire it was known from "*Broxbourne and many of the woods in the southern region, particularly Oxhey Wood, Bricket Wood and near Radlett*". The 1891 list by E.A. Fitch stated that the butterfly was abundant in Epping Forest and at Ongar Park Wood in Essex, and there was also a known colony near to Brentwood. Two more recent records of single butterflies from the Kent sector are given in Chalmers-Hunt (1979) for Badgers Mount on 2 June 1963, and Forest Hill "*a stray*" in about 1970. The Badgers Mount site is now a less than pleasing mix of conifers and motorway, and the butterfly is certainly no longer present.

The decline of the Pearl-bordered Fritillary seems to have begun during the 1950s, and continued into the 1960s, principally coinciding with the decline in woodland coppicing, but exacerbated by the loss of rabbits through myxomatosis. This caused an alteration in the herb layer of coppice woodlands which shaded out the violets on which the larvae depend. The decline still seems to be continuing across the country as a whole, and it would seem unlikely therefore that any reappearance of the species in our area will occur in the forseeable future.

QUEEN OF SPAIN FRITILLARY

Argynnis lathonia (Linnaeus)

The Queen of Spain Fritillary must be one of the most instantly recognisable butterflies in what can often be a very difficult group. The bright metallic silver-white "mirrors" on the under surfaces of its hindwings render it totally unique amongst the British butterflies. It is a rather rare immigrant to Britain, though a native of most of Europe including southern Scandinavia. There is evidence that it does breed here on occasions (though not in the London area) but the only evidence that suggests it may survive our winters is unreliable. De Worms (1950) states that this species has been reported annually in Britain, with as many as six individuals in 1945. In the London area however, there are only six authentic records altogether on record, four in the present century but only one in the present study period. These are as follows:

un-dated: Hertford (Stephens *Illustrations of British Entomology* (1828)
1868: Darenth Wood, Kent;
1934: Warlingham, Surrey, on 30 September;
1943: Sutton, Surrey, on 17 August;
1975: Radlett, Hertfordshire;
1982: Chiswell Green, Hertfordshire, on 29 May.

There was a possible seventh sighting during 1976, when one was reputedly seen at Symondshyde Great Wood in Hertfordshire.

Queen of Spain Fritillary *Photographer: Bryan Ceney*

HIGH BROWN FRITILLARY

Argynnis adippe (Denis & Schiffermüller) ssp. *vulgoadippe* (Verity)

The High Brown Fritillary is a rare butterfly in this country, and its status in Britain is now a vulnerable one. It is now almost certainly extinct in the London area. Nearly all the surviving colonies lie in the western half of Britain, though it is still quite common in most parts of Europe. During the late 1930s and early 1940s it seemed to be undergoing a tremendous range expansion, with butterflies appearing in a large number of suitable woodland localities. Until the early 1950s it was the commonest large fritillary in Hertfordshire, Buckinghamshire and Middlesex (Peachey 1980) and in Essex (Ford 1945). It was also "*generally common*" in parts of Kent (Scott 1950) and Chalmers-Hunt (1961) gives several localities including West Wickham in 1858, Abbey Wood in 1859, Darenth Wood in 1865, Keston in 1920, Wrotham and Oxted in 1946, Joyden's Wood in 1946 and 1947 and Hayes Common in 1947. The Woolwich Survey of 1909 also lists Sidcup. It is not without interest, however, that Petiver gave no localities for the London area, indicating that it may have been absent, or very rare, at that time. A dramatic decline was first detected in 1948, and it is now almost certainly extinct in all these county areas. Chalmers-Hunt (1979) states that there has been no record for Kent as a whole since 1971. In the London part of Kent, the butterfly became extinct much earlier: de Worms noted it as "*fairly common*" in Joyden's Wood, and in woods around Wrotham, Chelsfield, Shoreham Hill, and in Darenth Wood in 1945 and 1946, and seen on Hayes Common in 1947. Across the border in Surrey at the same period it was present at Banstead Downs and around Epsom, with a few at Box Hill in 1943. Ashtead Woods, and Prince's Coverts were also good localities for this butterfly, and in 1947 there was even one on Wimbledon Common. In 1953 it was said to be common on Bookham Common. In Middlesex it is recorded from Northwood, Copse Wood, Ruislip and "*near Harefield*", as well as one at Stoke Newington on 27 July 1924 and another at Finsbury Circus on 24 July 1928, whilst in Cockerell's 1891 list for Middlesex it is recorded from Isleworth. Hertfordshire localities given by de Worms were Broxbourne Woods, Whippendell Woods, Essendon, and Chorley Wood. More recently there have been sightings of vagrant individuals at Broxbourne Wood and near Hoddesdon in 1971, and at Cowheath Wood and Balls Wood in 1977. A colony at Bricket Wood died out in the early 1950s after having been first located in the mid 1930s. The last record for the London portion of Essex was from Thorndon Park in 1966, and was itself then the only Essex record since 1960. Elsewhere in Essex it occurred formerly in Epping Forest and at Ongar Park Woods. It will be most interesting to see whether the High Brown Fritillary can stage a comeback along the lines exhibited by the Comma during the present century, and indeed, if it, does, whether or not there will still be any suitable woodlands left in the London area to receive it!

DARK GREEN FRITILLARY

Argynnis aglaja (Linnaeus) ssp. *aglaja* (Linnaeus)

Whilst the High Brown Fritillary was essentially a woodland species in the London area, the Dark Green Fritillary is much more often seen in open situations, being found around woodland edges, along hedgerows and on grassland, particularly on the chalk downs. Although by no means as rare in Britain as the previous species, it is still not a common insect, its *comparative* abundance being due to the fact that the High Brown is declining at a faster rate than the Dark Green! The eggs are laid on a variety of species of violets: in calcareous grassland, apparently hairy violet *Viola hirta* is often chosen, whereas elsewhere the early dog violet *V. reichenbachiana* is also used. In Scotland the marsh violet *V. palustris* is apparently the foodplant of choice. Sadly, we do not have any data at all for preferences in the London area. Upon hatching during August, after about three weeks in the egg, the newly emerged caterpillar eats its eggshell and immediately enters hibernation at the base of the plant, not awakening to feed until March. With the warmer weather it feeds rapidly, pupating at the end of May to give adults in July and August.

Ungrazed, unimproved grasslands are the optimum habitats for this butterfly, and whilst the bulk of the North Downs in our area are no longer suitable for many butterflies since myxomatosis wiped out the rabbit population in the 1950s and 1960s, thus eliminating grazing over a wide area, certain select areas of this now neglected habitat still support small numbers of Dark Green Fritillaries. There were small numbers at Epsom Downs in 1980, when adults were seen on 17 July, whilst at Fairdean and Farthing Downs there are small numbers seen in most years, including 1986. It is most plentiful on the downs to the east of Shoreham, where the map shows a concentration of four post-1980 dots, though the word "plentiful" should be taken merely as a comparison with elsewhere in the region: nowhere is the butterfly common, and though adults may wander, the colonies seem to be extremely localised. Other recent records herald from the Biggin Hill area and Coulsdon Common. One seen on 14 July 1985 at Wimbledon Common (27T20) may have been a straggler, though it is just possible the insect has bred here undetected. The record for the Eltham area (47T44) is certainly a wanderer or a deliberate release. The Hertfordshire record for 09T22 relates to a single individual at Maple Cross on 27 July 1985, and most likely represents a wanderer from the small colony at Philipshill Wood in 09T04, just outside the London area.

As with so many butterflies, there are a number of localities reported in earlier years at which it is no longer found. Ashtead Woods and Box Hill are listed for Surrey, though it apparently does still occur on the part of Box Hill outside the London area recording circle. It was plentiful at Bookham Common in 1952 and 1953 whilst in Middlesex, Northwood, Copse Wood and Harefield

Dark-green Fritillary *Photographer: David Bevan*

were localities in the 1940s, and, earlier, Enfield Chase in 1883. In Kent it was formerly to be seen at Pett's and Joyden's Woods, and around Wrotham, with one being seen on a bombed site in Lewisham during July 1945. West (1906) also lists Darenth Wood. In Essex it was established in the Brentwood area by the 1950s, from where individuals were seen on three occasions between 1965 and 1971. This was the last known site for the Dark Green Fritillary in our part of the Essex area. In the west, it was numerous at Chalfont St Peter, in Buckinghamshire, during 1956. In Petiver's day it was apparently very rare: he gives (1717) only a Latin description without a name but with an excellent figure. Sadly we know too little about the overall ecology of this butterfly to be able to explain its decline in our area.

SILVER-WASHED FRITILLARY

Argynnis paphia (Linnaeus)

This third member of the larger fritillaries in this country is also a declining species in Britain, and is now more or less confined to a south-westerly distribution. It nevertheless does occur, albeit sparingly in the London area. The name "silver-washed" derives from the silver "wash" on the under side of the hindwings, which merges pleasingly with the green to make a most attractive butterfly. In the New Forest, a proportion of the females have their upper surfaces greenish brown instead of the normal bright orange-brown which is the norm in both sexes. This is known as form *valezina* Esper, and although it does occur elsewhere this is very rare, and may be the result of artificially assisted movements of New Forest stock by collectors. The decline had started by the turn of the present century, although there were years of increase and abundance in some areas. By the 1950s, however, the decline had gathered momentum and extinctions occurred in many areas. It had vanished from Suffolk by the end of the 1950s (Mendel & Pietrowski 1986). In Essex it began to spread from its stronghold in the north-east from 1930, and by 1950 it was widespread in the county. By 1962, however, it had apparently vanished from this entire area (Emmet, Pyman and Corke 1985) except for three isolated records in 1976, 1977 and 1983 which were all outside the London area. It has also become scarce in Kent, and there are only a handful of records for that county since 1960 (Chalmers-Hunt 1979) though it was formerly widespread in suitable woodlands.

Looked at more specifically in the London area, the first British record was made at the Physic Garden at Chelsea (Petiver 1699). During the present century the butterfly was particularly frequent in the woodlands in the south of our area, in Kent and Surrey. In the former county it was present in Joyden's Wood in 1946, in which year two were seen at Shooters Hill, and another one in Abbey Wood. The following year it was located at Darenth and Joyden's Woods, and also at Eynsford, Otford, Elmstead Woods, Hayes Common and "*round Keston*", with a singleton taken at Bickley in 1950. There is also an earlier record from Darenth Wood, in 1868. Since 1960, the records are sparse. A male was seen on *Buddleia* in a garden in Abbey Wood during 1976, in which year one was also seen at Farningham Woods. A female was noted at High Elms on 27 July 1961, where happily it has reappeared during the present survey. Other records were Meopham in 1976, and at Farnborough and Beechen Wood, Lullingstone in 1979. In Surrey, the localities were numerous, and included Colley Hill, Bookham Common, Oxshott Woods, Ashtead Woods, Banstead Woods, Claygate and Richmond Park, the latter locality during 1953. One was also seen at Balham in 1925. In Middlesex, Northwood and Harefield are listed, together with woods to the west of the reservoir at Ruislip (presumably the Bayhurst, Mad Bess and Copse Woods complex?). It was certainly present in this area during the 1950s. The 1899 list gives Hackney, but mentions no date. Cockerell gives a record for Enfield in 1883. One was also captured at Stanmore on 31 July 1894, whilst further towards town there was a male on some waste ground at the rear of the Natural History Museum, South Kensington on 11 July 1935 (Classey 1935) one near the Middlesex Hospital on 21 July 1949 and one other in the Temple Gardens (James 1940). Further north, in Hertfordshire, London area localities included Whippendell Wood, Bricket Wood, East Barnet, Watford,

Symond's Hyde, Broxbourne Woods, Hoddesdon, Beech Wood, Barnet and Chorley Wood. It is also listed from Chingford, in Essex. This presumably relates to Epping Forest, from where the butterfly had disappeared around 1874 (Fitch 1891). It made a brief appearance at Thorndon Park in the 1950s, disappearing almost as fast as it arrived. It was also noted at Woodford in 1926. The only records for our part of Buckinghamshire seems to be at Chalfont St Peter in 1957, and again in 1970.

The present-day distribution shows the butterfly to be widely scattered, but it is not common. In Hertfordshire, it was seen in Whippendell Woods during 1982, where it was previously recorded in 1956, but it has apparently not been noted here since the recent sighting. In July 1984, a very fresh, and almost certainly newly emerged adult was seen at Hoddesdon Park Wood, whilst in Balls Wood, there have been several sightings of odd individuals regularly from 1981 to 1986. During 1985, there was a casual sighting of an individual in a garden at Bushey on 27 July, and in the same month during 1984 three were seen on a bridleway east of Hatfield Park. In the south of our area, there appears to be small but nevertheless thriving colonies at Juniper Top and Mickleham Downs in Surrey, with casual sightings of individuals at Merton on 24 July 1983, and at Bushy Park on 7 July 1985. In Kent, there has been an apparent return to the High Elms area of Orpington, first noted in 1982, whilst on 10 August 1983 an individual was captured and released at Biggin Hill.

Silver-washed Fritillary — *Photographer: Michael Hammerson*

MARSH FRITILLARY

Euphydryas aurinia (Rottemburg) ssp. *aurinia* (Rottemburg)

This variable butterfly is another which has undergone a drastic decline in this country. This particular species' range contracted severely during the 1940s and 1950s, a little ahead of the other fritillaries, and it is now restricted to the south-west of England, western Wales and in small areas of north-west England and western Scotland. Unlike the other fritillaries, however, the Marsh Fritillary is somewhat scarce in Europe as a whole, having undergone a decline across its entire range, and it is now considered to be "vulnerable" by the Council of Europe (Heath 1981). The devil's-bit scabious *Succisa pratensis* is the principal larval foodplant, though it is also reported on other scabious species, and on plantains and, in captivity, it will accept honeysuckle *Lonicera*. Burton (1983) records the devil's-bit scabious widely in the non-urban parts of the London area, stating it to be a characteristic plant of old meadows and pastures on the London clay. In the Hertfordshire part of the London area there were "*three specimens*" of the butterfly from Haileybury (Foster 1937). In Middlesex, there is an old record for Neasden in Harris (1766) who states "*... accordingly, on the eighteenth of April, I went to Neesdon, near Welsdon, about seven miles from London where I was informed they were in great plenty, as indeed I found them to be*". There is a further record from Kingsbury, according to Cockerell (1891) whilst earlier Petiver had recorded it from Cain Wood (=Ken Wood) and Oak of Honour Wood. One was found at West Wickham, Kent in 1856 (reported in the *Entomologist's Weekly Intelligencer* for that year). In Surrey, Petiver recorded Dulwich in 1699. One was seen in Oxshott Woods in 1931, and another at Bookham Common in June 1950. It was very locally distributed in south-west Essex (i.e. the London portion) in the nineteenth century, with reports from Ongar Park Woods, High Beach and Wanstead Flats in 1839. In the 1950s there was also a colony "*near Broxbourne*". There seems to be no other records affecting our study area. Introductions were apparently made at Poors Field, Ruislip during 1959, 1963 and 1965, with more additions in 1976, but adults persisted at best three years beyond the release dates. There was also a former colony at North Harrow, TQ 136888 (an area now built over) but this probably stemmed from an introduction.

GLANVILLE FRITILLARY

Melitaea cinxia (Linnaeus)

The earliest British specimens of this butterfly were taken in Lincolnshire by Elizabeth Glanville and recorded by Petiver (1699) under the name of

Lincolnshire Fritillary. Later, Dandridge took the species in plenty in the London area at Dulwich, and Petiver promptly changed the name to Dullidge Fritillary. At that time this butterfly which we now call the Glanville Fritillary was widespread in southern England. There is then a huge gap in the records for the London area until, in 1964, according to the *Proceedings of the South London Entomological and Natural History Society* for that year, a number of Glanville Fritillaries were released in the area around Otford, Kent "*a few years ago*". Clearly they did not survive! As a breeding species it is now confined to the southern shores of the Isle of Wight in this country.

HEATH FRITILLARY

Mellicta athalia (Rottemburg) ssp. *athalia* (Rottemburg)

The Heath Fritillary is now confined in this country to isolated colonies in East Kent and in Cornwall, Devon and Somerset in the west country. Like the Swallowtail, it is afforded the protection of the law. Although this legal protection has the support of the author, it does seem a little illogical, since collecting the insect, which has had practically nothing to do with its demise, is a crime punishable by large fines, whilst the wanton and wholesale destruction of the habitats of this and many other rare insects is, in many cases, perfectly legal! Even where such action is not legal, as on Sites of Special Scientific Interest, the fines normally imposed upon offenders are miniscule in proportion to the fines which could theoretically be imposed on an individual collector.

In the London area it was quite a common species around 1700, and it was noted particularly from Cain Wood (=Ken Wood) and Hampstead Heath by Petiver. There is a record of Heath Fritillary at Epping Forest (Tyssen 1857) whilst Wilkes (1745) writes of its occurrence at Tottenham. It was recorded from Ongar Park Wood, Essex, as late as 1839 (Fitch 1891). There are no other reliable records. During 1952, attempts were made to introduce the butterfly at Park Wood, Ruislip. Adults were set down during that year, but the last record relates to two adults caught in 1954,and it is assumed that the project failed.

SPECKLED WOOD

Pararge aegeria (Linnaeus) ssp. *tircis* (Butler)

The Speckled Wood is perhaps one of our most interesting butterflies, at least from the point of view of its breeding biology. Although not universally accepted, evidence suggests that there is a rather peculiar double life cycle, with

Speckled Wood *Photographer: Neil Bowman*

both larvae and pupae overwintering, to produce two distinct, but considerably overlapping spring generations, each of which will produce a second brood of adults later in the year. Those which overwinter as pupae are said to produce adults in March, which survive through to mid May and produce a second generation of adults in late June, lasting to early August. The overwintering caterpillars pupate in April to give adults from mid May to mid June, and then a second generation from early August to early September. Much as the experts may debate this theory, what *is* certain is that the Speckled Wood can be seen on the wing in the London area from the end of March in an early spring to the middle of September in most years - usually without a discernible break. It may be this quite unique ability to maintain a continuous presence of the adult, and therefore mobile, stage, which accounts for the recent tremendous spread of the insect.

The range of the Speckled Wood in Britain has fluctuated considerably. In the last half of the nineteenth century and in the first years of the present one, the butterfly was a declining species. Since about 1940 however, it has spread again and now has recolonised most of its old haunts south-west of a line from London to Liverpool, and is now spreading slowly beyond here. In the London area, it was first met with by Petiver during the early 1700s at Enfield, who called it the "Enfield Eye" in his illustrated work *Papilionium Britanniae* (1717) and stated that it was not common. It later became known as the Wood Argus

(Wilkes 1749) and eventually , as at present, as the Speckled Wood (Harris 1766). As with the Wall butterfly, tracing its past history has proved difficult. In 1887 one was seen at Shoreham, Kent, and in 1892 a few were reported from the Sevenoaks district. But in 1895 it was no longer present in the districts around Lee, Eltham and Bexley (Fenn 1895). It is interesting that de Worms (1950) considered that the butterfly "*has increased in the south, but apparently disappeared from some localities in the northern part of the region*". This agrees well with the present-day situation, presented on the distribution map here which, whilst probably not entirely complete, reflects the true situation during the period from 1980 to 1986: the Speckled Wood butterfly is spreading and increasing in number in the London area from the south to the north. This also seems to tie in nicely with the national picture. The map presented by Heath, Pollard and Thomas shows a curious gap in the records where it appears that the butterfly has looped around London through Surrey, then Kent, then Essex, and on the other side through Buckinghamshire and into Hertfordshire. The London evidence suggests that it is now encroaching upon the Capital principally from the Surrey and Kent side.

Urbanisation appears to be little obstacle to the spread of this species, which seems to be quite happy in the dappled sunlight provided by the secondary sycamore and other "woodland" of parks, cemeteries, and waste sites of London, although in many of these areas it may have been artificially introduced, such as those at Wanstead, Essex, (48T06, 48T08 and 48T26). Here the caterpillars thrive on the coarse grasses which abound in such sites, notably *Dactylis glomeratus* and *Agropyron repens*.Grass plants chosen by the female for egg-laying are always in a shaded situation, and the caterpillar feeds both by day and by night.

WALL

Lasiommata megera (Linnaeus)

The vernacular name of the Wall was bestowed upon this insect by Harris in 1766, and has been adopted by both South (1906) and Frohawk (1934). Bradley and Fletcher (1979) also use the name Wall. The name "Wall Brown" was an invention of Heslop in his 1959 list, and is seldom used today. Petiver's 1699 name reads "the golden marbled butterfly with black eyes", but he later (1717) changed this to "The London Eye". Alternative names for this butterfly have included the great argus butterfly (Wilkes 1749), the orange argus (Lewin 1795) and, confusingly, the gatekeeper (Samouelle 1819). It is an insect which seems to love the sunshine: on hot sunny days it will be seen in a number of situations,

Wall *Photographer: Neil Bowman*

including along hedgerows, roadside verges, field edges, woodland rides and clearings, open grassland, and larger gardens. In Essex it is one of the few butterflies seen in the narrow strips of coarse grass that follow the former field boundaries where once stood hedges. The adult butterflies are on the wing first during May and June, the females laying eggs singly on the leaves of grasses growing in the shelter of hedge banks or under bushes. This gives rise to a second generation of adults during late July, which often live on until mid-September. The larvae from this generation hibernate, but will often feed during milder spells. In most years, they will then pupate during April to produce the spring brood but, if the winter has been particularly mild, and the spring is not too cold and wet, they will pupate earlier (as a result of their ability to wake up and feed during the milder weather) paving the way for a third generation of adults later in the season. In the London area, evidence suggests that there was such a third brood during 1983, though during the remaining six years of the survey there were probably only two. The caterpillar feeds at night on grasses, including *Brachypodium sylvaticum*, *B. pinnatum* and *Holcus lanatus*, but in more urban areas seems to prefer *Dactylis glomerata*, the cock's-foot grass.

In spite of its ability to utilise coarse grasses as a larval food plant, the Wall does not appear to have colonised the urban parts of London to the same extent as the Speckled Wood. Further, and instantly apparent from a comparison of the maps for these two species, the Wall Brown is found predominantly in the northern half of the London area, whilst the Speckled Wood is found largely in the south. It is highly unlikely that the two species are mutually exclusive – first because several sites support both species, and second, because if this were the case one would expect there to be a more uniform, but patchy, distribution of both species across a larger part of the London area. So, alternative explanations must be sought. Tracing older records however, has proved difficult. It seems possible that the Wall has always been less common at least in the Kent portion of our area. Chalmers-Hunt (1979) states that "*According to the Kent Biological Archives and Records Centre, since 1971 it has been recorded from every ten kilometre square in the county, excepting that area of Kent encroached upon by the County of London*". The records for metropolitan Kent which then follow that statement also seem to indicate a comparative scarcity in that area during the years since 1960. Certainly it is most unlikely that under-recording could account for many of the gaps in the present distribution, though inevitably it will account for a few. Great care should be taken, when recording the butterfly from new areas, to ascertain whether or not it has arrived there since the present survey was completed. In the more urban areas of London the distribution pattern is confusing. The butterfly is absent from the highly urbanised "South Bank", and the "West End", yet it *is* present in Tower Hamlets, Haringey, much of Hackney and even in the City of London, though whether or not it breeds in all of these areas is uncertain. Many records may in fact relate to wanderers.

[*Opsiphanes tamarindi* Felder & Felder

This large butterfly, placed by some authors in the Brassolidae, but considered here to belong to the Satyridae, ranges naturally from Mexico to southern Peru, the larvae sometimes becoming a pest on bananas. There are just five records from Britain, all relating to importations, including one in London (Thompson 1937 and Bristow 1986).]

MARBLED WHITE

Melanargia galathea (Linnaeus) ssp. *serena* Verity

To the surprise of many people, the Marbled White belongs to the family of "browns", and not to the "whites". The confusion results from the simple mistake, particularly prevalent amongst Lepidopterists, of classifying an insect according to its general appearance, without recourse to proper taxonomic examination. Detailed examination of the Marbled White reveals that it has only four walking legs (the front pair are vestigial) whereas the "whites" use all six legs for locomotion. The caterpillars have two conspicuous "spines" at the rear end, a feature absent in the Pieridae, and they have a totally different range of food-plants. The British "whites", with the exception of the Brimstone, overwinter as chrysalids, whilst the Marbled White, in common with the other members of the family Satyridae, hibernates as a caterpillar.

The Marbled White is a butterfly of central southern England, and parts of the south-west, and therefore largely misses the London area. As with most grassland butterflies, it has declined greatly during the last forty years because of the extensive losses of natural grasslands to ploughing, general agricultural "improvement" and other land uses. However, rather than suffering through

Marbled White *Photographer: Michael Hammerson*

cessation of grazing, this butterfly is actually helped by this particular alteration in land use, and now thrives in areas that would once have been better suited to Adonis Blues and Silver-spotted Skippers! In the London area it is sparsely distributed along the remains of the chalk grassland on the North Downs in Surrey, often quite numerous where it occurs, though becoming progressively less common into Kent, where there are only two recent records, both in the Borough of Bromley. Old records from the southern sector include Hinchley Wood in 1949 and by the River Mole at Cobham in 1947, both Surrey, and in Kent at Chislehurst Common, mostly as single specimens from 1932 to 1946. It is possible that many of the current records from Kent and Surrey stem from introductions: adults are regularly released in the New Addington area, (36T80) whilst the colonies in TQ 15 and TQ 25 may have been assisted at least by the introduction of the butterfly in the Dorking area (TQ 15 south of our boundary) during the late 1940s. The record from 15T24 relates to a casual sighting of an individual butterfly at Bookham Common on 20 July 1985. Elsewhere in London, there are old records from the Brentwood area of Essex, and during the early part of the last century it was apparently common in Epping and Hainault Forests in the same county. Hampstead Heath, Middlesex, provides us with the first London area record: Petiver recorded it here, under the name "our half-mourner" around 1695. From Hertfordshire, Foster (1937) lists Watford in 1878, and Haileybury in 1921, whilst Newman (1869) gives Woodcock Hill, Elstree. De Worms later noted "*a flourishing colony*" in Whippendell Woods (de Worms 1959) and added that it was taken regularly at nearby Chalfont St Peter in Buckinghamshire. The present-day records do not indicate any active colonies in our part of Hertfordshire, except possibly at Jacott's Hill (09T86) where three were seen in 1983. The other sightings in this region of the map relate to casual sightings of individuals at Oakend Wood (08T08) – 27 July 1985; Denham Golf Course (08T28) – also on 27 July 1985; Poors Field, Ruislip (08T88) – 28 July 1984; Hoddesdon Lodge (30T48) – 30 July 1984; and Stanstead Abbots Gravel Pit (31T80) during 1982.

GRAYLING

Hipparchia semele (Linnaeus) ssp. *semele* (Linnaeus)

The Grayling was said by de Worms in 1950 to have "*only a limited distribution in the London area, mainly on the chalk downs and heaths*". In the Surrey sector, it was "*very abundant*" at Colley Hill in 1945, where it outnumbered many common species, whereas in 1943 only two were seen in this locality. It was also numerous on the downs round Box Hill, common on the heaths round Oxshott, and at Wisley Common and Surbiton Golf Course. In Kent it was noted at Lewisham in 1871, and it was abundant in 1946 and 1947 on Hayes Common, Dartford Heath (last seen in 1968), Keston Common, around Shoreham, Eynsford and Otford, common in Darenth Wood and at Blackheath. De Worms concluded that "*It definitely shows signs of spreading in north-west Kent*". Chalmers-Hunt (1979) added Badgers Mount, where it was last seen in 1957. There is also a single old record from Haileybury in Hertfordshire, where the Haileybury School list of 1888 gave it as "*very rare*". The first available record for the London area appears in Petiver's *Papilionum Britanniae*, published in 1717

Grayling Photographer: Peter Gasson

where, under the title of "the Tunbridge Grayling" it was said that "*it is very rare about London*".

However, although the losses have been slight for this butterfly on a national scale, it has in fact suffered a far more drastic decline on the North Downs than it has elsewhere in the country. Today, the butterfly is limited to one small colony in our area, at a locality in Kent where it was first noted during July 1982. This must remain confidential for the time being as the colony would be very quickly eliminated by collecting. There was, in addition, a casual sighting of an adult at Grays Chalk Quarry SSSI in Essex during 1985, and a possible sighting of two at Rainham Marsh during the following year. There is no evidence of breeding at either of these two sites.

Graylings are single-brooded butterflies, and adults are on the wing in the second half of July, through August, and in to September. They lay eggs on the sheep's fescue grass *Festuca ovina* on chalk grasslands sites, or other grasses elsewhere, which hatch after about three weeks. The caterpillar hibernates in the third instar, awakening to feed again in the spring. Before hibernation they will feed by day or night, but afterwards they seem to be entirely nocturnal. Pupation occurs underground in late June, and the butterflies emerge after a month. The adult butterflies possess cryptic patterning on the under sides of their wings, and can be extremely difficult to spot when settled.

[WOODLAND GRAYLING

Hipparchia fagi (Scopoli)

A male of this south and central European butterfly was captured in July 1946 at Oxted, Surrey. It was doubtless an escape from captivity.]

[THE HERMIT

Hipparchia briseis (Linnaeus)

A single specimen of this "brown" butterfly was said to have been reared from a larva found near Newington on 11 August 1838 or 1839. It is an insect of southern Europe, eastwards to Russia and its claim to a place on the London list is extremely doubtful: two other 'Newingtons' exist in southern England, and the one near Folkestone is the most likely of the three if the record is genuine.]

GATEKEEPER

Pyronia tithonus (Linnaeus) ssp. *britanniae* (Verity)

Also known to many as the Hedge Brown, the Gatekeeper is one of our commonest summer butterflies in many parts of the London area. It is widely distributed in southern England, extending into Yorkshire and Lancashire but avoiding the central high ground of the Pennines. It is also widely distributed in Wales, except on the mountains, though in Ireland it is restricted to the south coastal area. Adult butterflies normally appear in July, slightly earlier than the often similar Meadow Brown from which the present species can, usually, be distinguished by the presence of two white dots in the black "eye-spot" on each fore wing: in the Meadow Brown there is normally only a single white spot here. Eggs are laid on grasses, including annual meadow grass *Poa annua* and cock's-foot *Dactylis glomerata*, though there are no discrete colonies as with so many other butterflies; rather the adult butterflies from a wide area will attend the same patch of flowers in search of nectar, giving the impression of a local abundance. Bramble *Rubus fruticosus* flowers are particularly attractive to Gatekeepers in the London area. The nocturnal caterpillar eats little on hatching, and from October enters hibernation whilst still very tiny. In the spring it recommences feeding when the weather warms up, and pupates during June. There appears to be only the one brood each year, unlike the Meadow Brown which is double-brooded, or even triple-brooded in exceptional years.

Heath, Pollard and Thomas (1984) remark in the national atlas that the Gatekeeper "*... is almost absent from London, and in this respect contrasts sharply with the closely related Meadow Brown*". We shall discuss the latter mentioned species presently, but their observations on the Gatekeeper are essentially true, even though the present work records a presence in every ten-kilometre square of the grid, a feat not achieved by those other authors. Indeed the present map is particularly interesting. Not only does it show the presence of the butterfly all around, and only very rarely within, the urban portion of the London area, it also portrays the insect as the only fully circum-urban species recorded during the present survey. Indeed, there is little interpretation neccessary for the reader to obtain a full idea of the situation. Penetrations into the urban area are worth examining however. There is a line of records along the length of Epping Forest, reaching into Redbridge in TQ 48, with isolated records at East Ham (48T22 - St Marys Nature Reserve) and at Barking (48T62 - Thamesside Park). This may be a recent invasion. There is an isolated record in Tower Hamlets at Cable Street, E1 (38T40) on 23 July 1984. The St Pancras and Islington Cemetery (29T60) and Highgate Woods (28T88) provide another point of entry, and the records in east Haringey and south Enfield are all on or

Gatekeeper *Photographer: Stuart Holdsworth*

adjacent to railway embankments. In the south-west, Wimbledon Common, Mitcham Common and other eminently suitable areas allow the Gatekeeper to creep nearer to town, whilst in the Kent sector, much of the Borough of Bromley contains suitable habitat. It will be particularly interesting to discover whether or not the Gatekeeper will be able to occupy some of the larger urban sites which are currently being developed with wildlife in mind, and if so, whether the populations will thrive. Certainly there is no reason why they should not do so, provided there is a route by which they can gain initial access, and there is powerful argument in favour of an ecological survey of linear sites such as railway lines and the like with a view to possible management as wildlife corridors, connecting the urban zone with the countryside.

MEADOW BROWN

Maniola jurtina (Linnaeus) ssp. *insularis* Thomson

The Meadow Brown must surely be the most widespread and familiar of British butterflies, occurring the length and breadth of the British Isles, apart from in mountainous regions. It is by no means the commonest, however: in London at least, that place is taken by the Small Tortoiseshell. Subspecies *insularis* is the most widespread, and the one which occurs in our region, but there are different subspecies in Ireland (*iernes* Graves) the Scillies (*cassiteridum* Graves) and on the west side of Scotland (*splendida* White). Confusion is possible with the Gatekeeper in some instances, but the larger size and the single-pupilled eye-spot on the wing of the Meadow Brown usually serves as a ready method of separation. The present-day distribution map for London indicates that the butterfly occurs just about everywhere, and to a large extent this is true. There are, however, one or two blank patches where it has not been recorded. Beyond doubt, many tetrads which are not already "dotted-in" will have Meadow Brown butterflies resident within their boundaries. This is particularly the case in the tetrads in the more rural border areas of Kent and Surrey, which are the least well recorded areas by virtue of the fact that they are the furthest tetrads from the author's home base! Never the less there are a number of more central areas to consider. These blank areas in fact follow the line of the River Thames as it passes through the heart of the city area. Working from west to east, there are blank areas in Hounslow, Richmond, Hammersmith & Fulham, Kensington & Chelsea, Westminster, and the northern parts of Lambeth and Southwark. Here the trail ends courtesy of the derelict docklands in the south of Newham, after which we return to a large and unexpected gap in Barking & Dagenham. There are, however, Meadow Brown butterflies seen regularly in the heart of the area, including in the City of London itself, and, during 1984, two on separate

Meadow Brown *Photographer: Peter Gasson*

Small Heath *Photographer: Ian G. Johnson*

dates in July at a minute backyard garden in Bradbourne Street, Fulham (not seen there before or since). It is quite likely that time will see these insects in every tetrad of the London area, though whether this will be as breeding insects, or merely as wanderers (such as the Bradbourne Street individuals) only time will tell.

Caterpillars of the Meadow Brown overwinter when quite small, and recommence feeding in the spring. Grasses are the foodplants, and it seems that whilst many are taken, smooth meadow grass *Poa pratensis* and other species of *Poa*, as well as *Agrostis* species, are preferred. The larvae feed alone, nocturnally, then generally pupate in May, and, though there are thought by many to be two broods it is far more likely that there is a protracted emergence of a single brood throughout the summer. What little evidence there is available for the London area favours the latter view, with adult butterflies recorded continuously from 14 June (1983) to 20 October (also 1983), more normally from the last two weeks of June to the last week of September or just beyond into October.

SMALL HEATH

Coenonympha pamphilus (Linnaeus) ssp. *pamphilus* (Linnaeus)

The Small Heath is a widely distributed butterfly in Britain, but one which tends to be local in its distribution within a given area. Its overall British distribution has apparently not changed over the last three hundred years or so, so clearly it has the recipe for success! There is a single brood in some years, with a partial second brood during favourable seasons. The first adults of the year emerge in May/June. Some of the caterpillars from these adults will feed slowly, and hibernate almost fully fed the following winter to produce pupae early the next spring, giving adults in May and June again. Other caterpillars from the same parents will, it seems, feed very rapidly, and pupate in July to produce adults in August/September. The caterpillars of these adults hibernate whilst still small and produce adults the following June/July. Thus there is a complicated system whereby the Small Heath may be seen for most of the summer in the London area, with just the briefest of gaps in some years at the start of August. The evidence from the present survey seems to hint that in unfavourable seasons, such as 1986, many caterpillars will favour the idea of feeding slowly and not pupating until the following spring. There were certainly extremely few Small Heaths seen during that year.

An examination of the London area map shows a widespread and patchy distribution in keeping with statements made above. In general, the truly urban areas are avoided, though areas of semi-wilderness within this type of terrain may support colonies. The butterfly does not appear to be very mobile, and there seems to be little movement even between adjacent colonies. As far as actual populations are concerned, numbers are far higher in the Hertfordshire, Essex, Kent and Surrey areas than they are in urban Middlesex (there is no such information from our part of Buckinghamshire). A colony along the River Roding at Redbridge during 1981 occupied about 30 metres of one bank of the river only (the opposite bank was unsuitable in any case) and extended into the rough grassland only two or three metres away from the river. Here the larvae fed on *Poa annua* and there were approximately fifty individuals on the wing during July. In the ten-acre derelict churchyard which forms St Marys Nature Reserve, East Ham (48T00) an isolated colony surrounded by housing and separated from other suitable areas by a five-lane main route into London produced few more than a dozen examples during the same period.

It is quite likely that more sites for this little butterfly will be discovered over the years, but given the generally sedentary nature of the individual insects, and the stable status of the animal as a whole in Britain, it seems unlikely that it will be recorded from the majority of the tetrads currently blank.

RINGLET

Aphantopus hyperantus (Linnaeus)

The Ringlet butterfly, seen from above, is rather a drab-looking insect, along with others such as the Green Hairstreak. But like the Green Hairstreak, when it closes its wings and reveals its under surfaces, the true meaning of its vernacular name becomes apparent: a series of black eye-spots, each with a distinct white pupil, and each surrounded by a ring of golden-yellow. It is almost entirely a woodland butterfly, preferring rides, clearings or adjacent lanes, which are slightly damp. The female scatters her eggs at random amongst grasses growing about two feet in height in damp situations, and, upon hatching two to three weeks later, each caterpillar must select its own foodplant upon which it will feed by night. A number of species of grass are recorded, though there are clear preferences amongst different batches of caterpillars. There is no data to hand for the preferences of London caterpillars, however. During October, the caterpillars hibernate, though they emerge to feed during mild weather, and do not become fully fed until the following June. Pupation takes place on the ground amongst the grasses, and the chrysalis is not attached to anything, remaining loose on the floor. Adult butterflies are on the wing in a single brood from early July to the end of August, a little earlier in the Kent and Surrey sectors.

The distribution during 1980 to 1986 in the London area reflects the woodland nature of the butterfly. It is confined to woodlands in the south in Kent and Surrey, and in the north in Hertfordshire, with four isolated sites in Essex, and a cluster of sightings in the Highgate Woods area of Middlesex. The only exception relates to a single adult at Northolt (18T24) doubtless either a wanderer or a release. There are, of course, a number of woodlands where the Ringlet butterfly does not occur, and some of these do apparently contain suitable habitat in the form of damp rides with coarse grasses. Doubtless the butterfly has been simply missed at some sites, but a comparison of its distribution map with that of other species surely cannot indicate under-recording as the real reason for such a huge gap in the records for, say, Essex. Chalmers-Hunt (1979) states that it is largely absent from the eocene soils of north-west (suburban) Kent, north of the chalk and west of the Darent, which is essentially our portion of that county. The present results bear out that statement, with the Ringlet in our part of Kent being restricted to woods on the chalk. It is perhaps not without significance that the soils of Essex in our area are rather acid, and certainly produce woods which are quite dissimilar to those of Kent and Surrey where the Ringlet does occur.

MILKWEED

Danaus plexippus (Linnaeus)

Also known as the Monarch, this is the classical migrant butterfly: in America its long-distance flights to its hibernation site has many times been the subject of television natural history programmes. In Britain however, immigrants reach us also from the population in the Canary Islands, probably as strays. They never establish here, simply because their foodplants, milkweeds of the genus *Asclepias*, do not grow naturally in Britain. During 1981, escaped individuals from Syon House Butterfly Farm established themselves temporarily on *Asclepias* just across the river at Kew Gardens, but this was only a short-term affair. The butterfly is popular with breeders, and there are many records of escapes and deliberate releases. There are also a number of accidental importations on record, as for example two which flew out of the cargo hold of a ship at Tilbury Dock in 1920! There are records of only nine genuine immigrants in the London area, all occurring between 1937 and 1982. In chronological order these are:

> Harrow, Middlesex – 2 October 1937; West Wickham, Kent – 22 August 1950; Norbury, Surrey – 25 September 1957; Godstone, Surrey – one each on 21 and 29 October 1967; New Cross, Surrey – 24 October 1968; Oxted, Surrey – 19 October 1973; Epsom, Surrey – a male on 11 September 1977; and Loughton, Essex – late July 1982.

Ringlet *Photographer: Andrew Merritt*

Milkweed *Photographer: Michael Hammerson*

[THE TIGER

Danaus chrysippus (Linnaeus)

An example of this large butterfly was captured at Chislehurst, Kent, and its photograph appeared in the *Kentish and Eltham Times* Newspaper for 15 July 1983. There is no doubt whatsoever that this was a released individual.]

DISTRIBUTION MAPS

SMALL SKIPPER 1980-1986

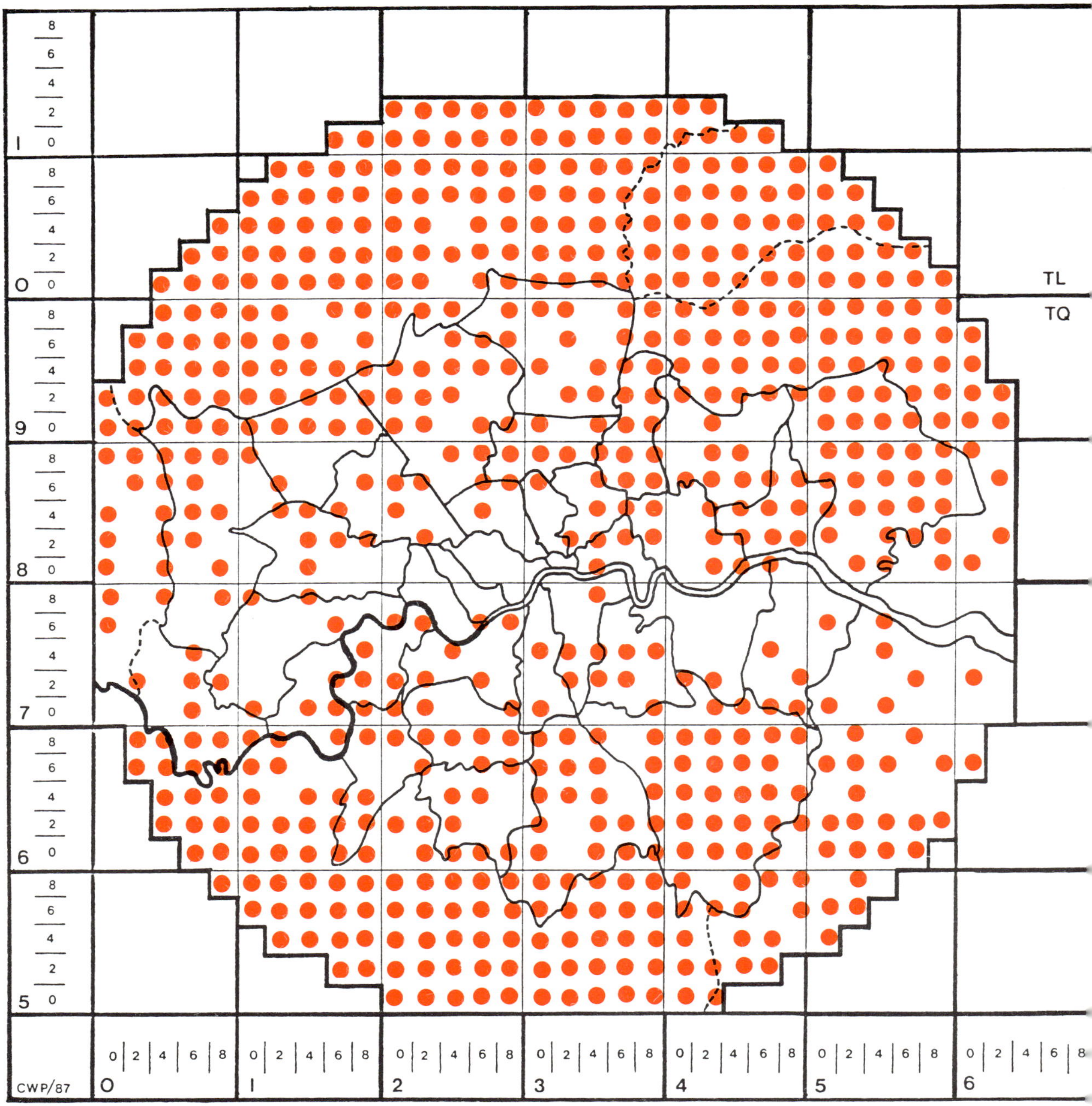

ESSEX SKIPPER 1980-1986

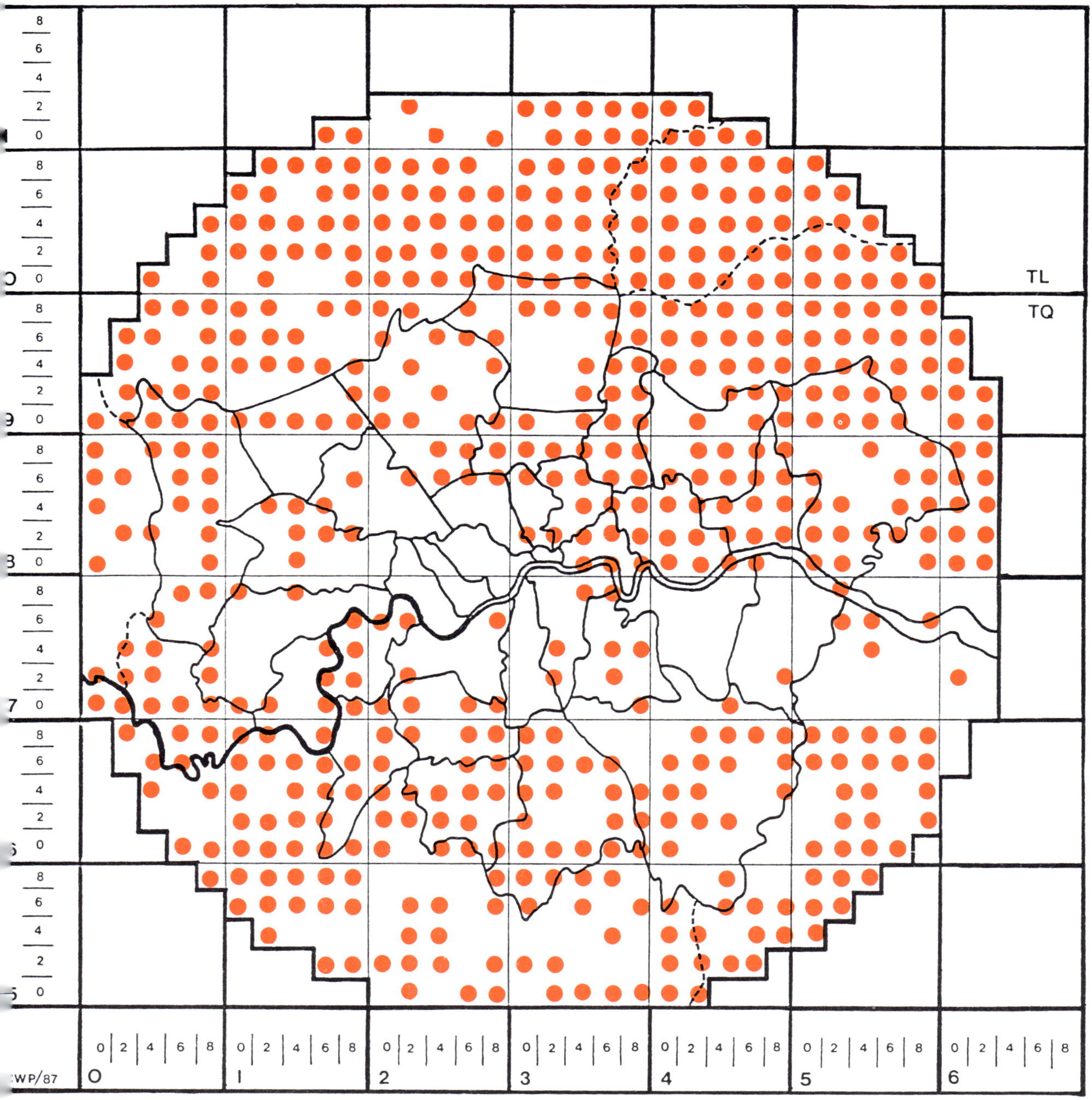

SILVER-SPOTTED SKIPPER 1980-1986

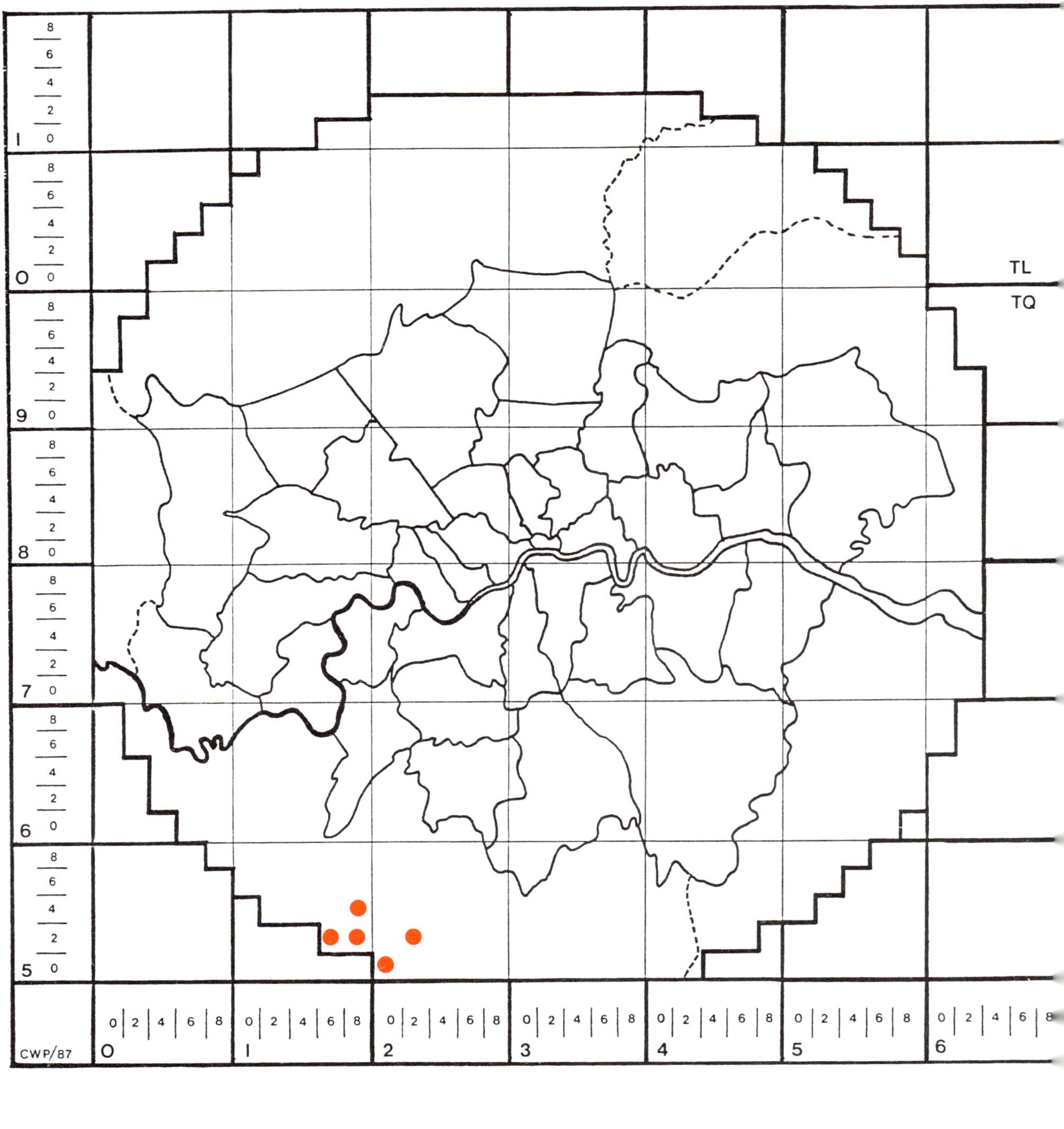

LARGE SKIPPER 1980-1986

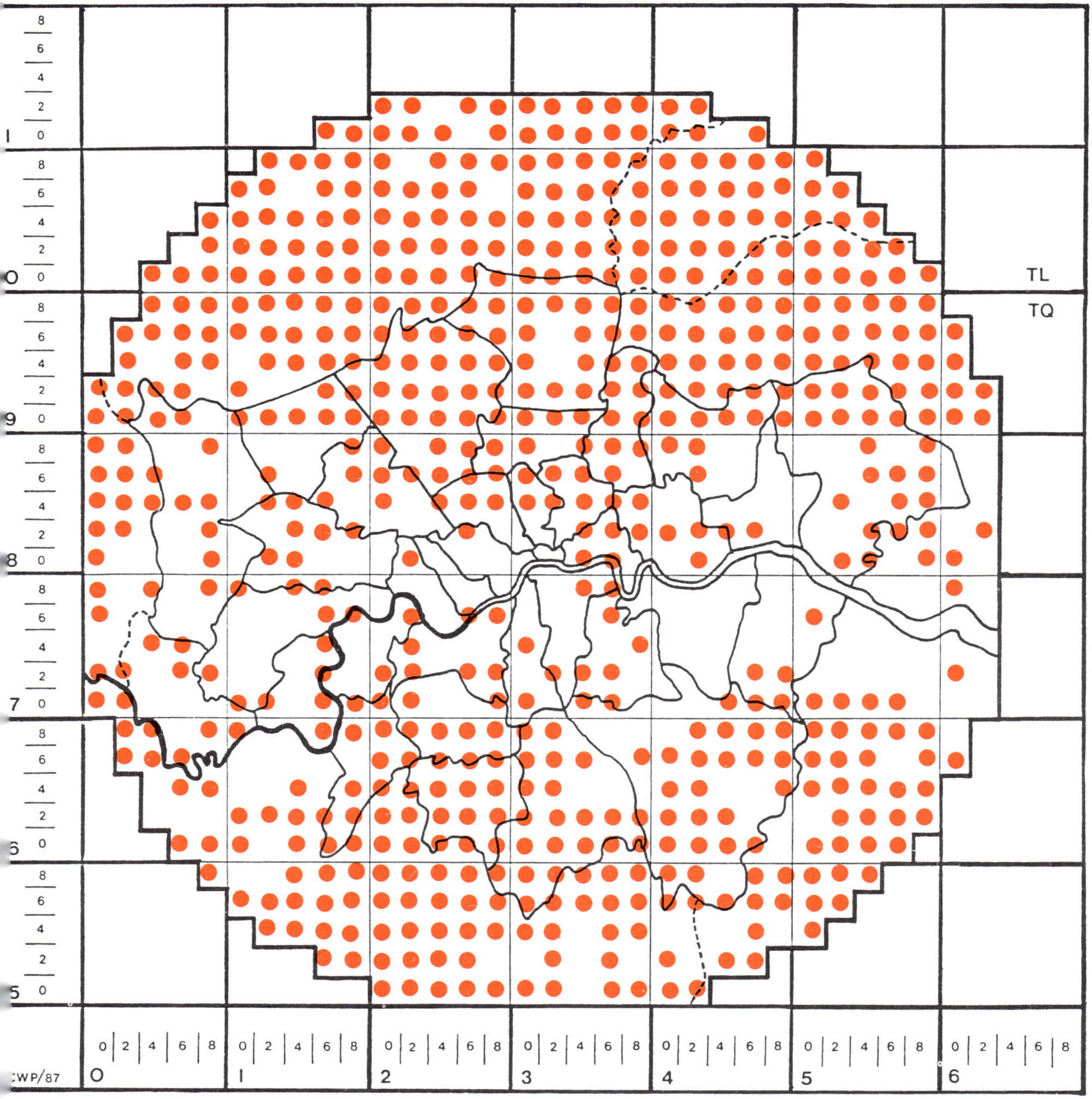

DINGY SKIPPER 1980-1986

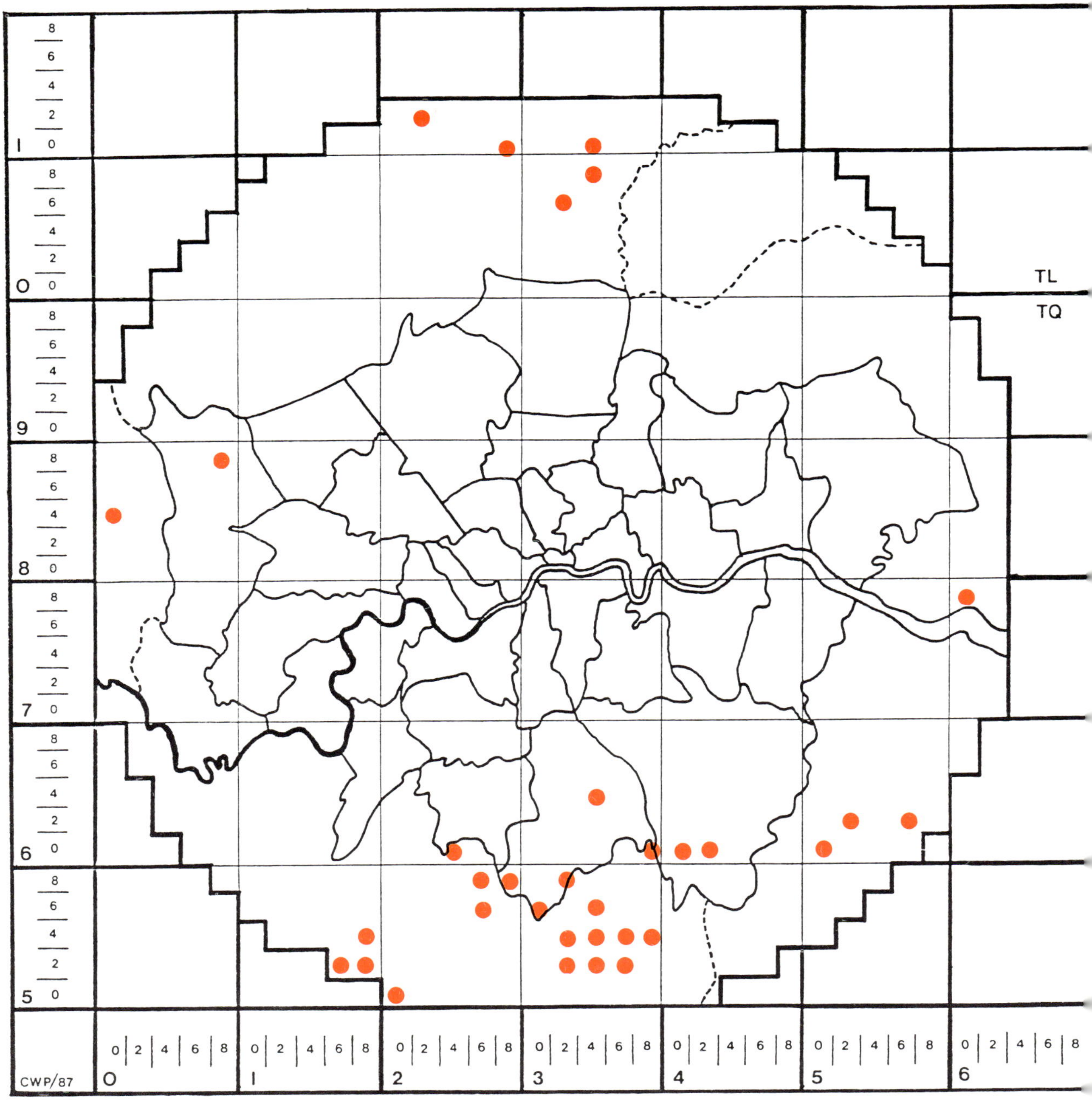

GRIZZLED SKIPPER 1980-1986

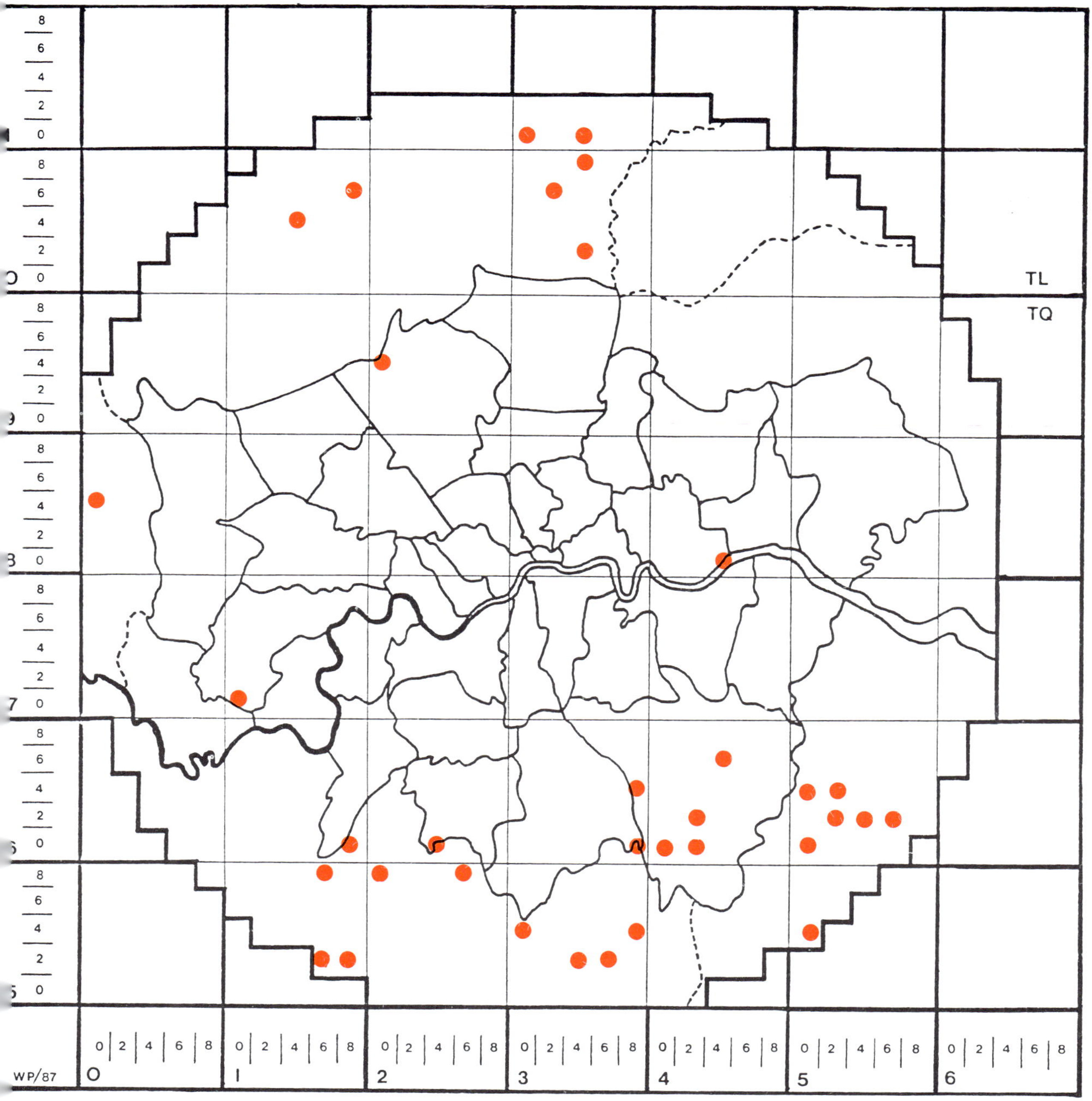

CLOUDED YELLOW 1980-1986

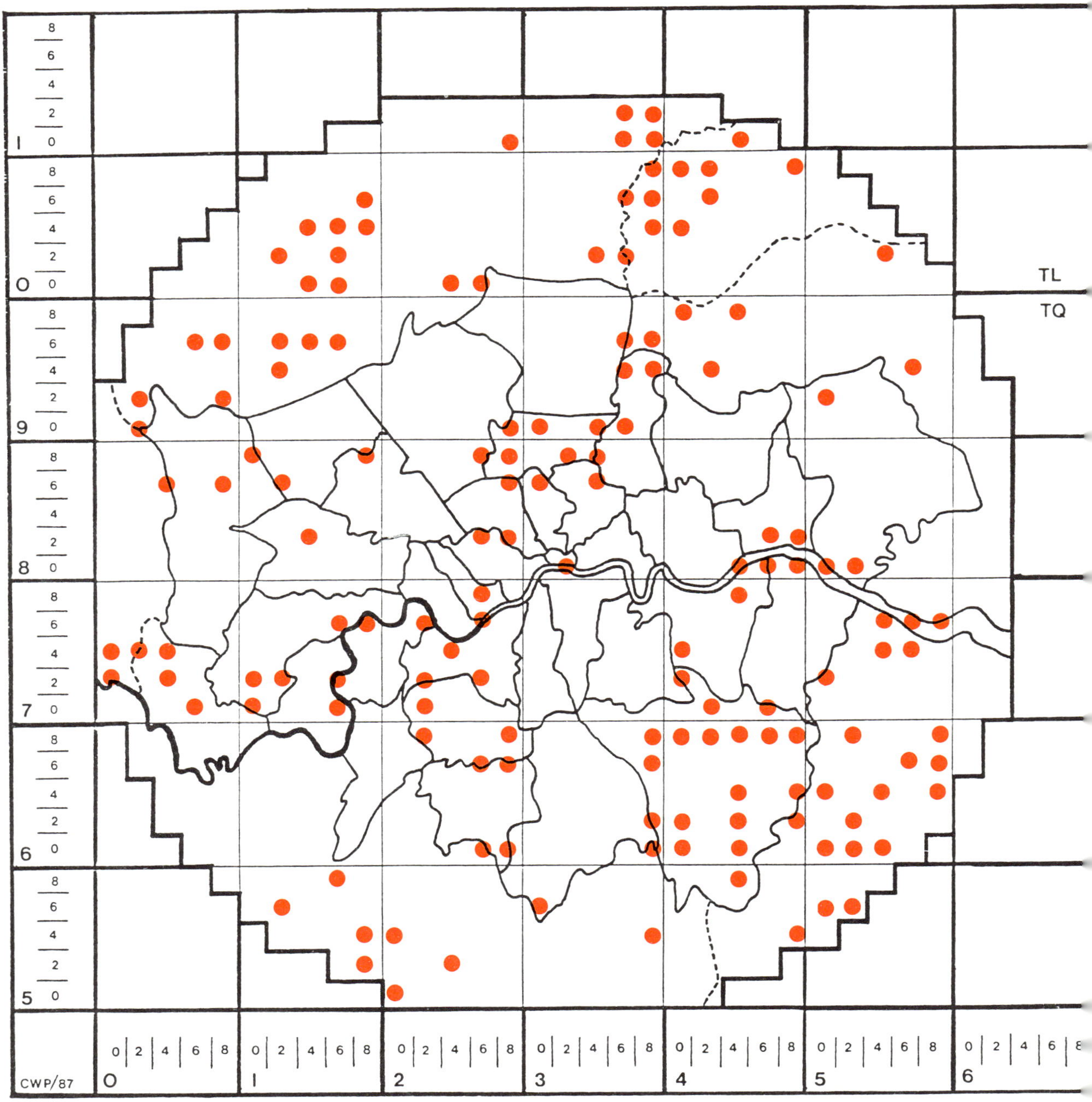

BRIMSTONE 1980-1986

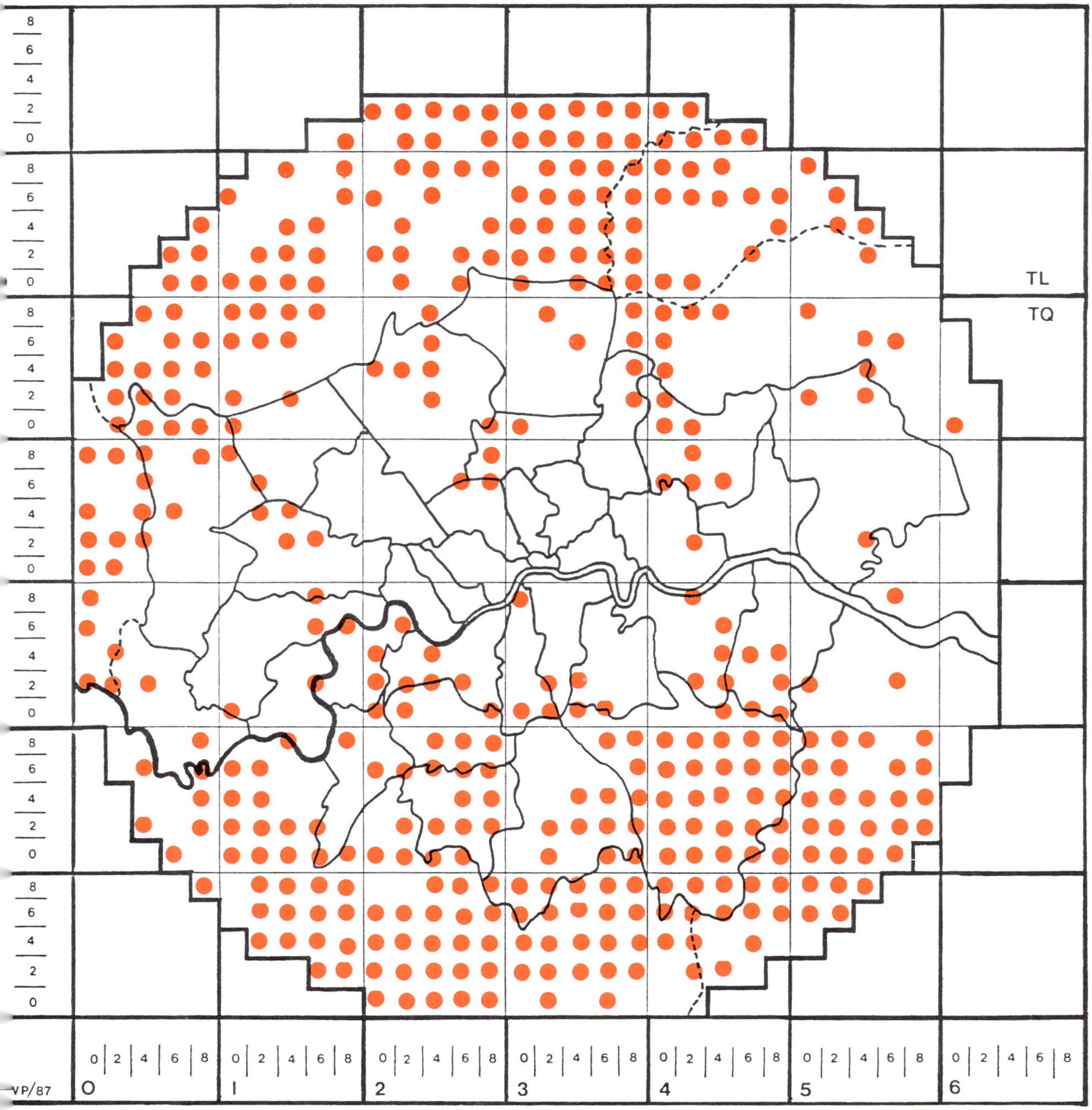

LARGE WHITE 1980-1986

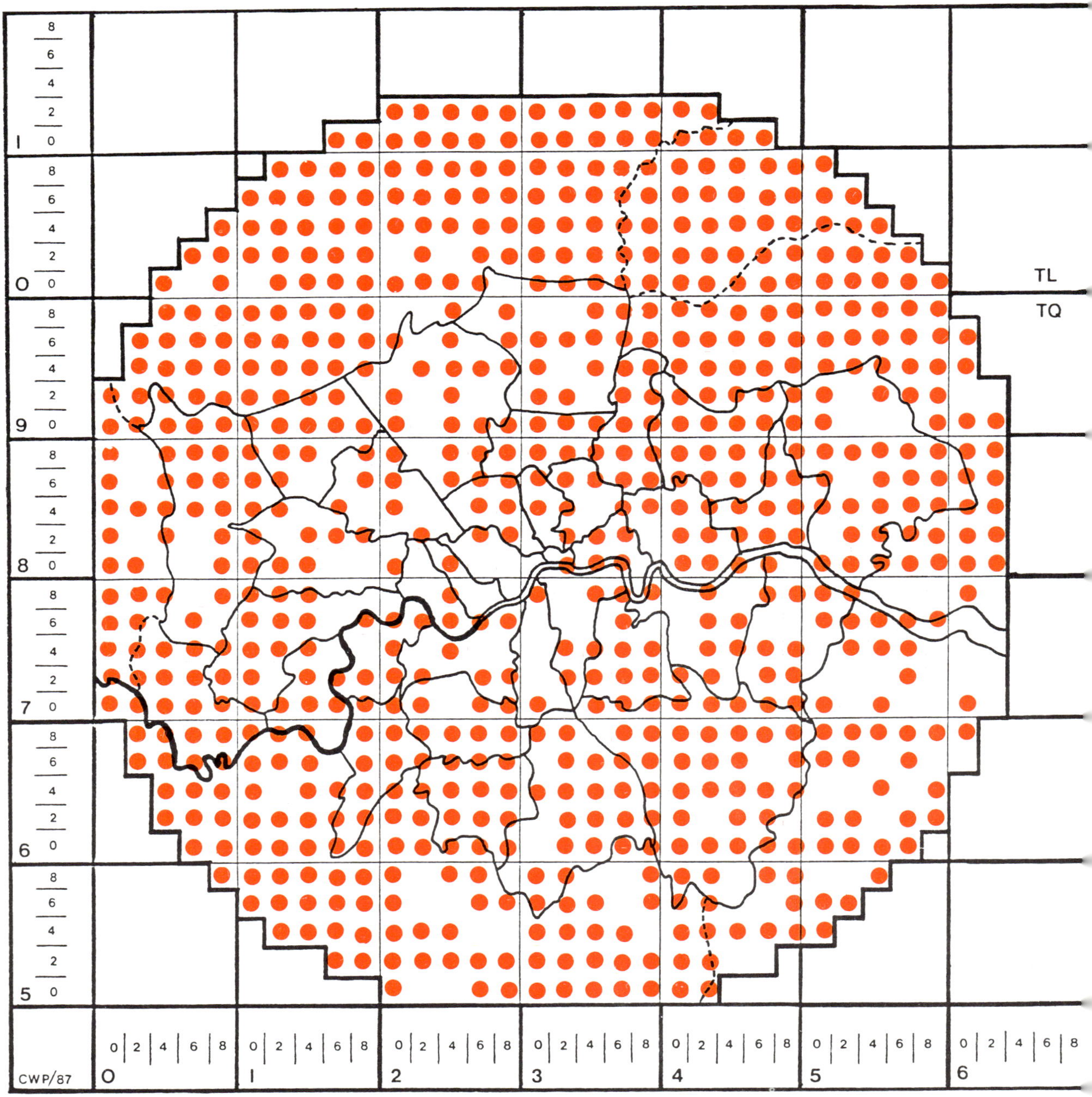

SMALL WHITE 1980-1986

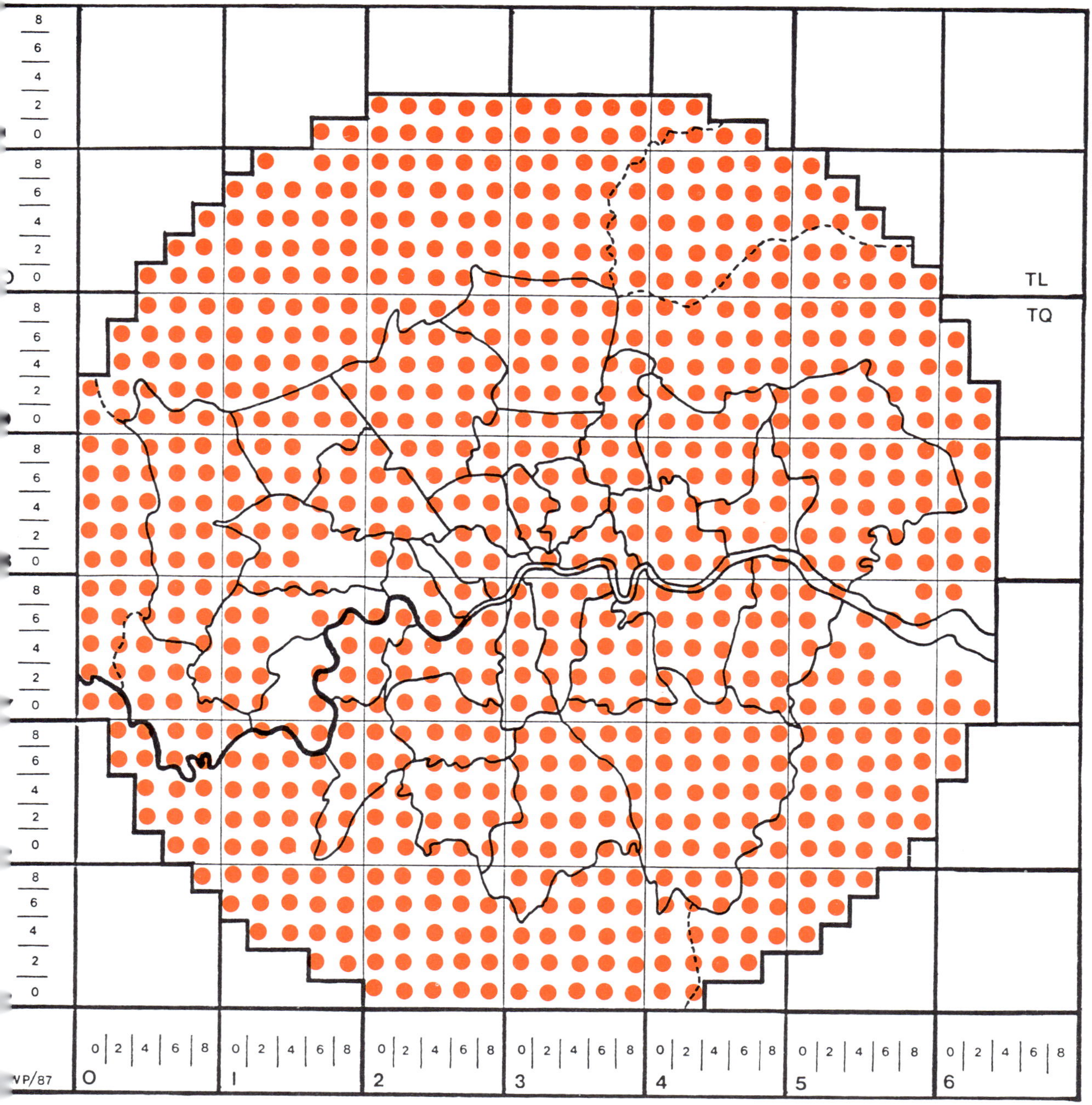

GREEN-VEINED WHITE 1980-1986

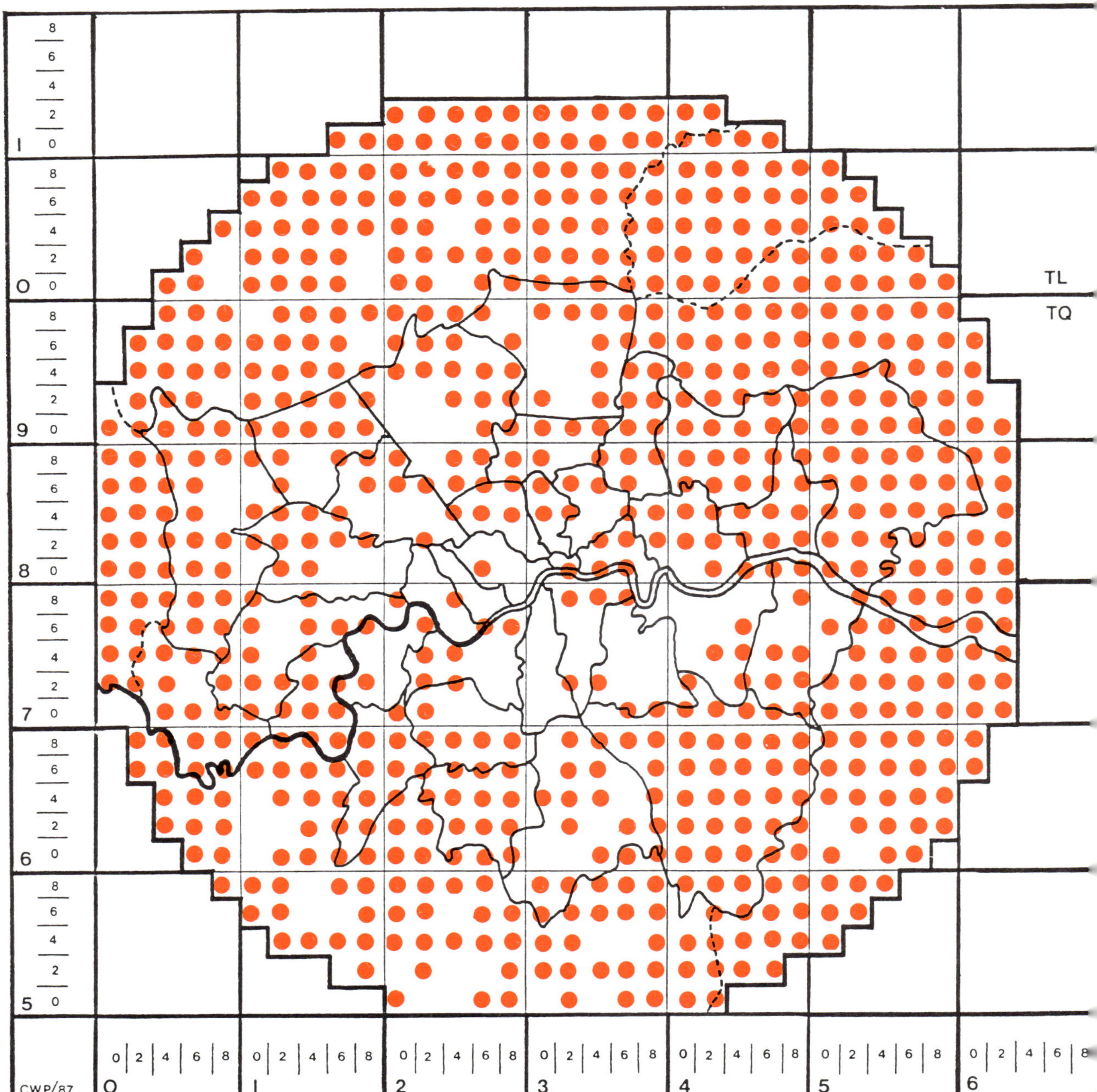

ORANGE-TIP 1980-1986

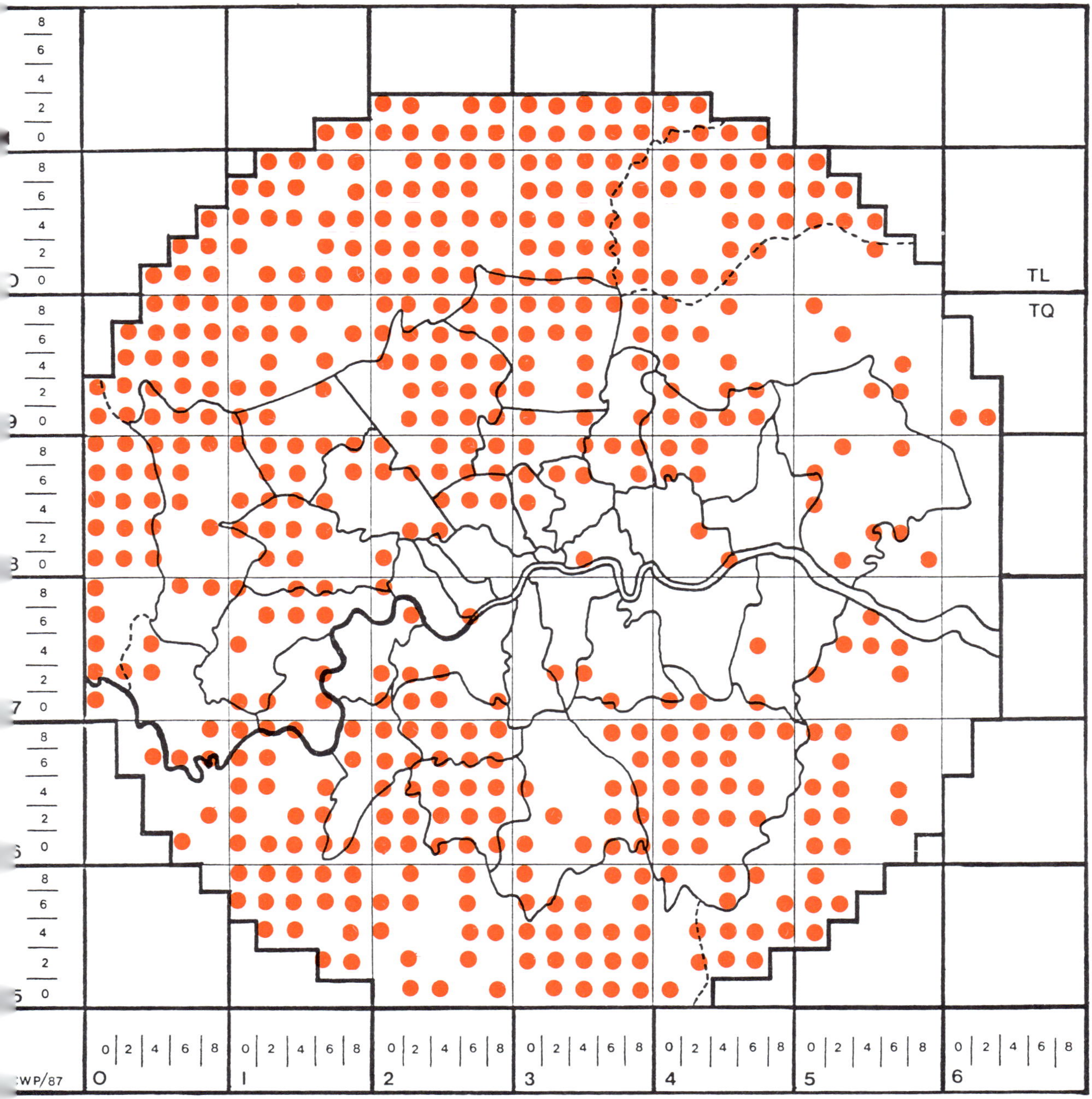

GREEN HAIRSTREAK 1980-1986

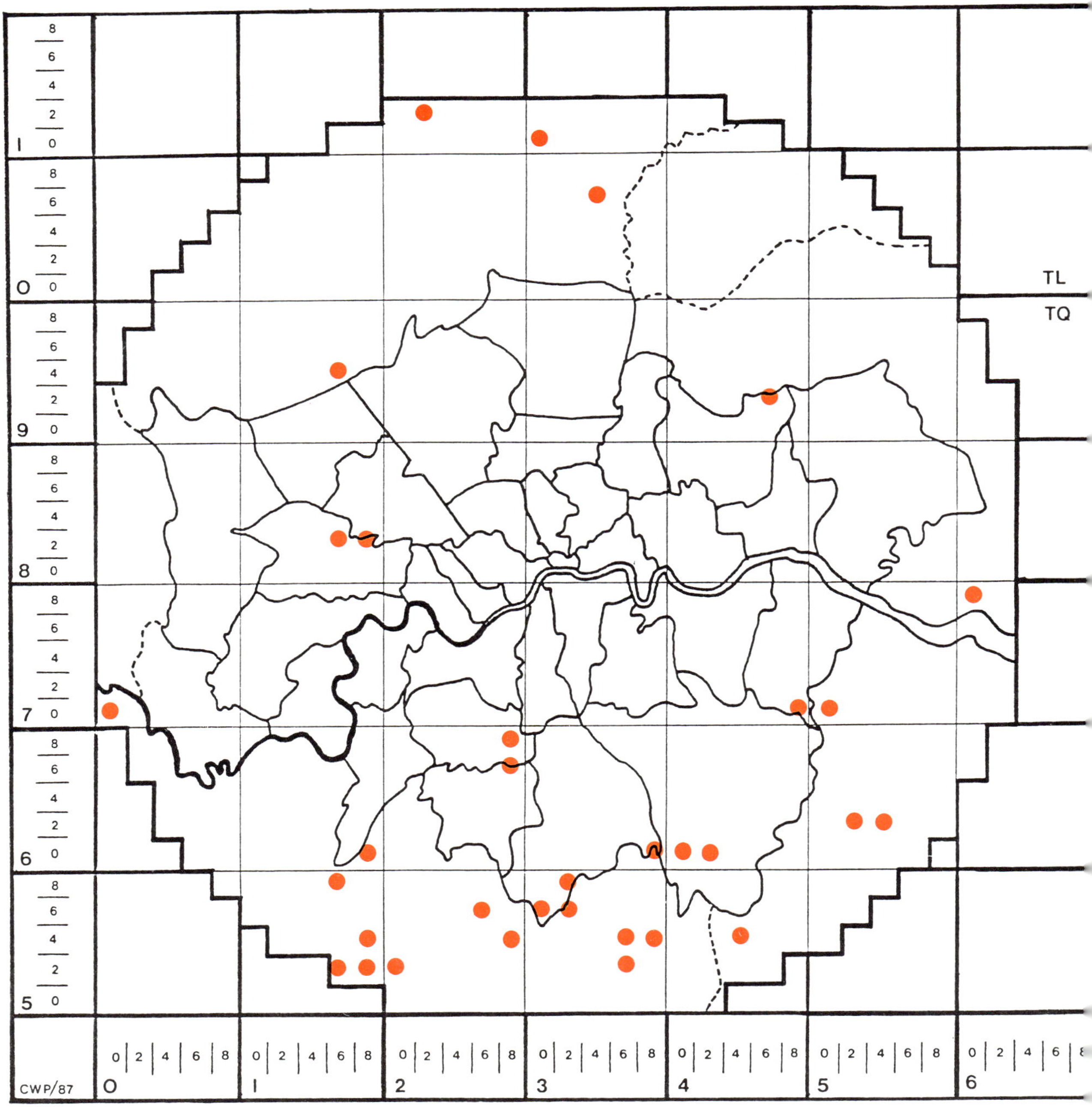

BROWN HAIRSTREAK 1980-1986

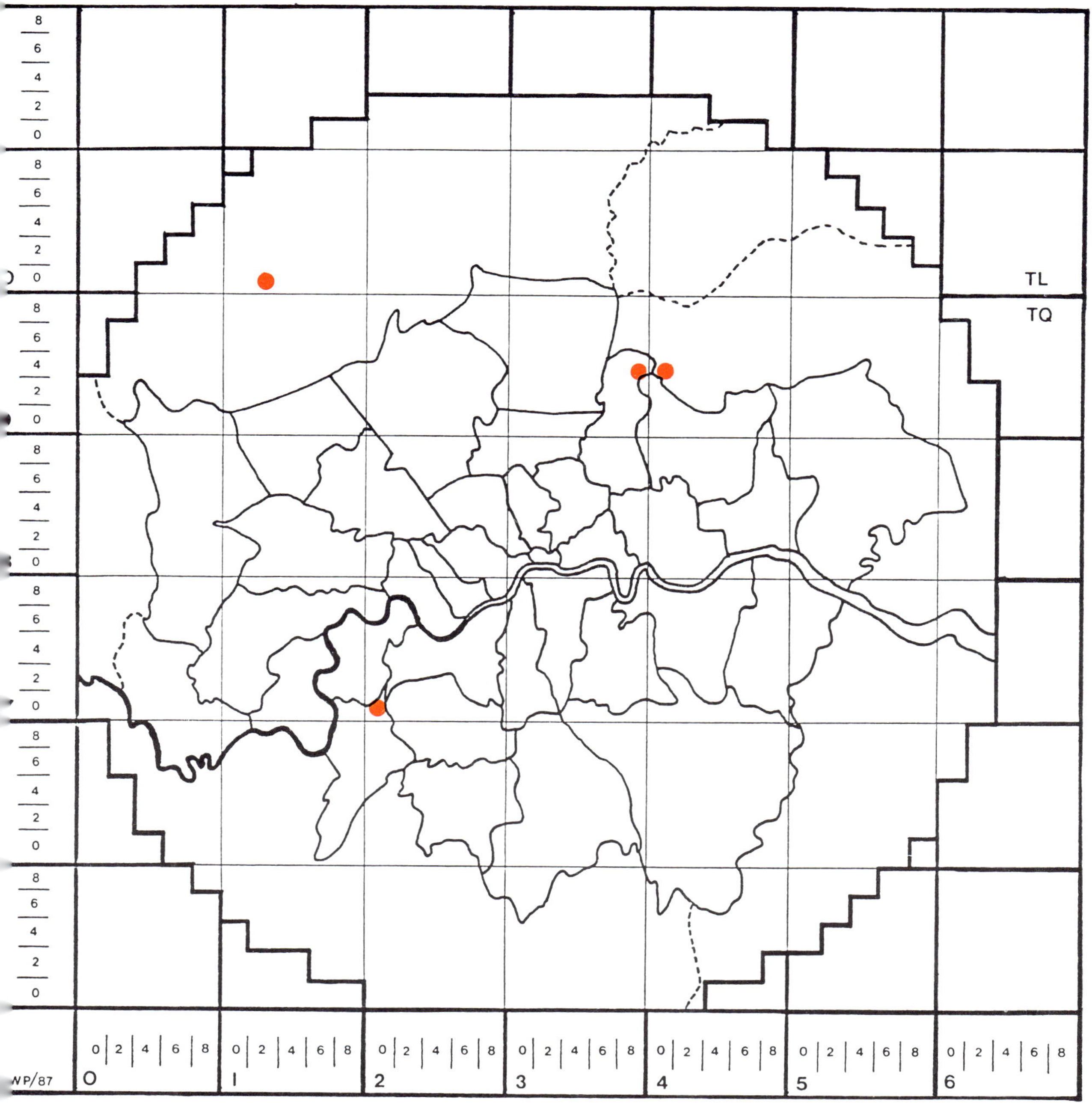

PURPLE HAIRSTREAK 1980-1986

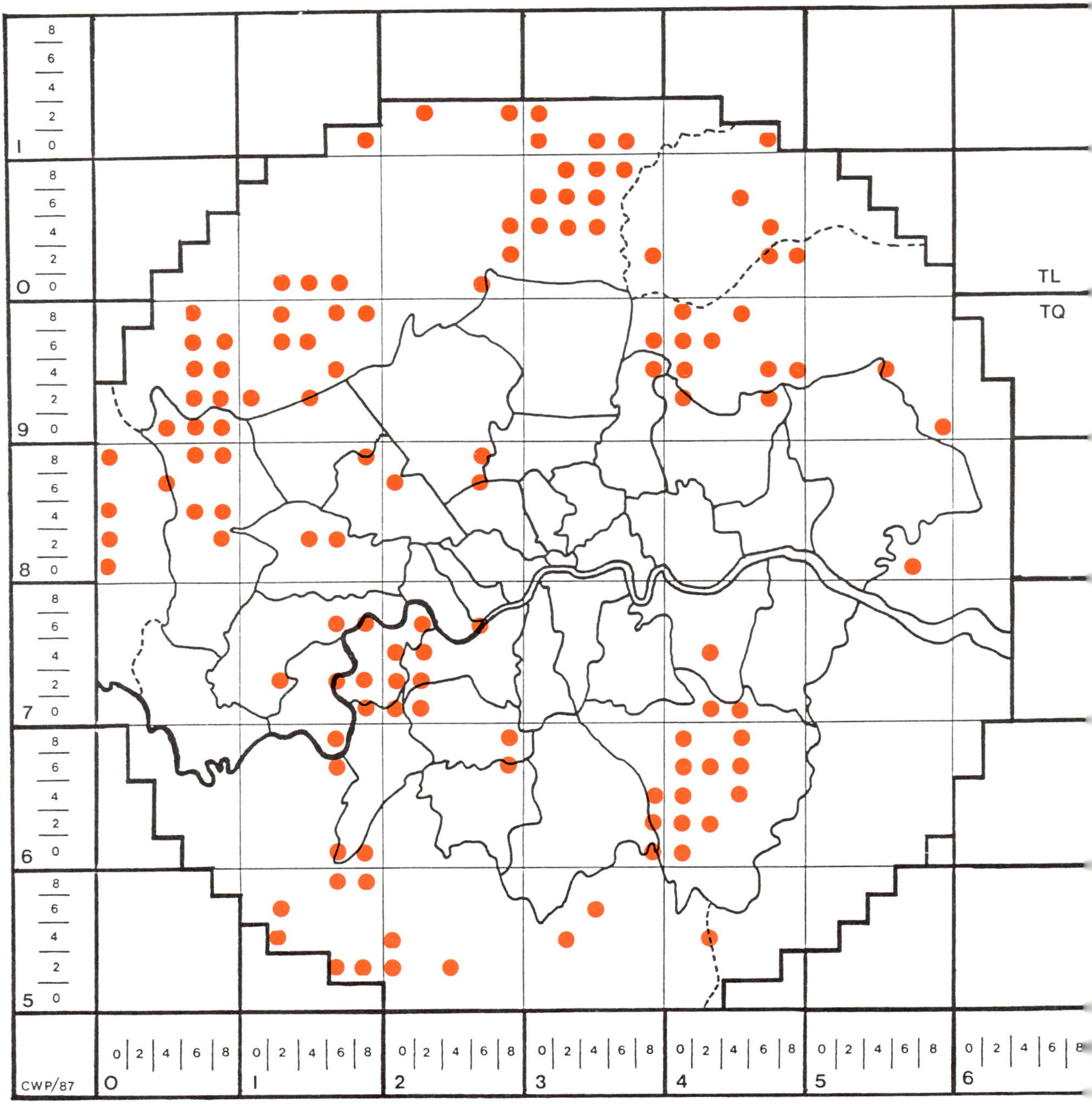

WHITE-LETTER HAIRSTREAK 1980-1986

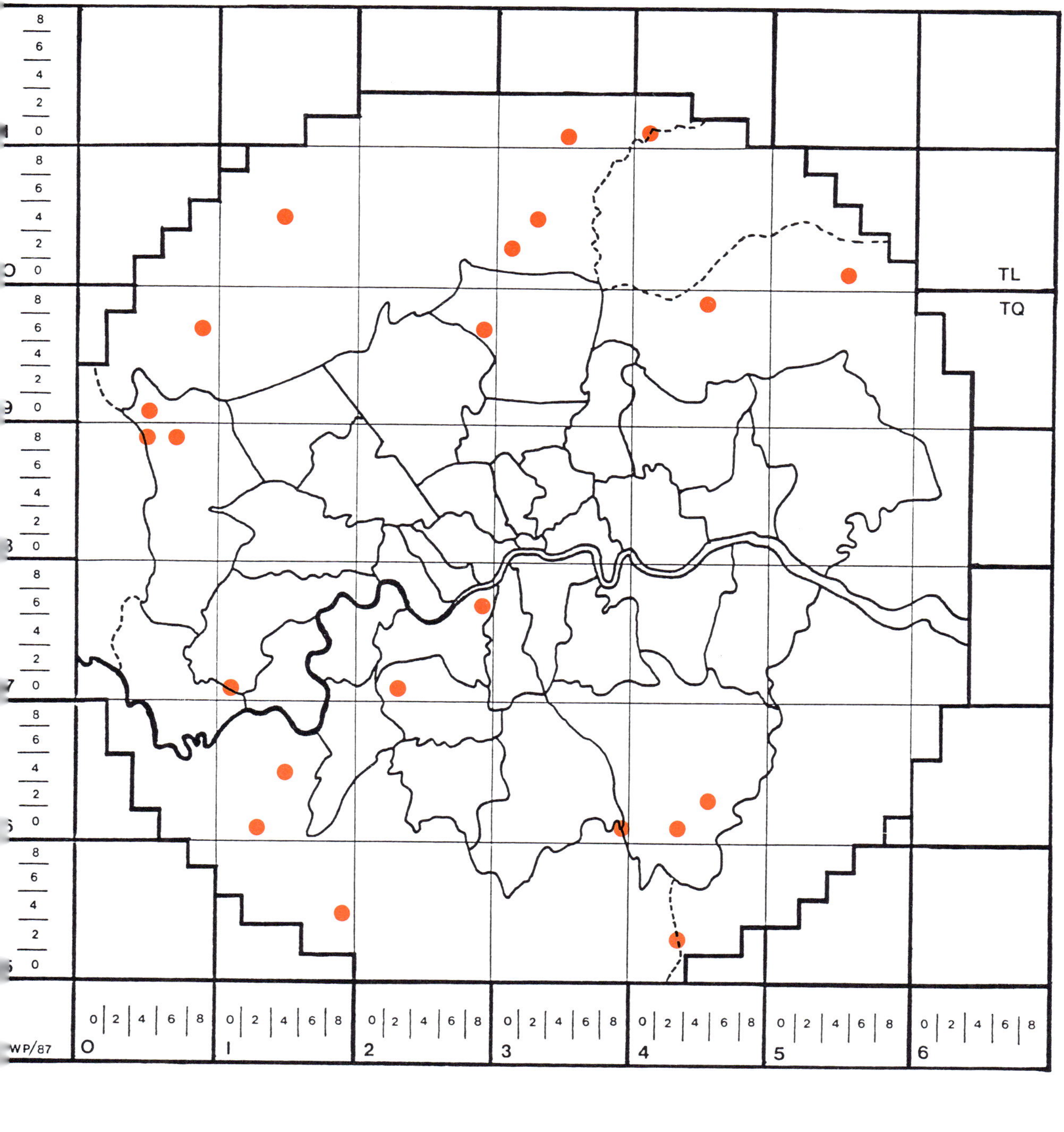

SMALL COPPER 1980-1986

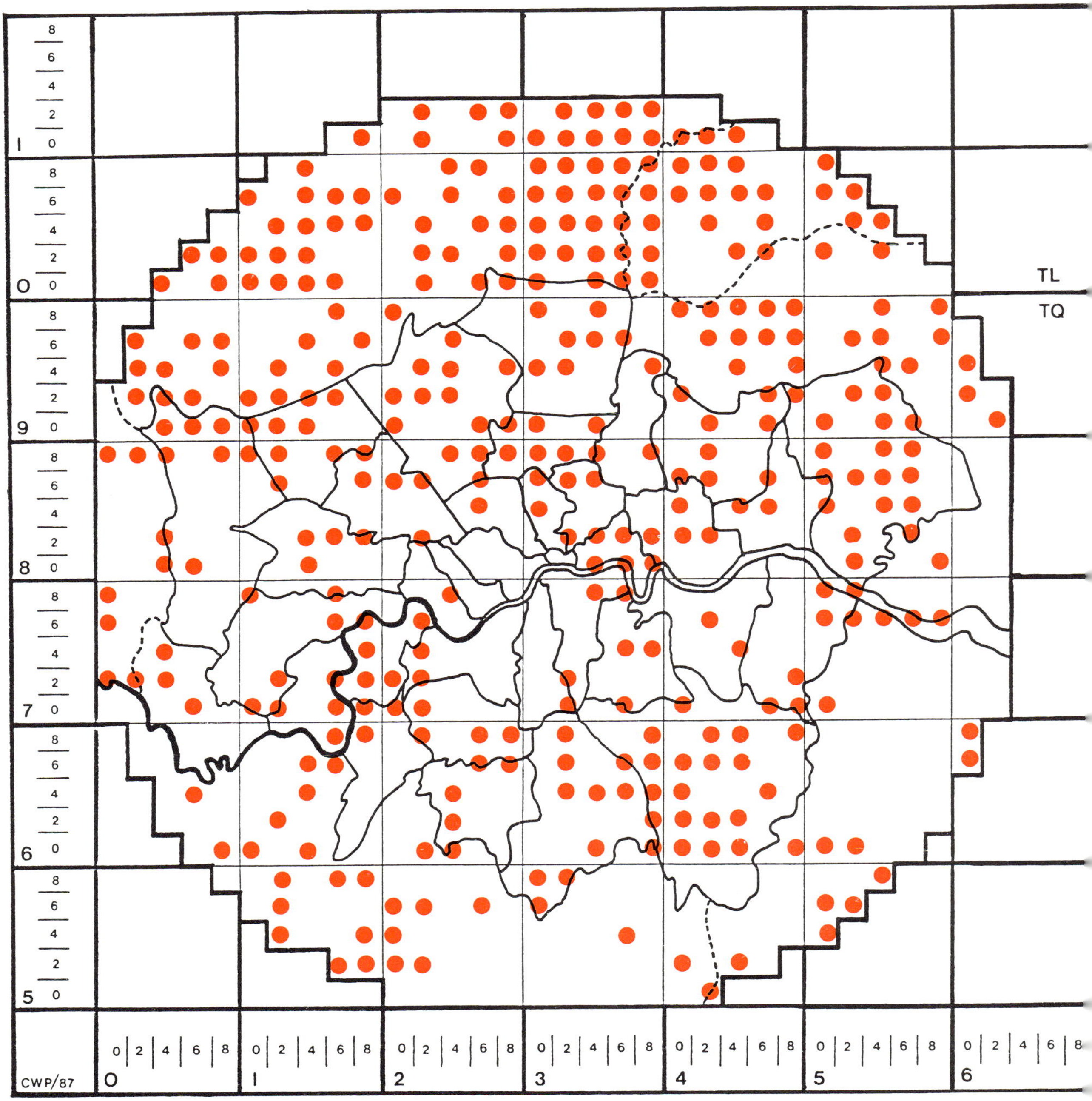

SMALL BLUE 1980-1986

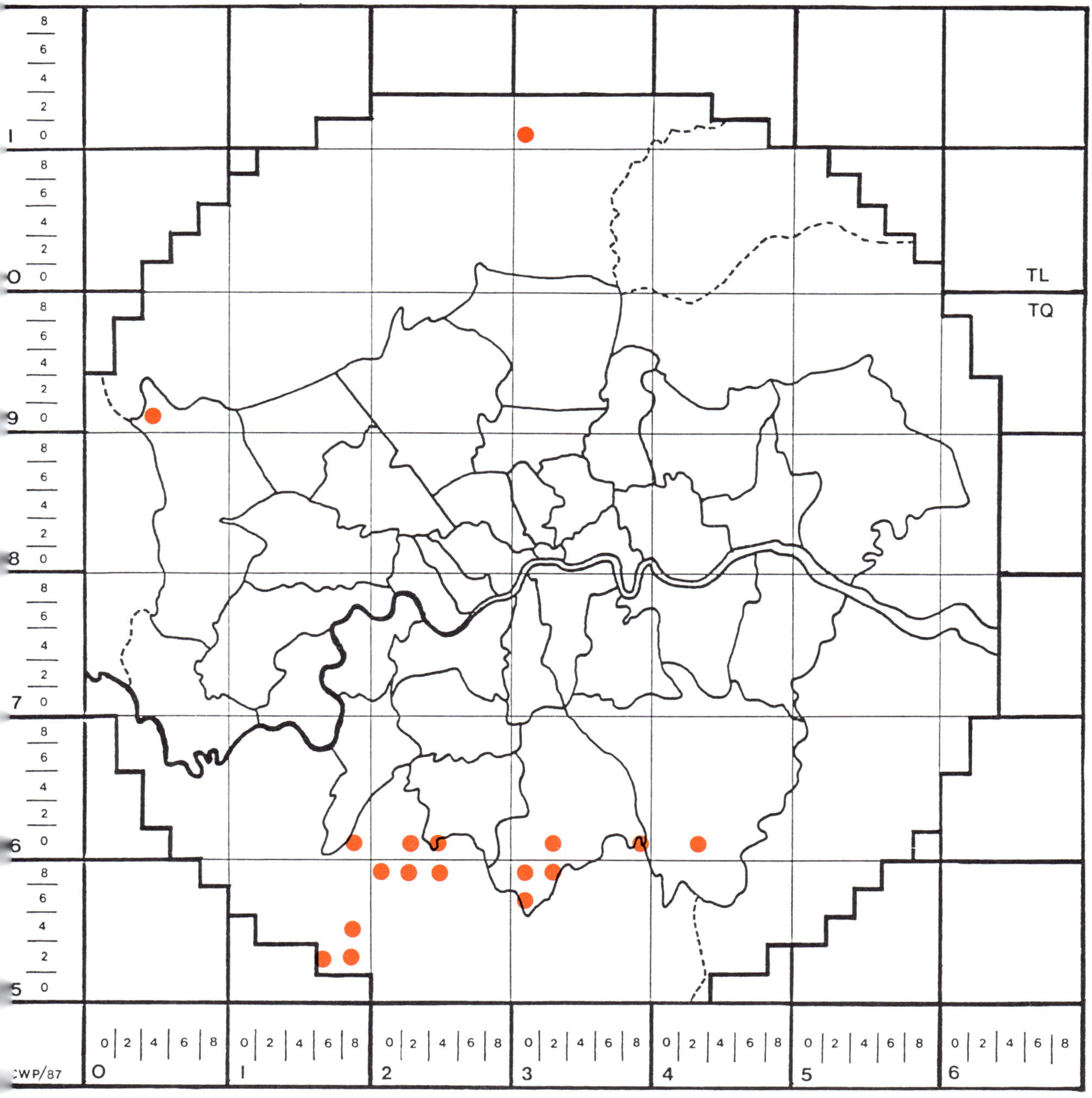

SILVER-STUDDED BLUE 1980-1986

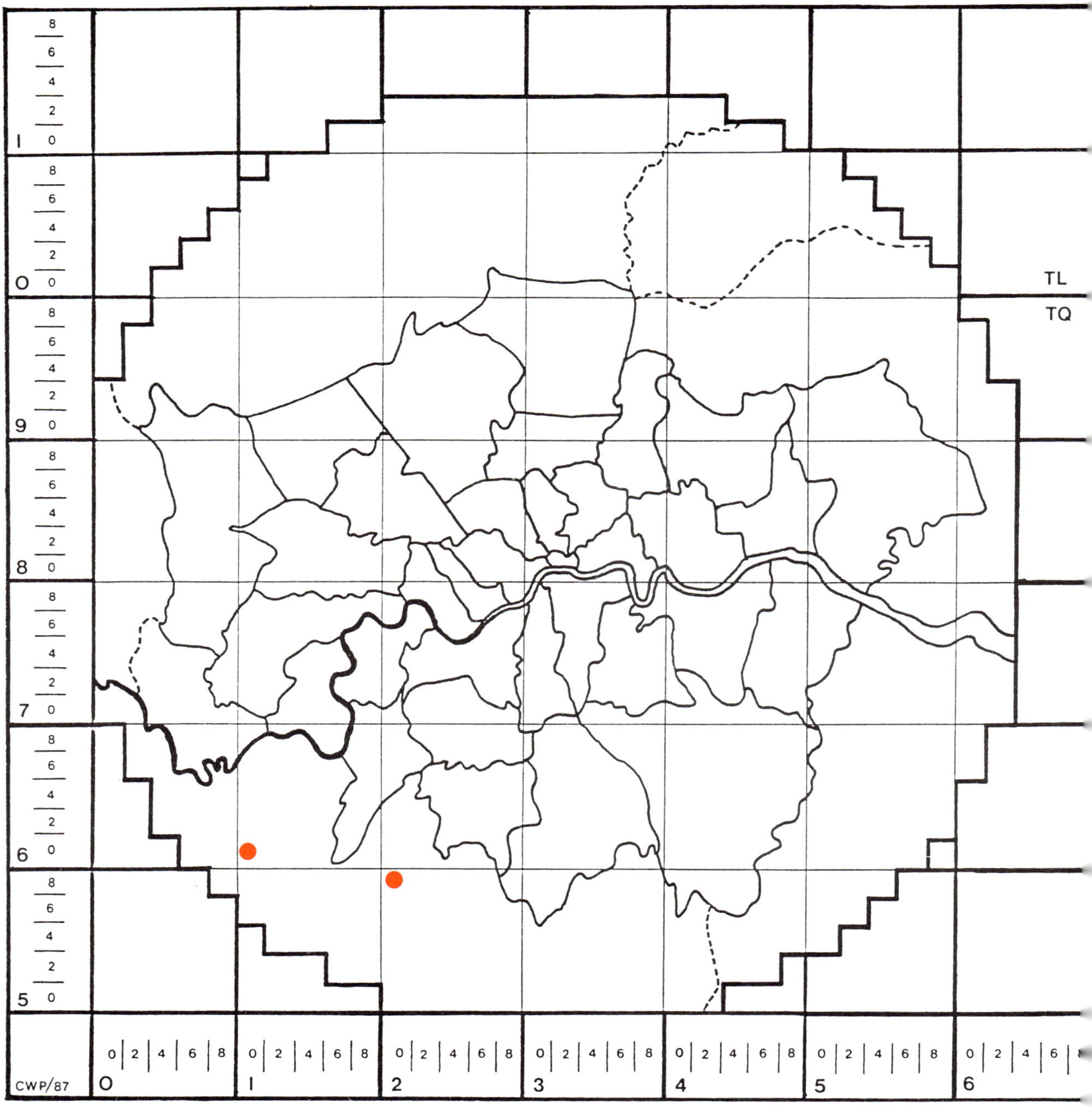

BROWN ARGUS 1980-1986

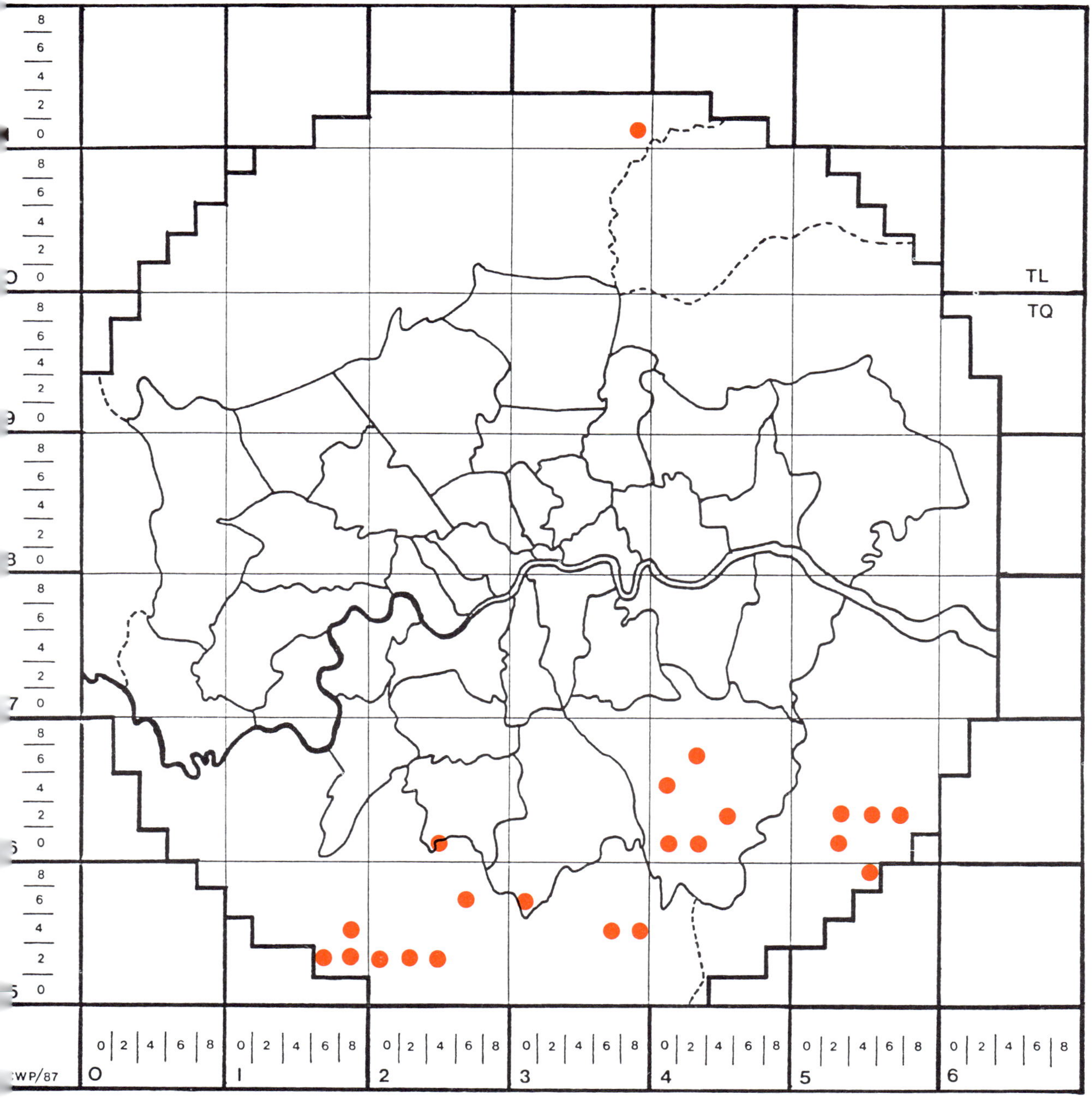

COMMON BLUE 1980-1986

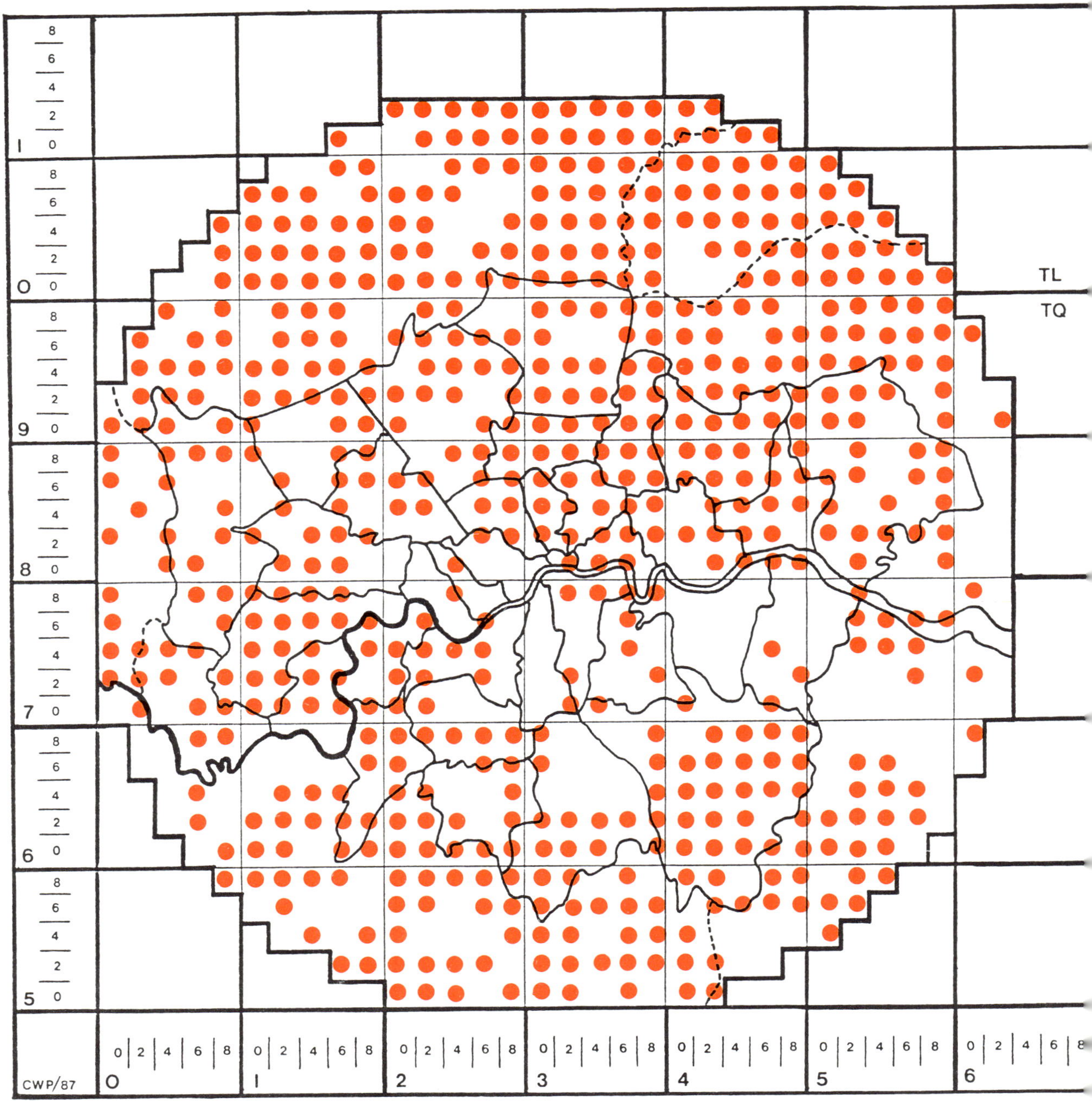

CHALK HILL BLUE 1980-1986

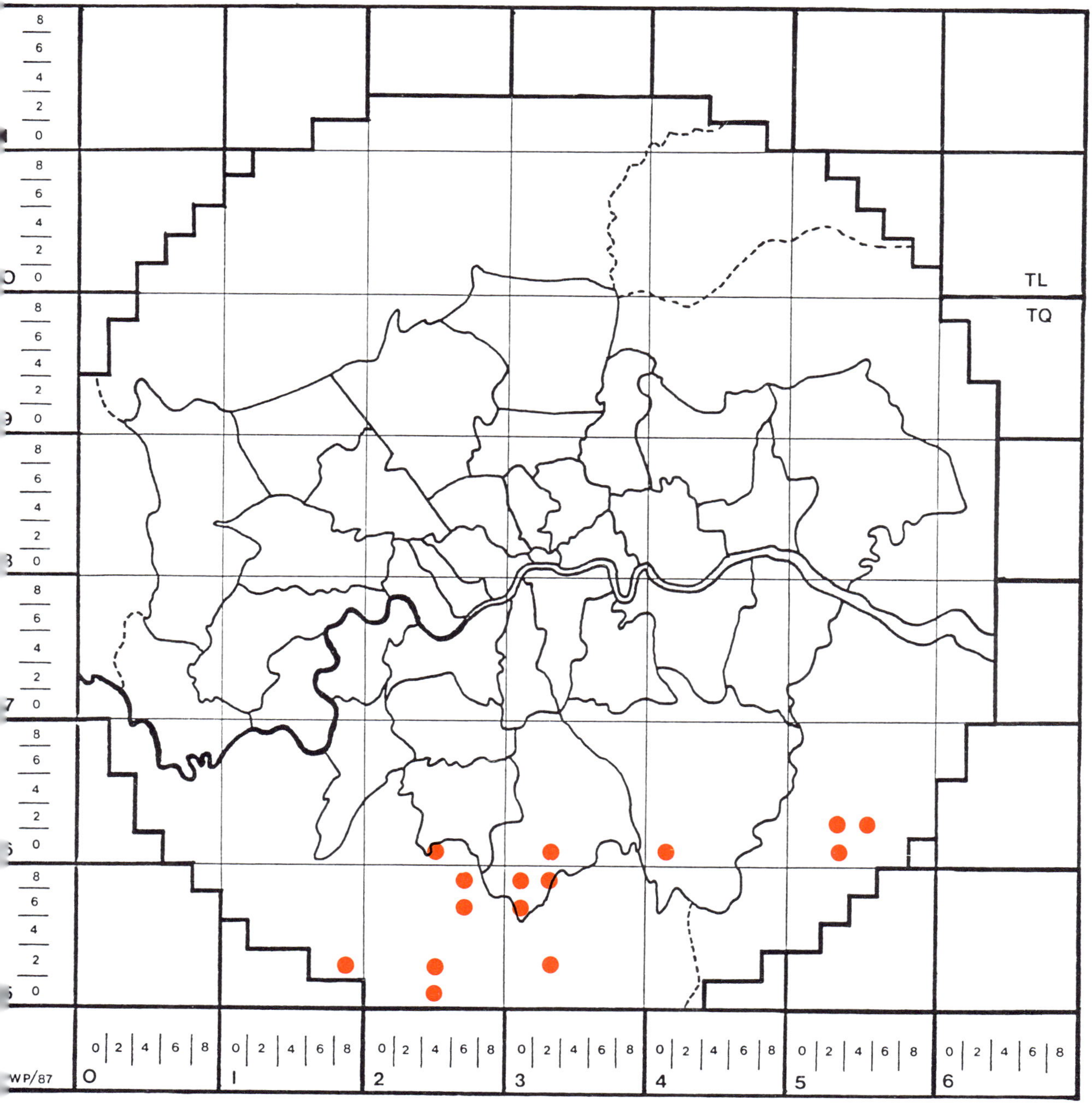

ADONIS BLUE 1980-1986

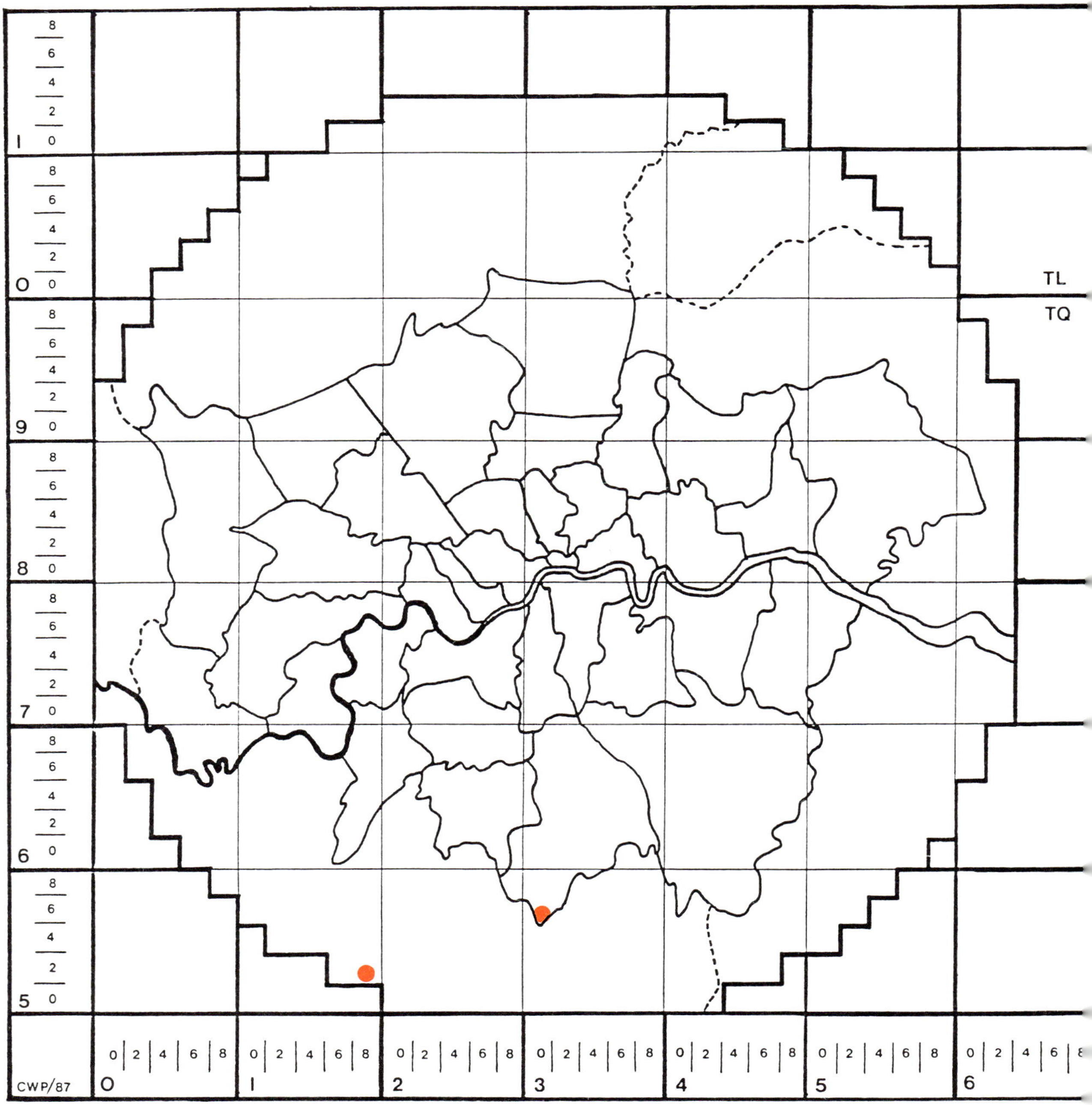

HOLLY BLUE 1980-1986

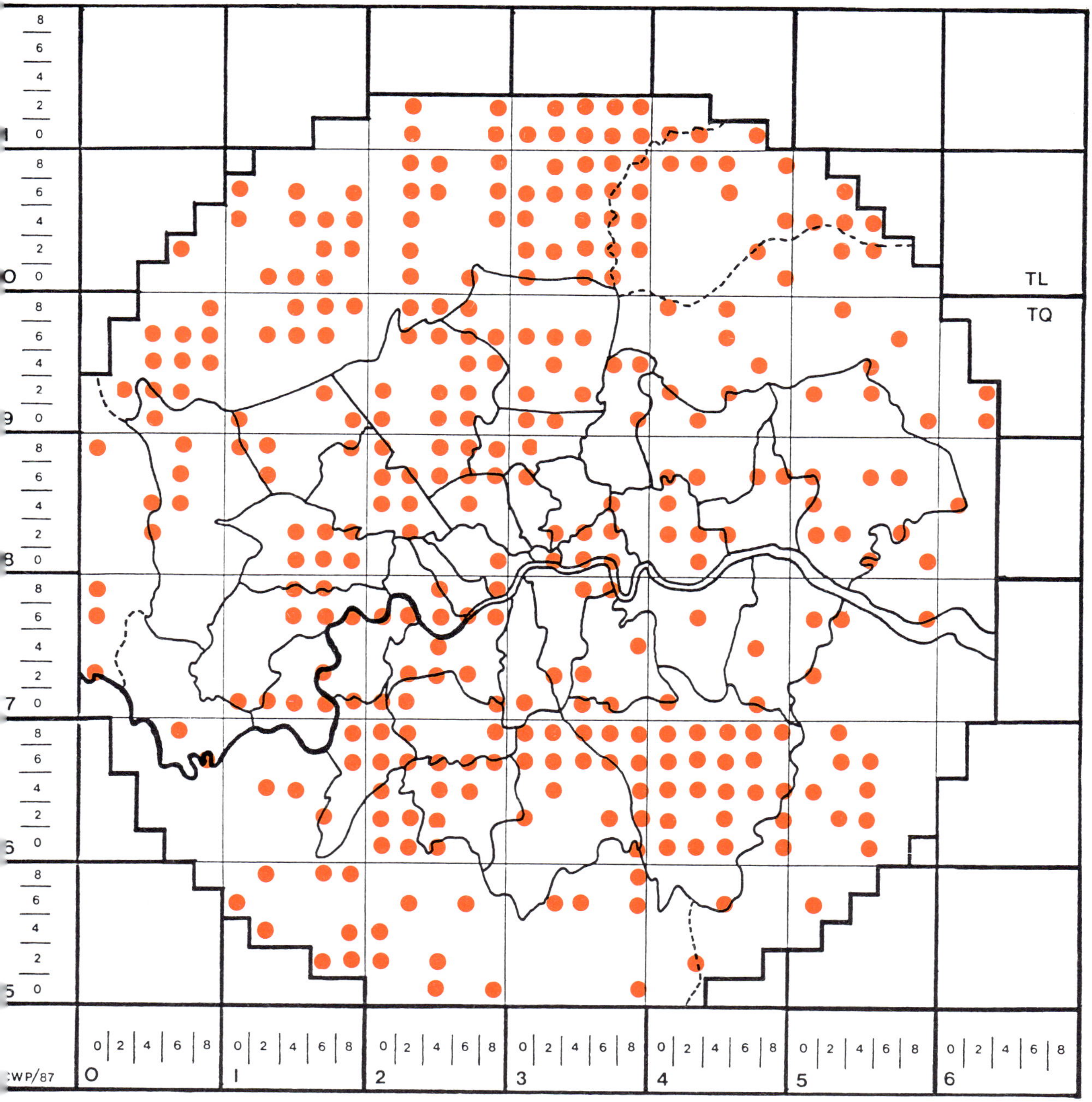

DUKE OF BURGUNDY 1980-1986

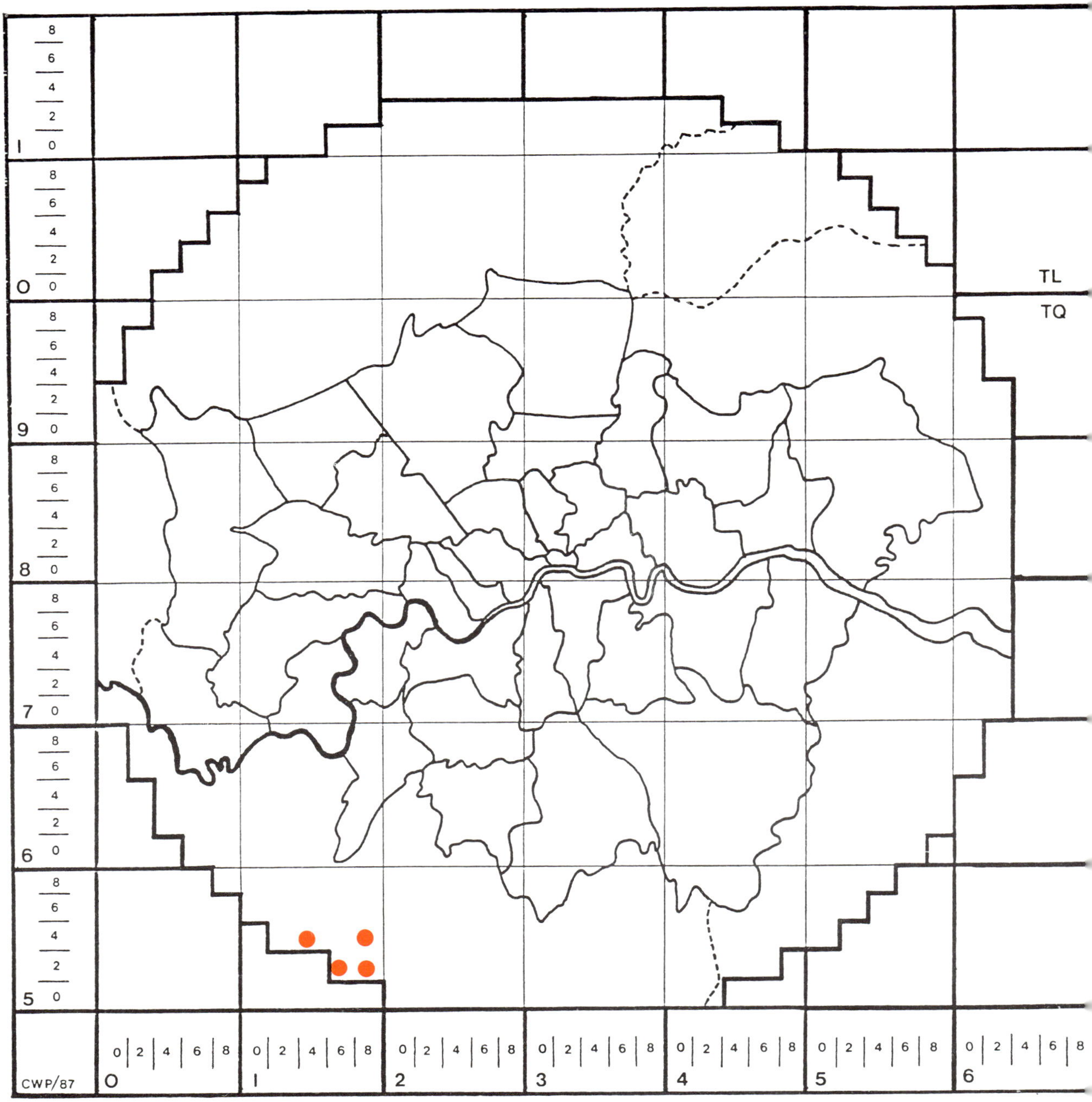

WHITE ADMIRAL 1980-1986

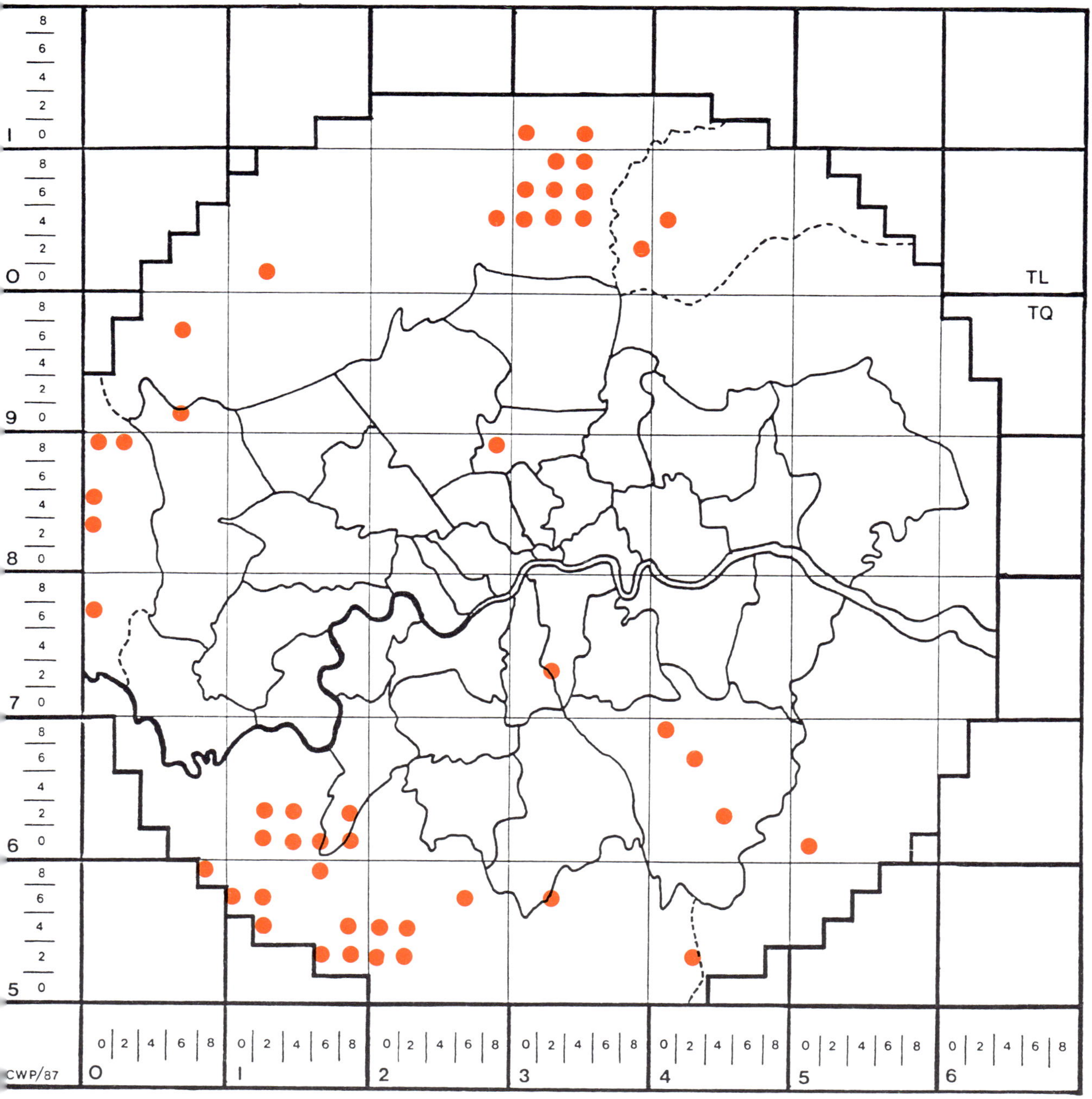

PUPLE EMPEROR 1980-1986

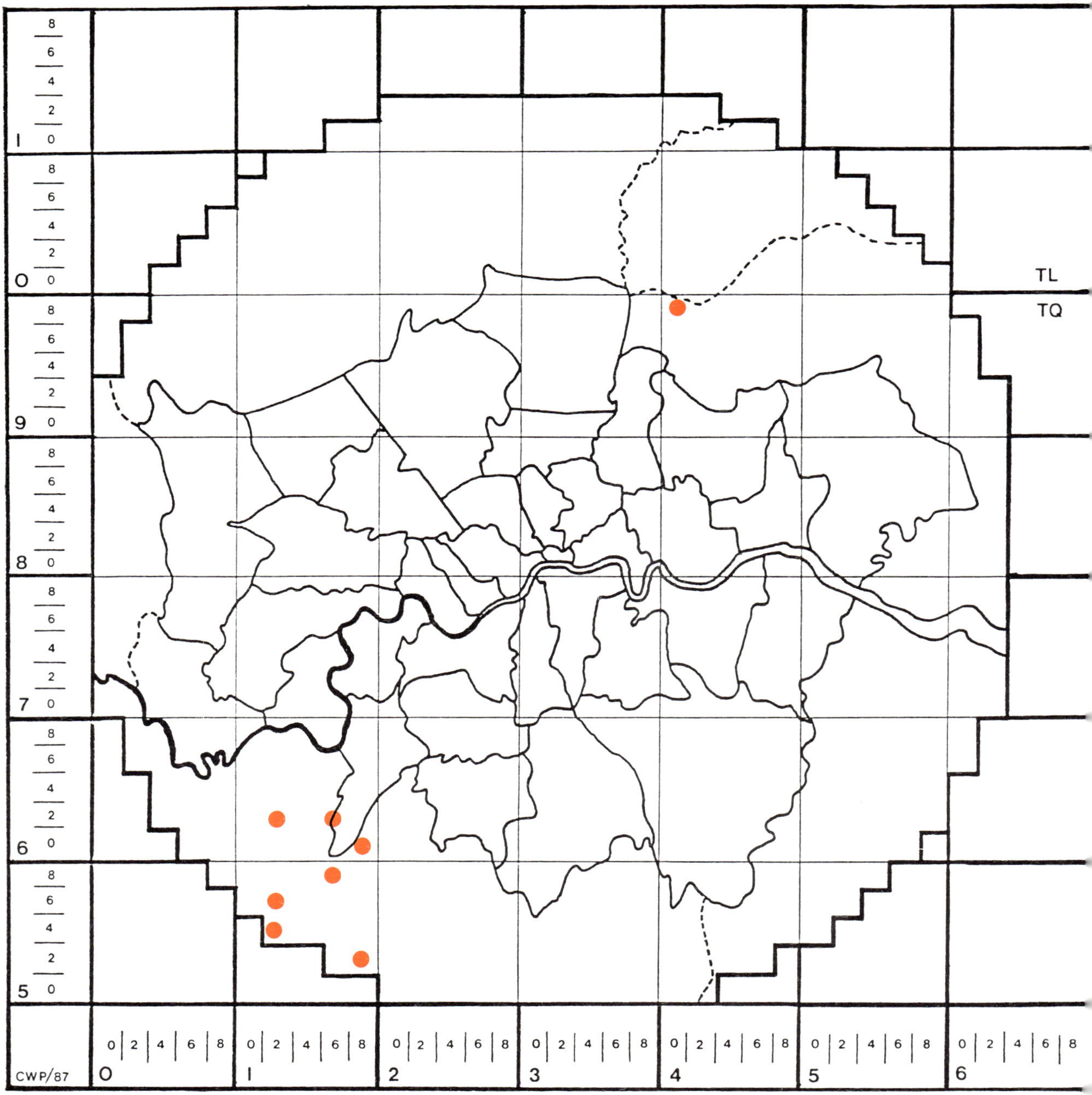

RED ADMIRAL 1980-1986

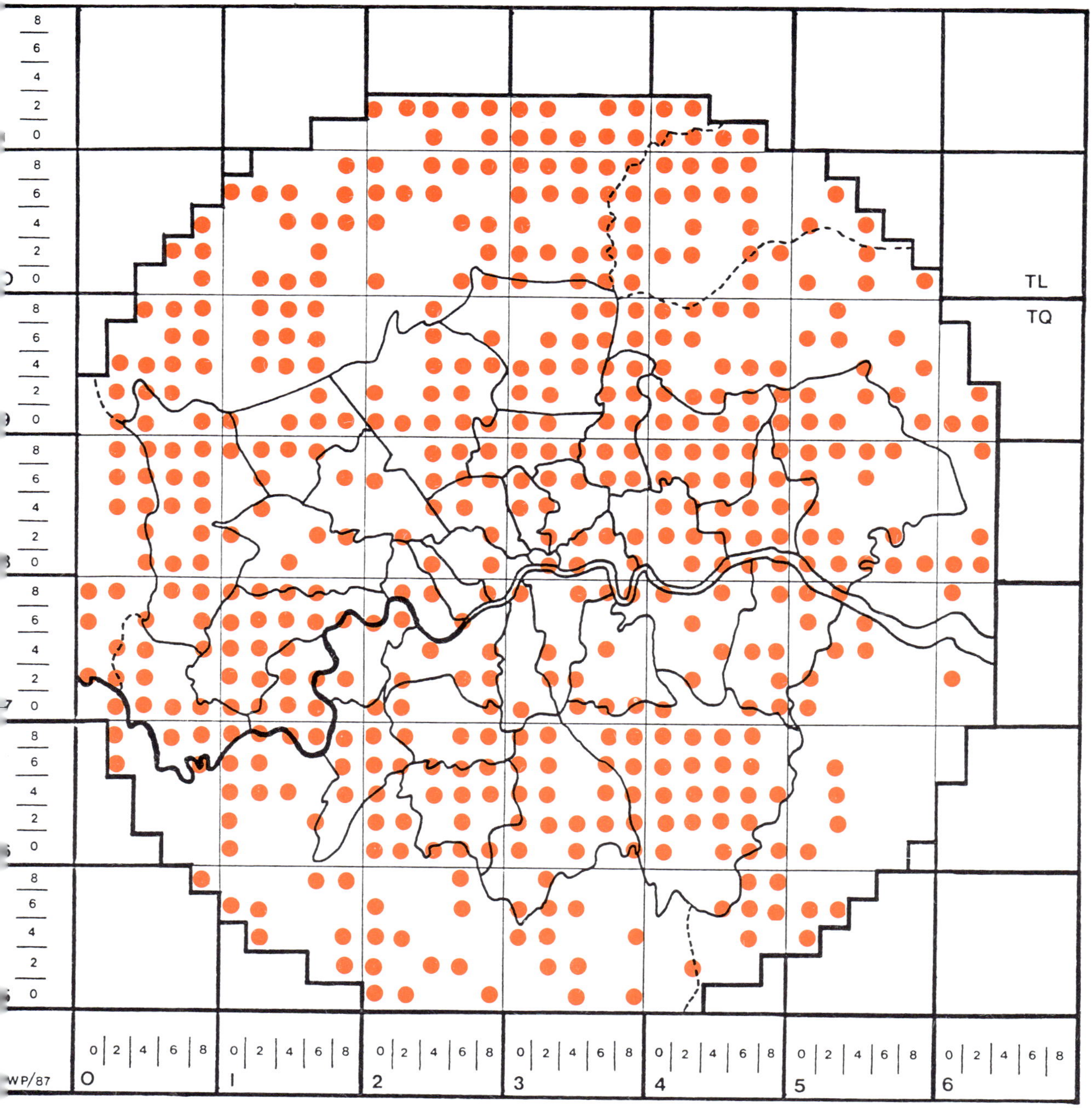

PAINTED LADY 1980-1986

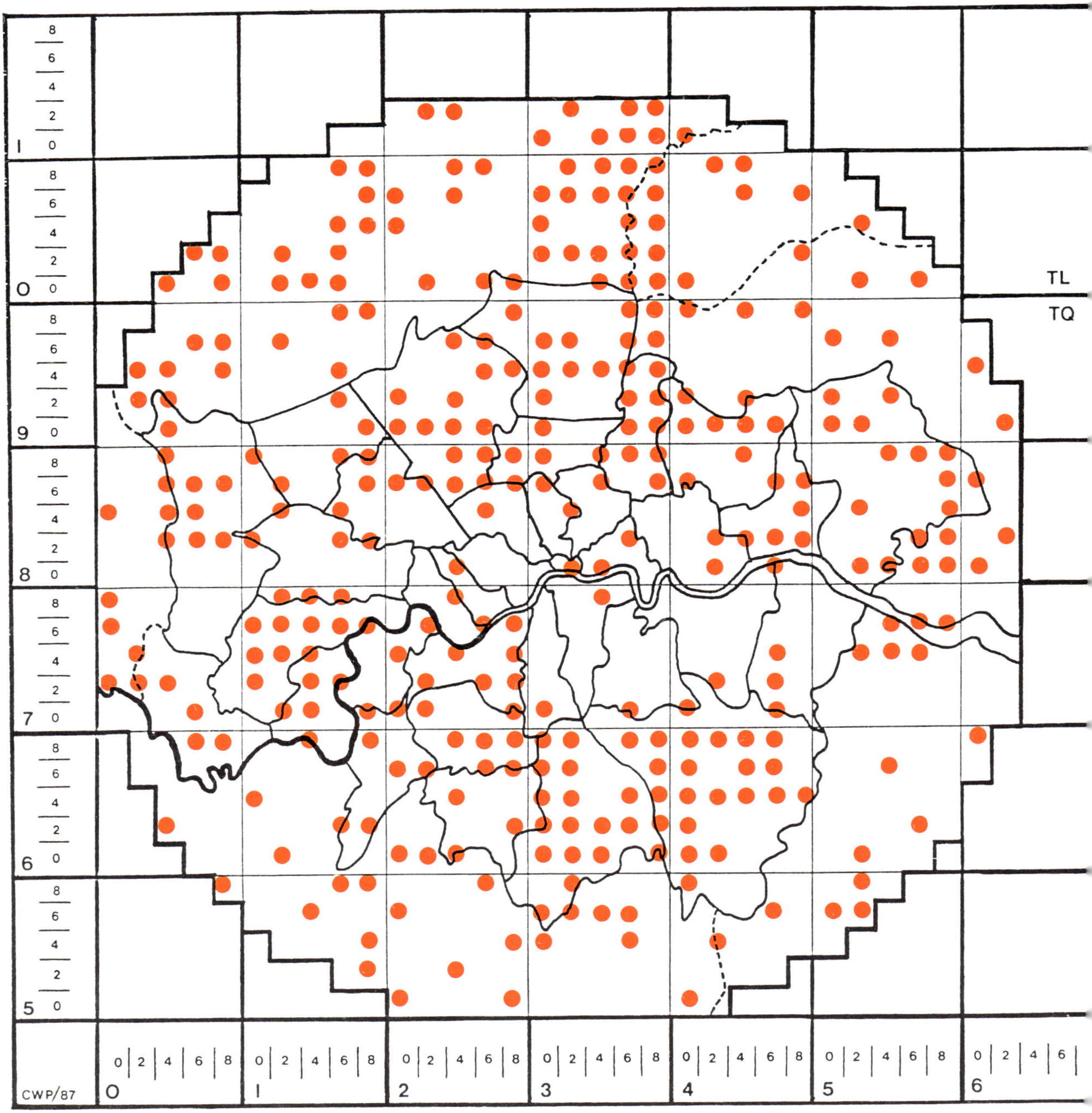

SMALL TORTOISESHELL 1980-1986

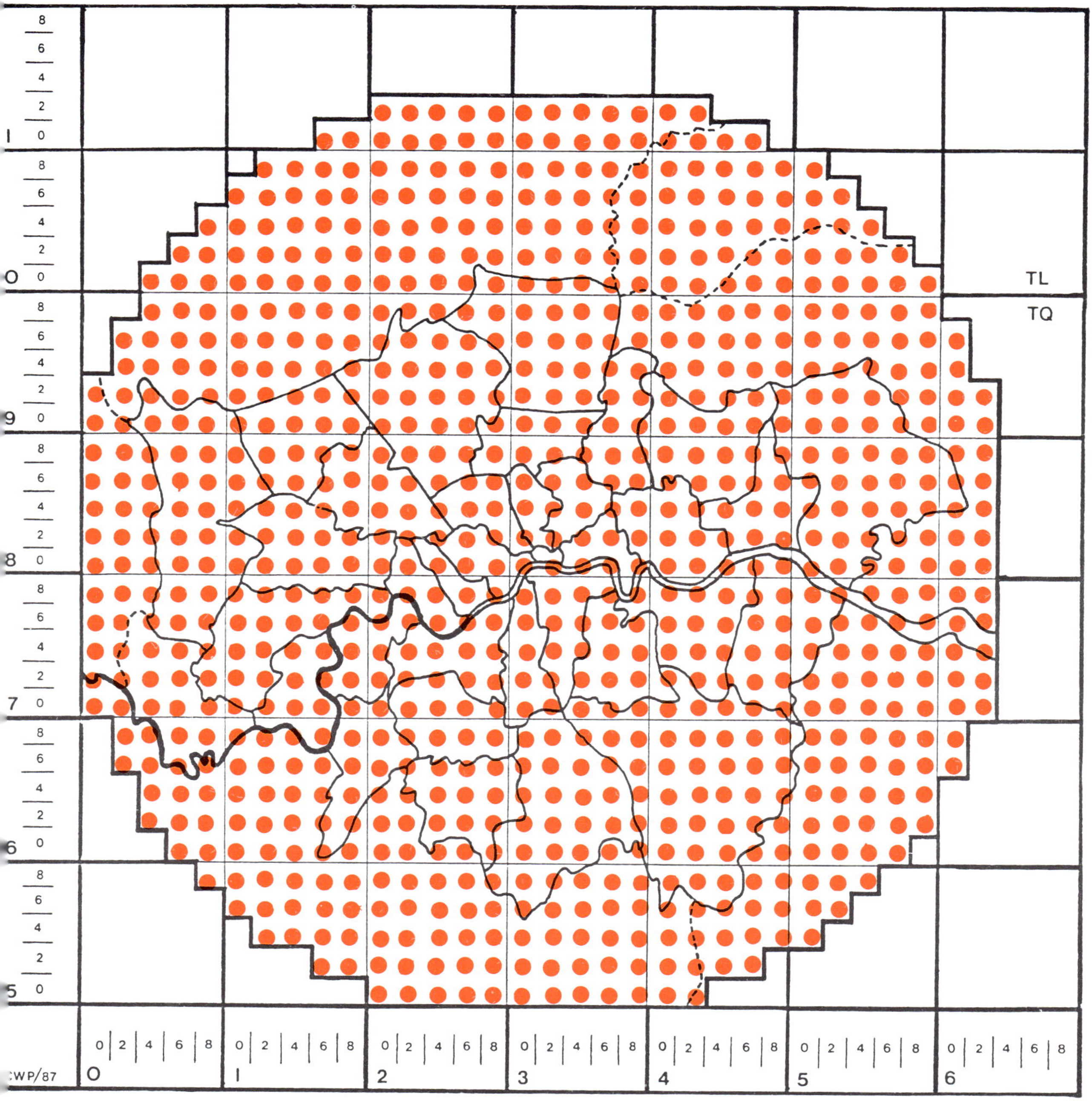

PEACOCK 1980-1986

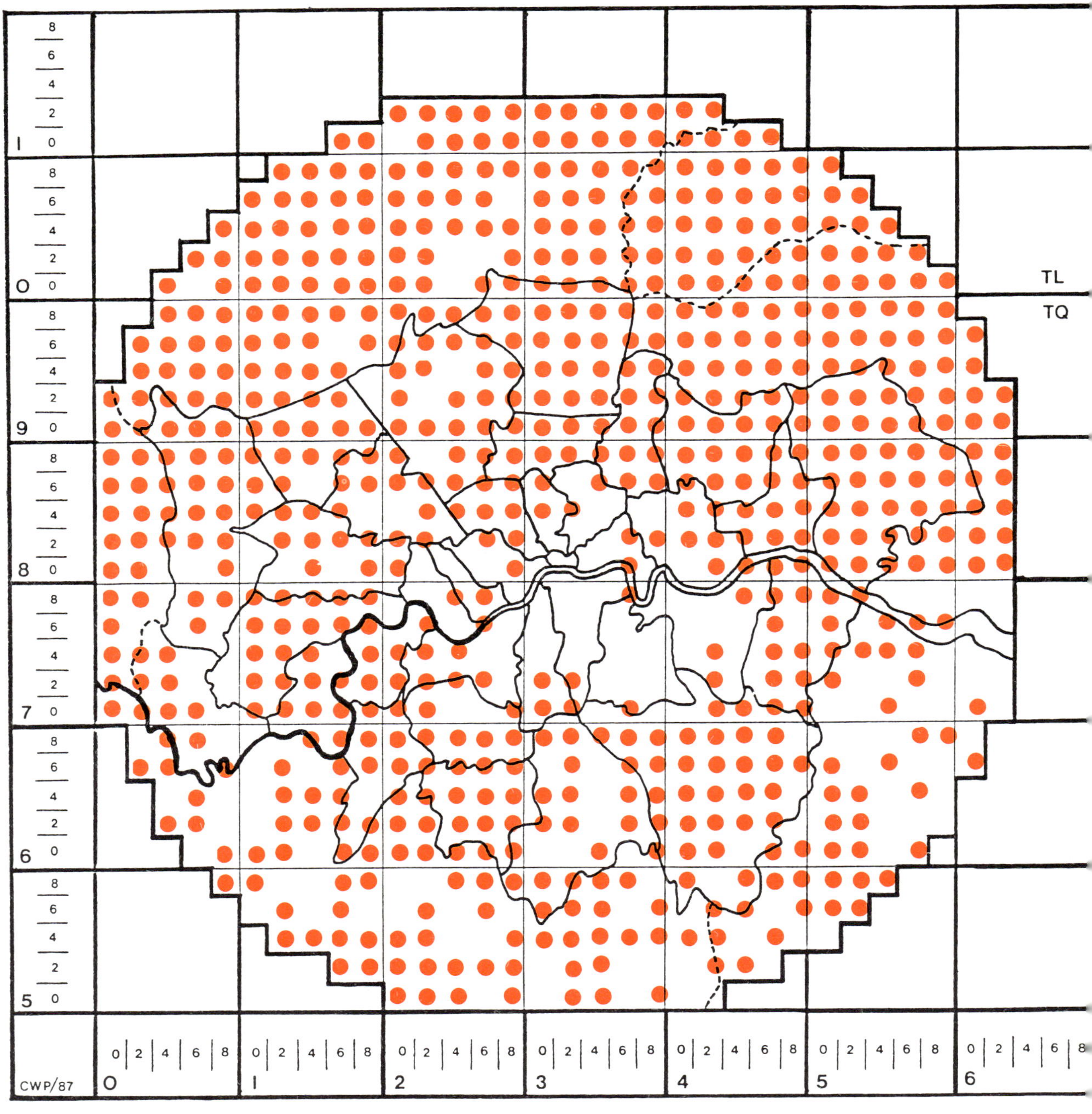

COMMA 1980-1986

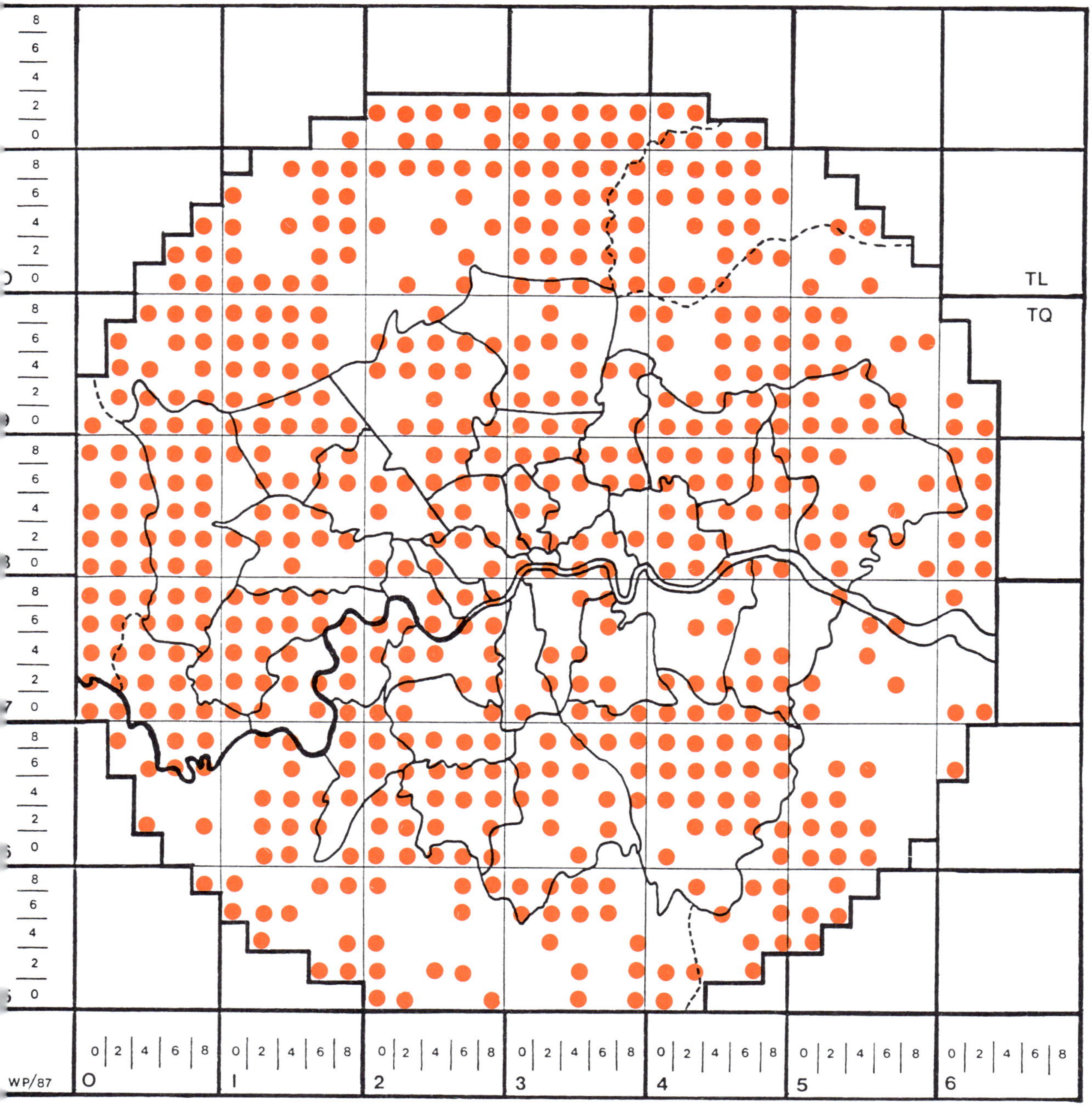

PEARL-BORDERED FRITILLARY 1980-1986

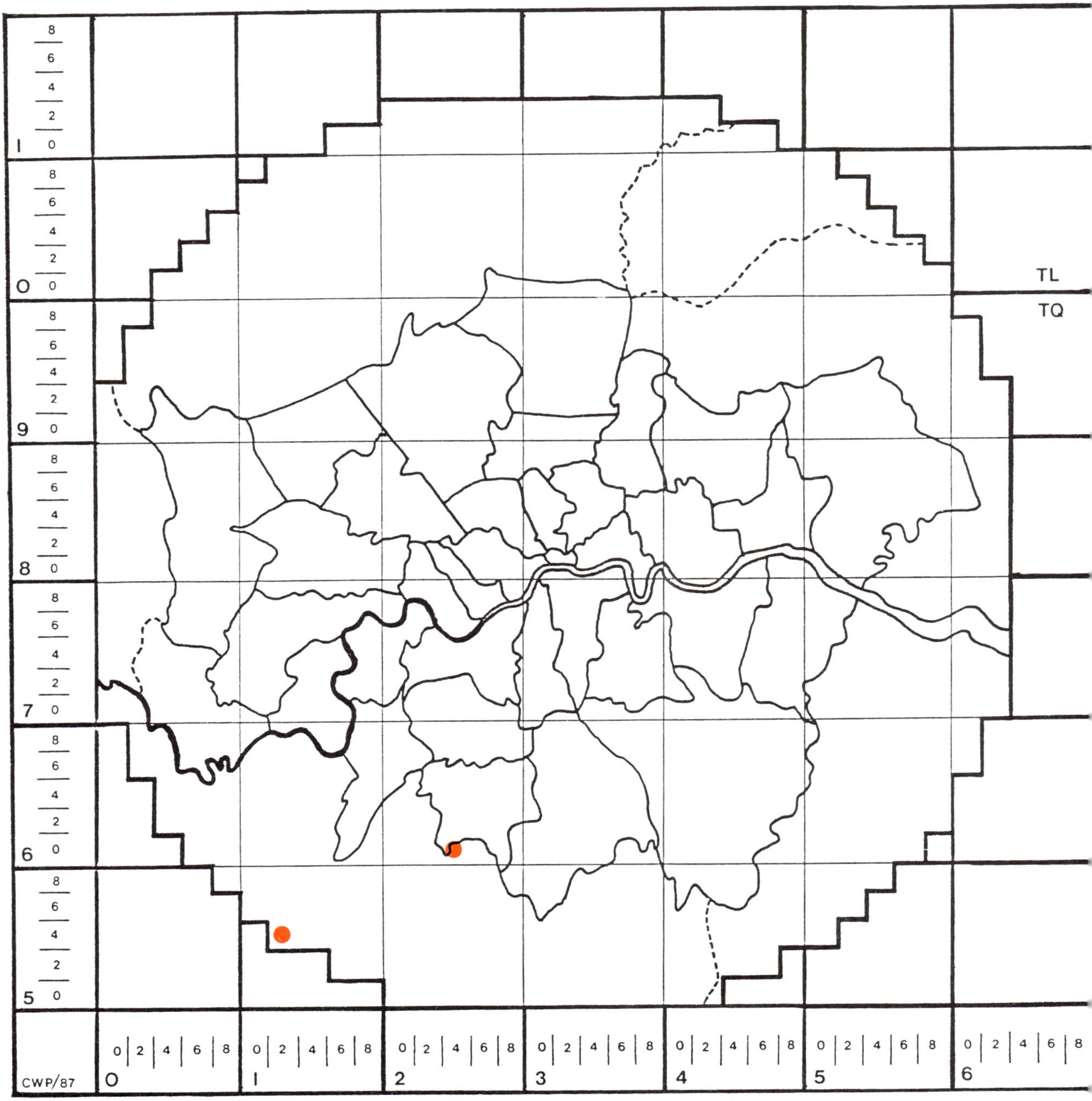

DARK GREEN FRITILLARY 1980-1986

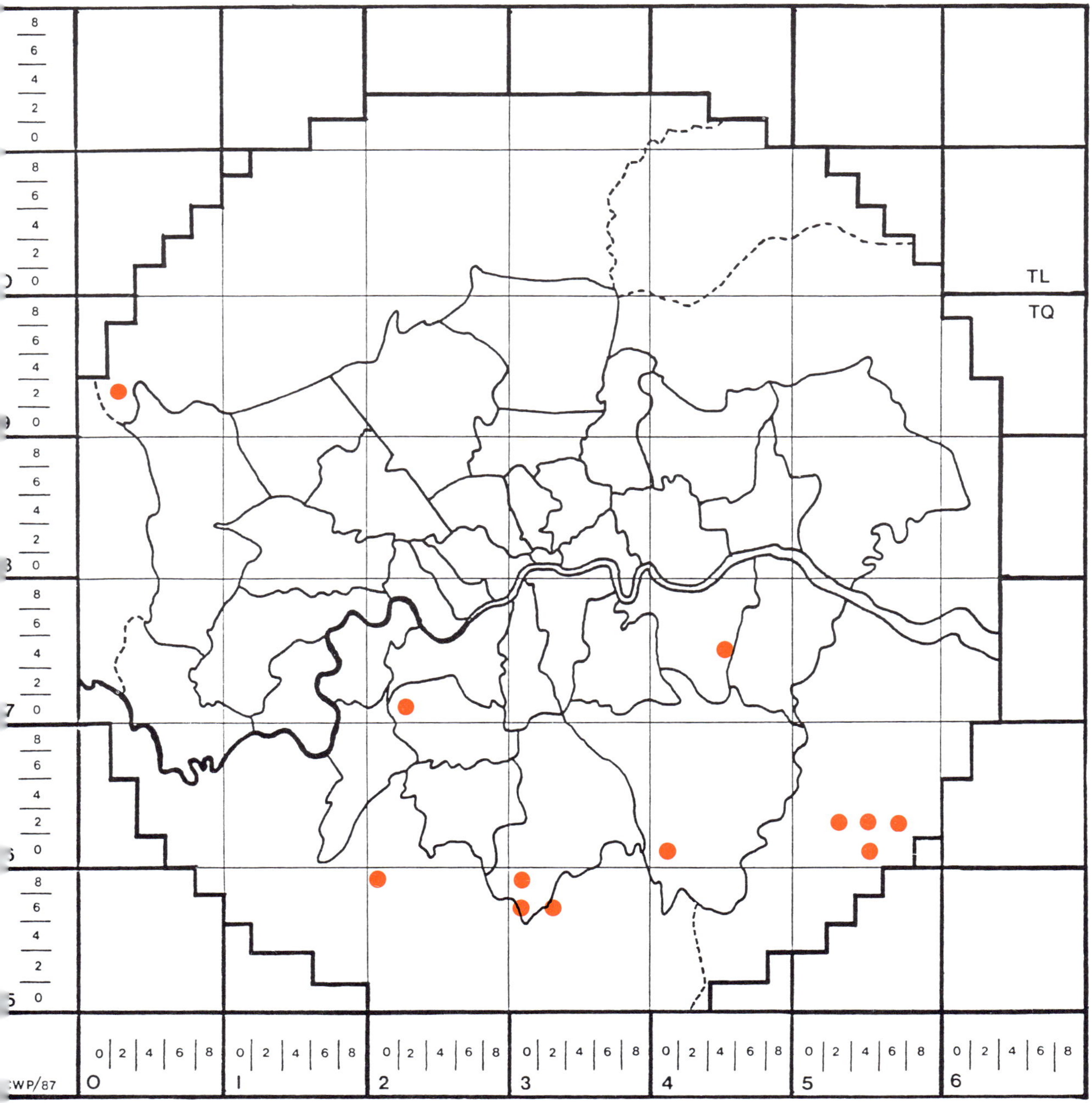

SILVER-WASHED FRITILLARY 1980-1986

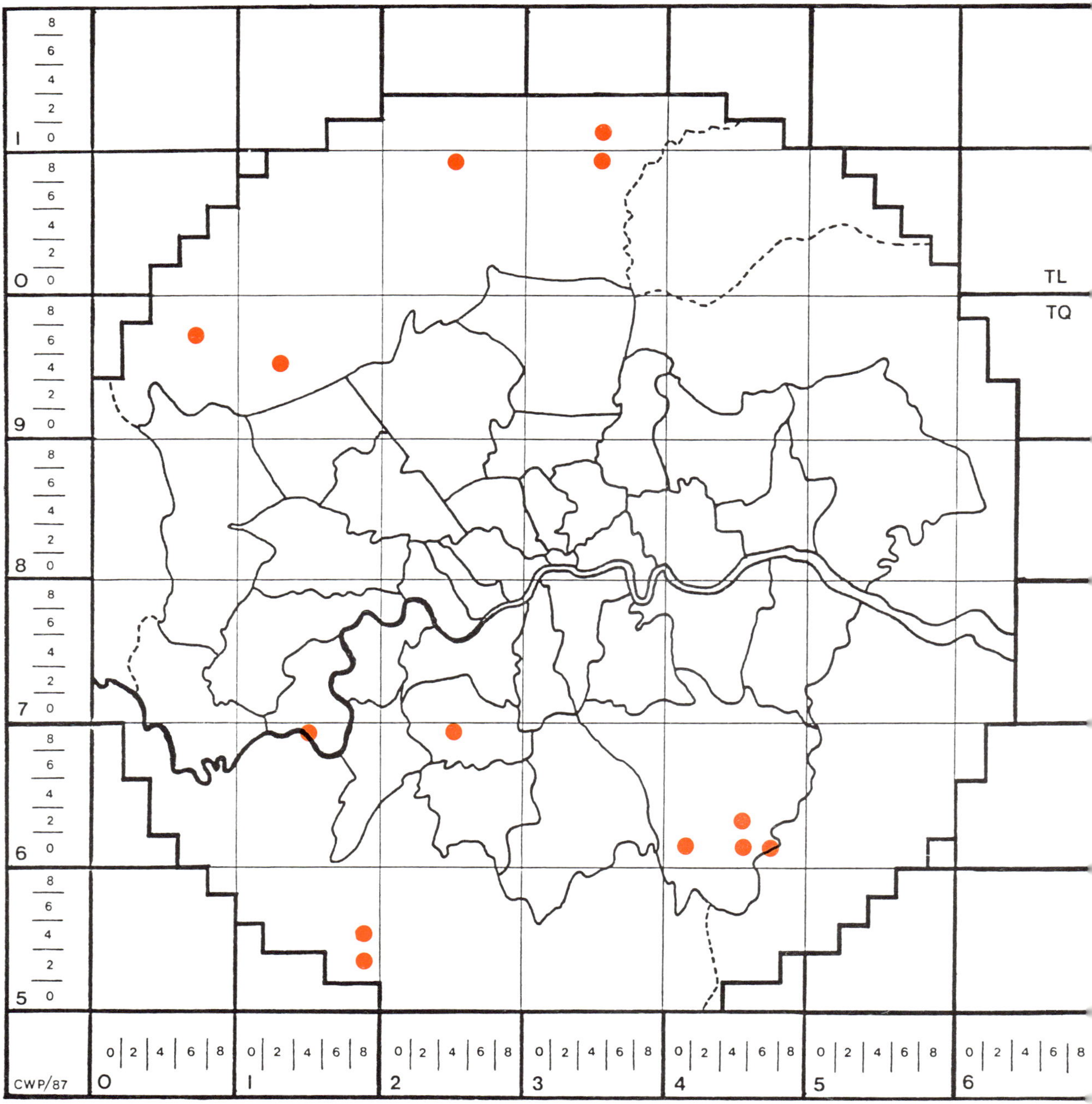

SPECKLED WOOD 1980-1986

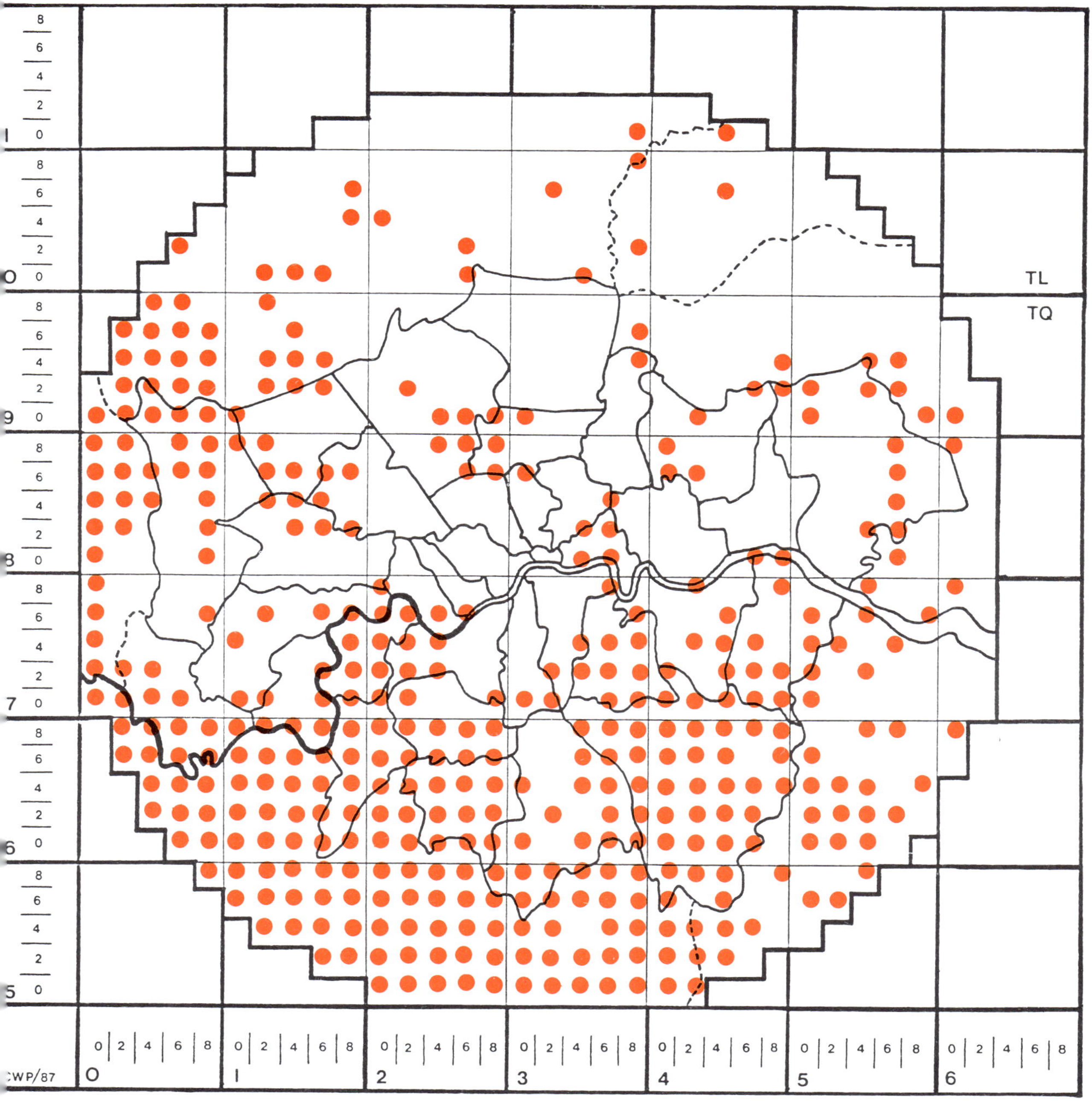

WALL 1980-1986

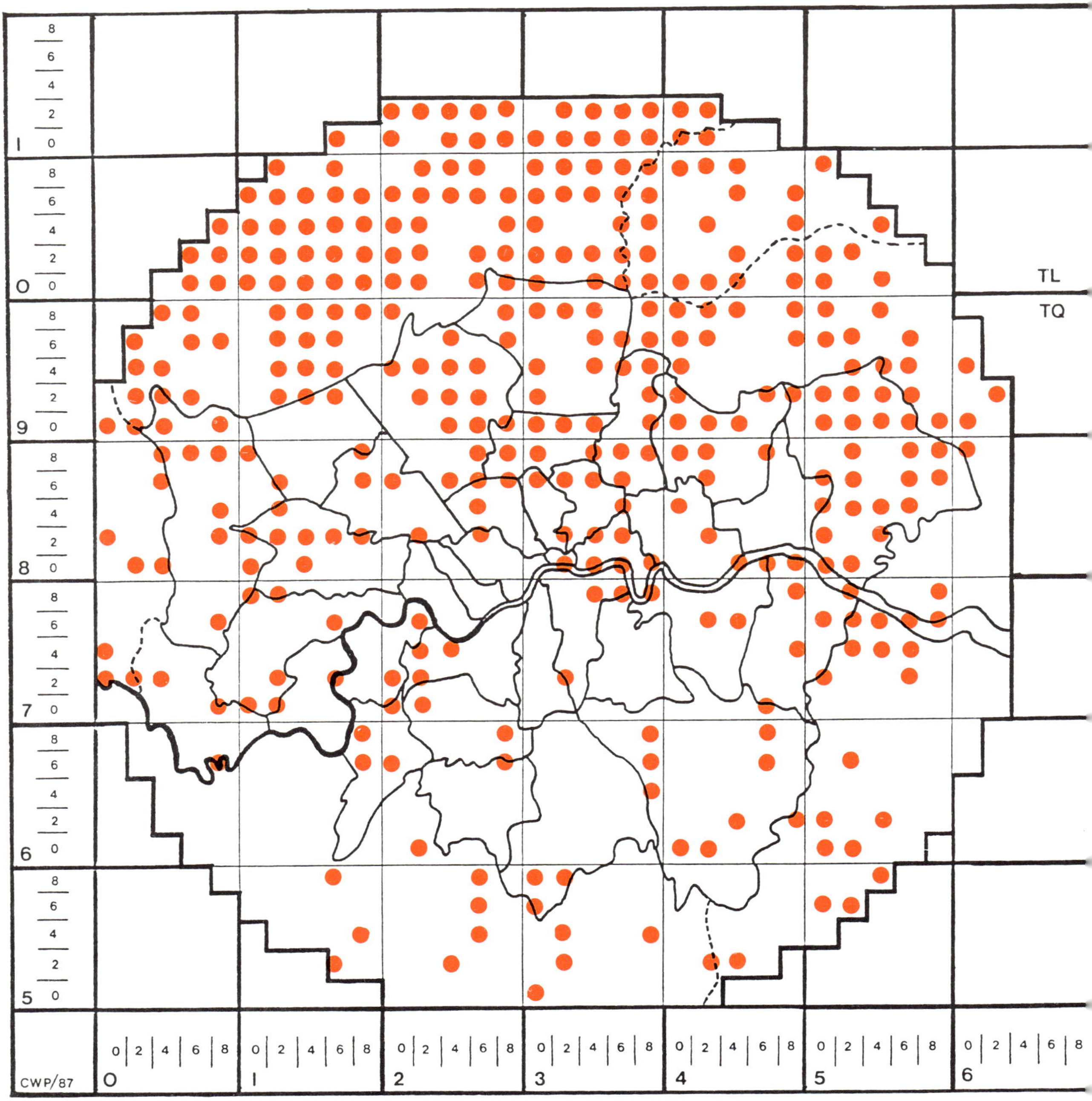

MARBLED WHITE 1980-1986

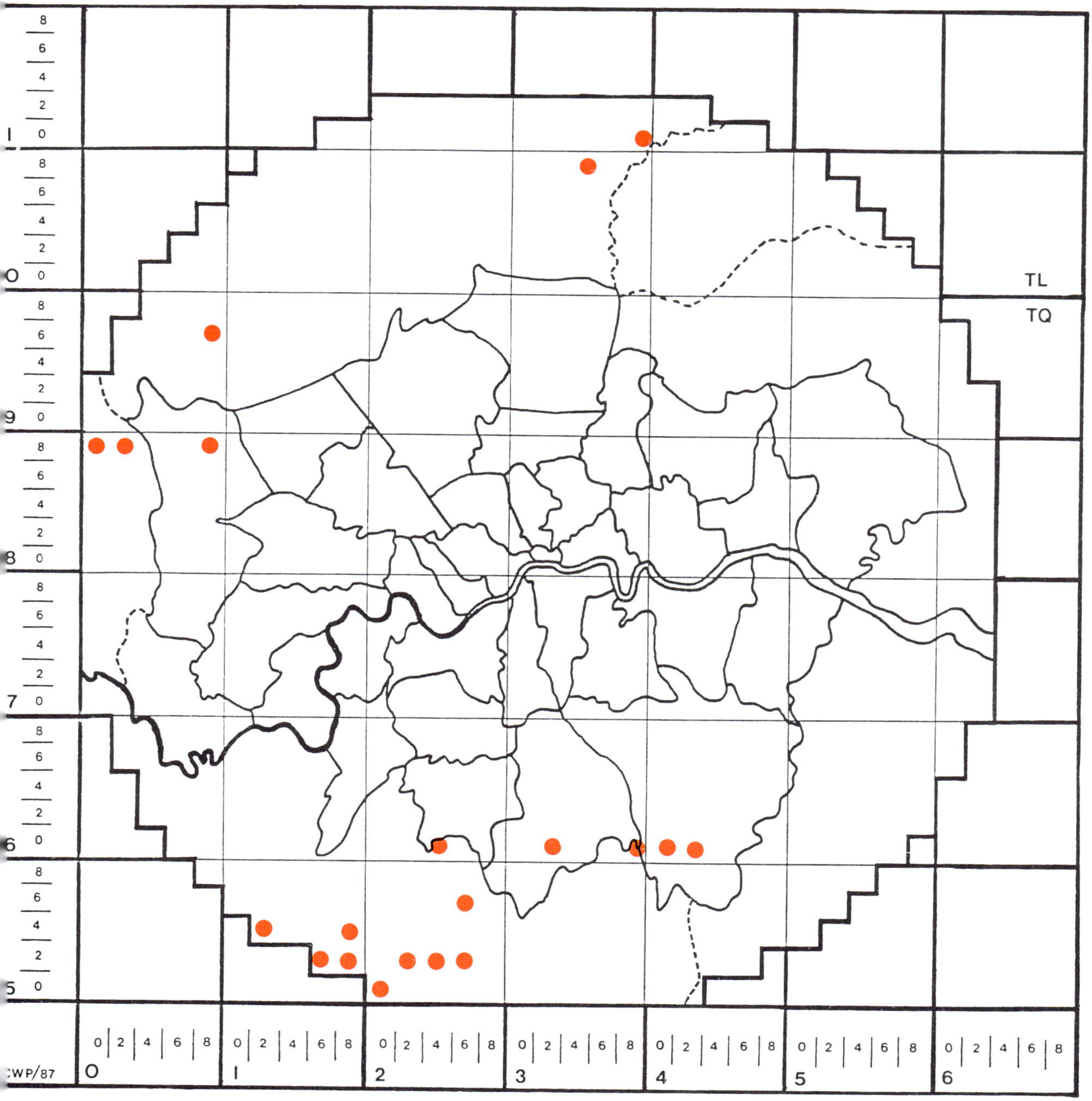

GRAYLING 1980-1986

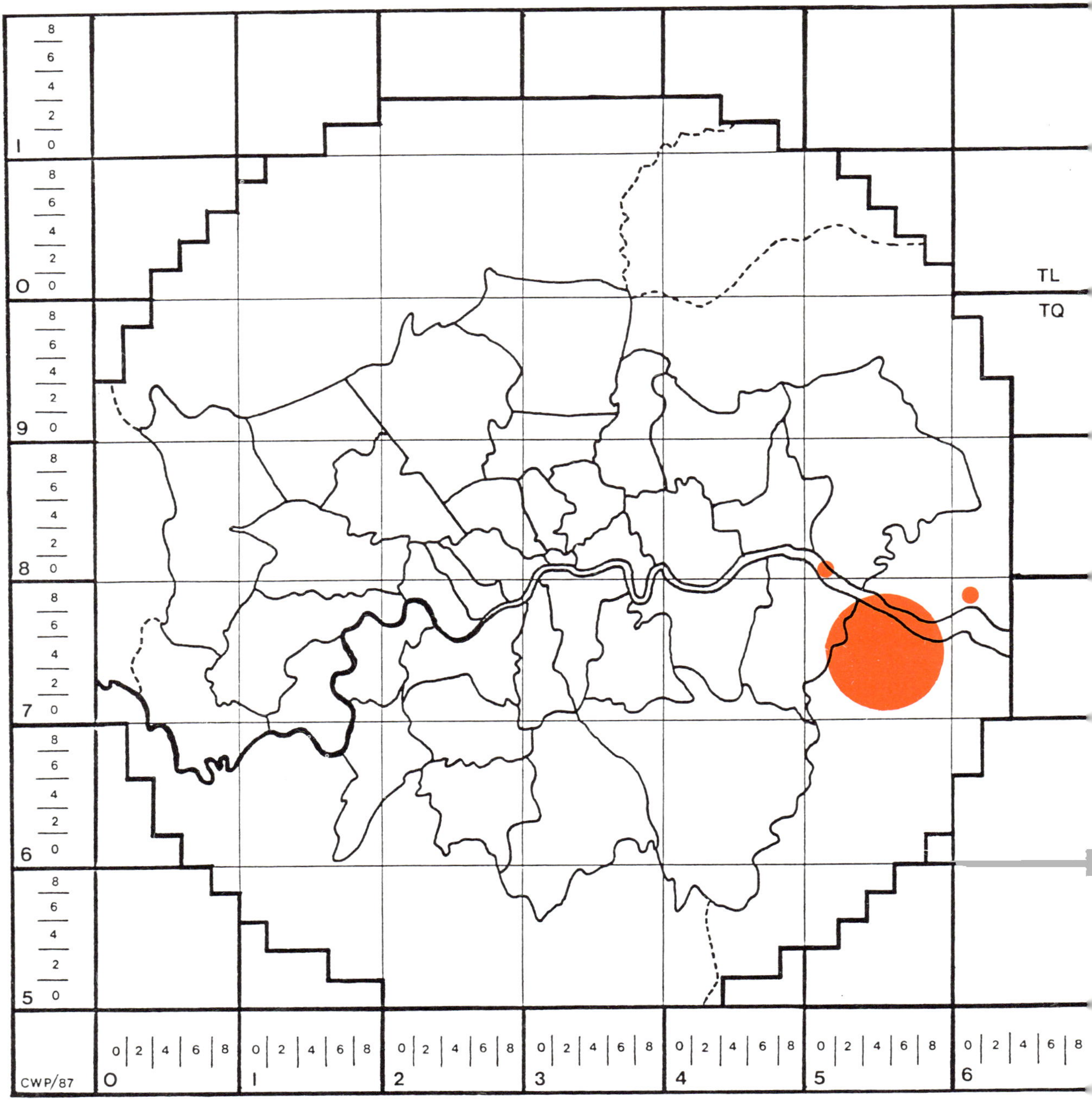

GATEKEEPER 1980-1986

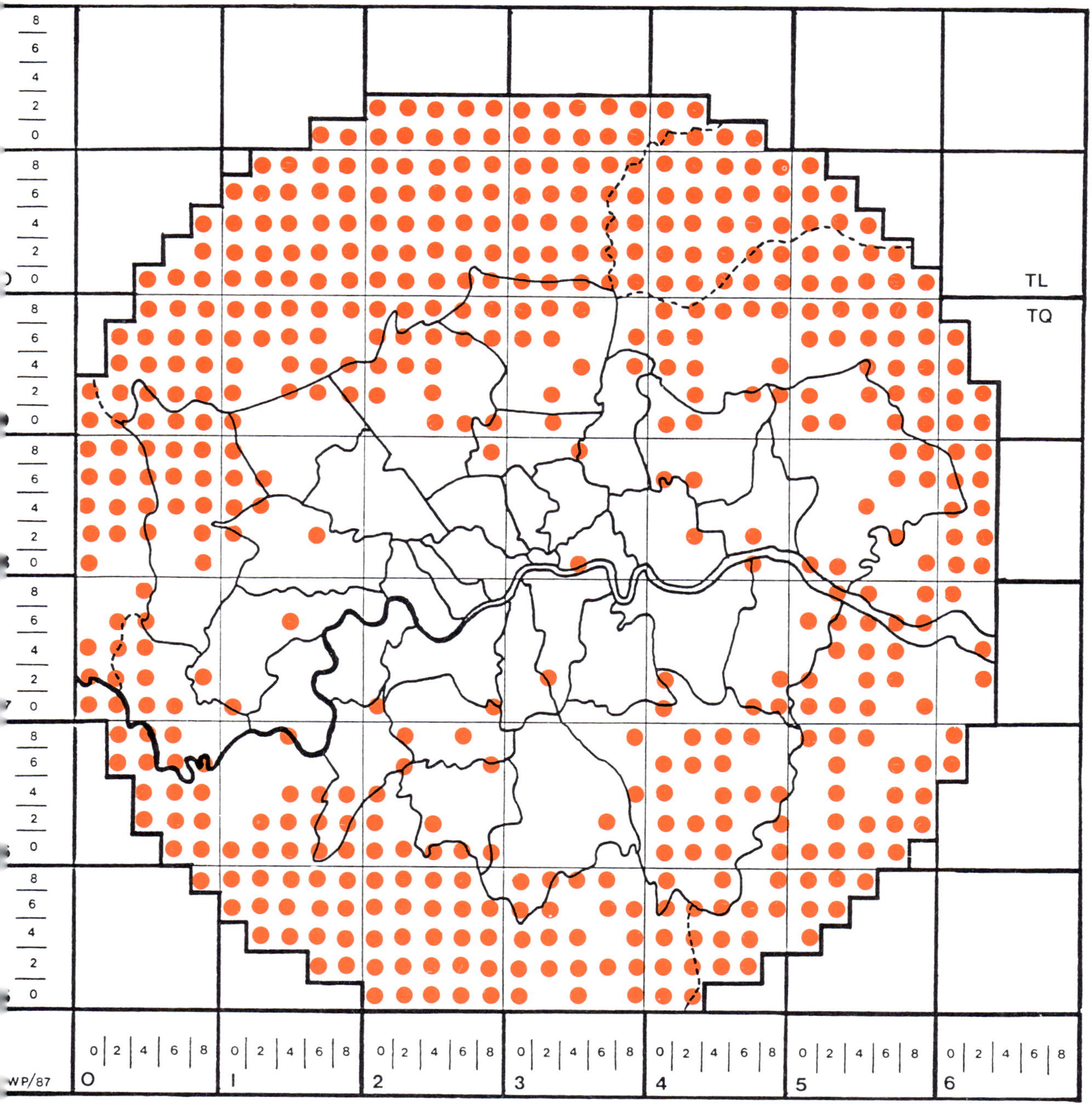

MEADOW BROWN 1980-1986

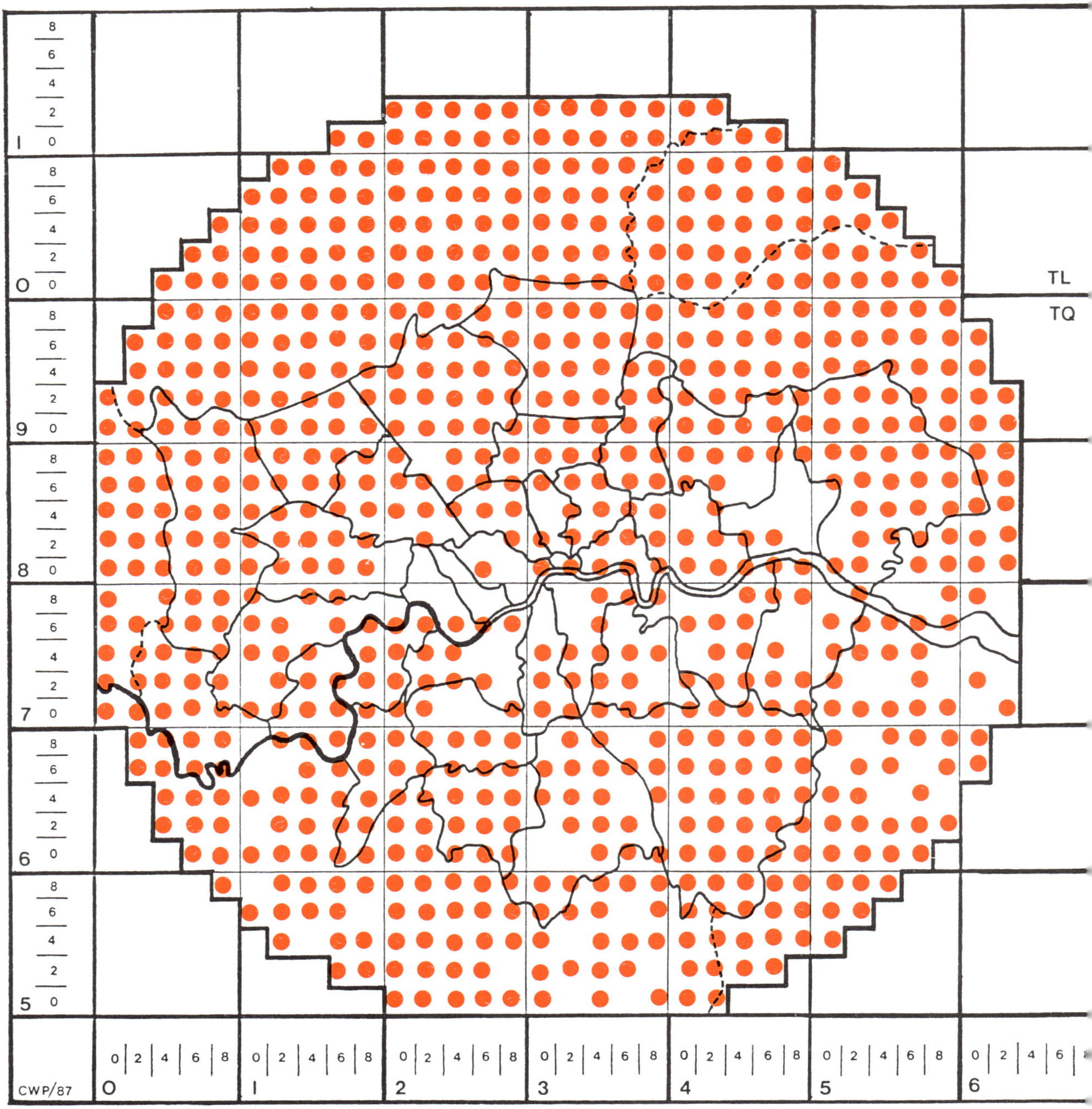

SMALL HEATH 1980-1986

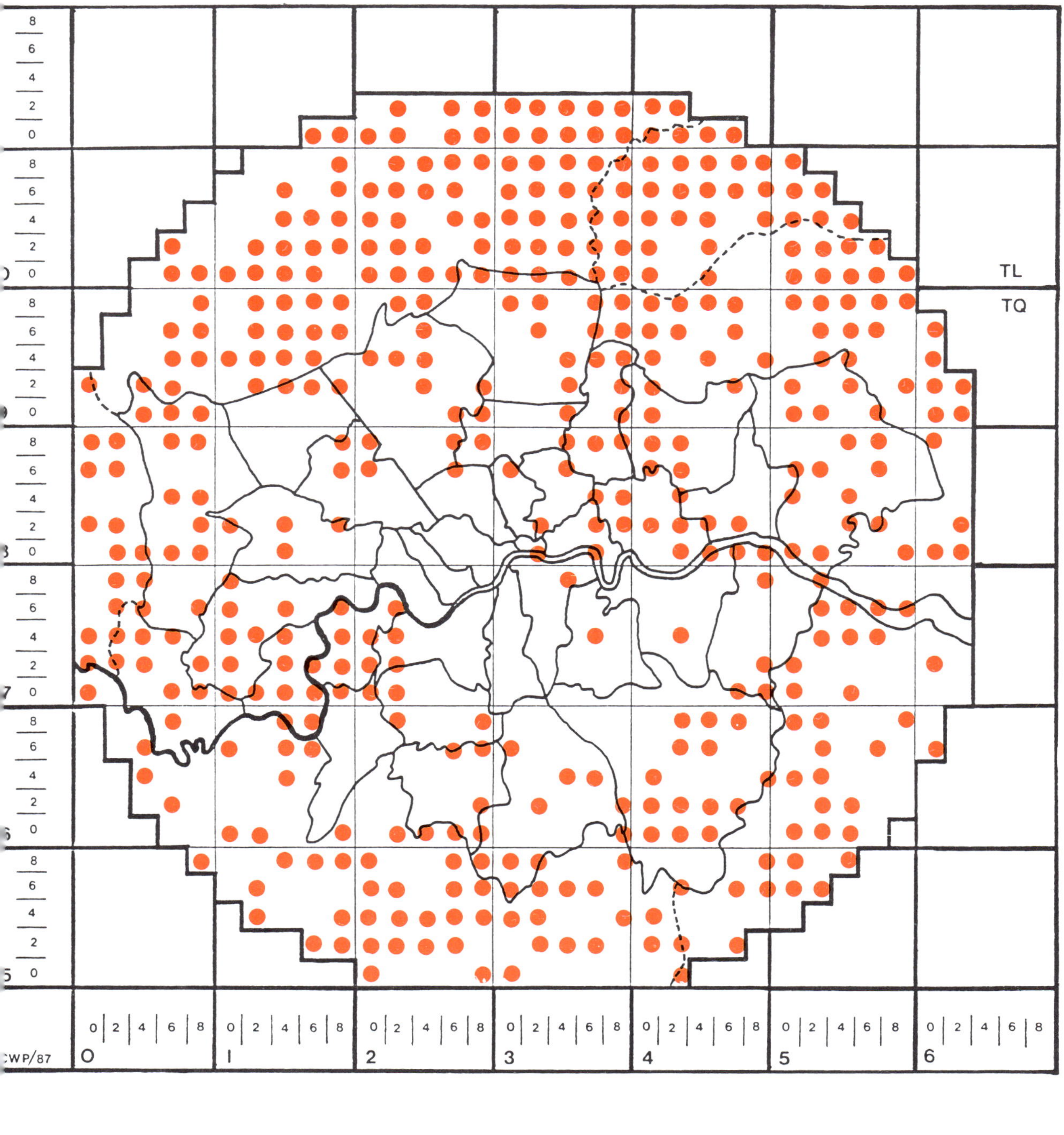

RINGLET 1980-1986

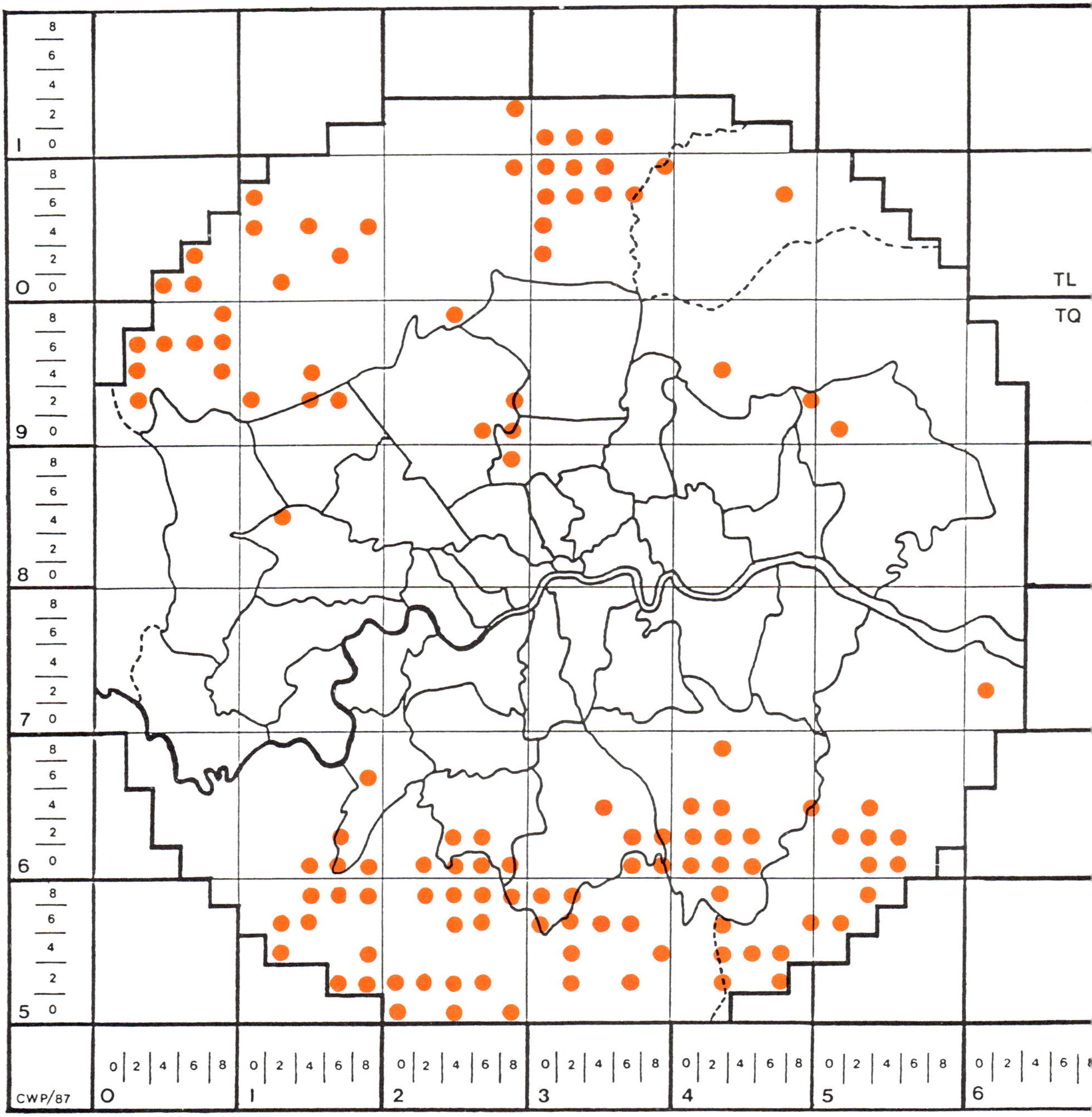

REFERENCES

Alderson, H.,	1900	*Papilio machaon* larvae in Kent. *Entomologist's Rec. J. Var.* **12**:274 -275.
Allan, P.B.M.,	1949	*Larval Foodplants. London: Watkins Doncaster.*
Allen, A.A.,	1969	Notes on a few garden butterflies at Blackheath, 1968. *Entomologist's Rec. J. Var.* **81:**149-150.
Allen, A.A.,	1970	Butterflies and a few moths at Blackheath etc. *Entomologist's Rec. J. Var.***82**:61-62.
Allen, A.A.,	1978	*Thymelicus lineola* Ochs., *Nemophora fasciella* F. etc., at Blackheath, 1977. *Entomologist's Rec. J. Var.* **90**:220-221.
Allen, A.A.,	1980	An unlikely find in a N.E. Surrey garden. *Entomologist's Rec. J. Var.* **92**:6.
Ansorge, E.,	1961	Macrolepidoptera of the Chalfont area, Buckinghamshire. *Entomologist's Gaz.* **12**:11-18.
Argent, J.B.,	1892	*Lycaena coridon* and *Colias edusa* and *helice* in Epping Forest. *Essex Naturalist* **6**:140-141.
Aston, A.,	1960	Lepidoptera observed at Dulwich, 1957-1960. *Entomologist's Rec. J. Var.* **72**:238-243.
Ashton, A.,	1962	Lepidoptera observed at Dulwich in 1961. *Entomologist's Rec. J. Var.* **74**:67.
Baker, P.J.,	1977	The polyphagous habits of *Polygonia c-album* (L.). **89**:157-158.
Baker, R.R.,	1972	Territorial behaviour in Nymphalid butterflies *Aglais urticae* (L.) and *Inachis io* (L.). *J. Anim. Ecol.* **41**:453-469.
Bantock, C.,	1981	Butterflies in North London. *British Butterfly Conservation Society News* **26**:45
Barrett, C.G.,	1892-95	*The Lepidoptera of the British Isles.* London.
Barrett, C.G.,	1905	Lepidoptera. *Victoria County History of Buckinghamshire* **1**:87-106.
Bell, A.,	1972	Camberwell beauty in Hertfordshire. *Entomologist's Rec. J. Var.* **84**:285.
Bower, R.W.,	1888	List of Macro Lepidoptera of Haileybury School. *Trans. Herts. Nat. Hist. Soc. Fld. Club.* v:23.
Bradley, J.D. & Fletcher, D.S.,	1979	*A recorder's log book or label list of British Lepidoptera.* London: Curwen.
Bradley, J.D. & Mere, R.M., in McClintock, D.,	1964	Natural History of the Garden of Buckingham Palace. *Proc. Trans. S. Lond. ent. nat. Hist. Soc. 1963*:55-74.
Bretherton, R.F.,	1951	Our lost butterflies and moths. *Entomologist's Gaz.* **2**:211-240.
Bretherton, R.F.,	1961	First records of *Thymelicus lineola* (Och.) and *Chlorissa viridata* (L.) in Surrey: a correction. *Entomologist* **94**:37.
Bretherton, R.F.,	1971	*Lampides boeticus* L. and *Thecla betulae* L. in Surrey. *Entomologist's Rec. J. Var.* **83**:326.
Bristow, C.R.,	1986	The occurrence of *Opsiphanes tamarindi* Felder & Felder (Lepidoptera:Satyridae) in Britain. *Entomologists Rec. J. Var* **98**:96-97.
Brooks, M. and Knight, C	1982	*A Complete pocket guide to British butterflies.* London: Jonathan Cape.

Brown, D.C.G., 1977 *Nymphalis antiopa* L. in November. *Entomologist's Rec. J. Var.* **89**:54.

Buckell, F.J. and Prout, L.B., 1899-1902 The Fauna of the London District. *Trans. City of Lond. ent. & nat. Hist. Soc.* **8**:51-63; **9**:66-80; **10**:62-74; **11**:54-68.

Buckstone, A.A.W., 1935 *Nymphalis antiopa* in Surrey. *Entomologist* **68**:15.

Buckstone, A.A.W., 1945 *Pontia daplidice, Lampides boeticus* and other migrant Lepidoptera in Surrey. *Entomologist* **78**:157.

Buckstone, A.A.W., 1946 *Nymphalis polychloros* in Surrey. *Entomologist* **79**:90.

Burrows, D., 1973 *Nymphalis antiopa* (L.) the Camberwell Beauty in Kent in 1973. *Entomologist's Rec. J. Var.* **85**:269.

Burton, J.F., 1955 The butterflies of the north-west Kent marshes with special reference to the 1953 floods. *London Naturalist* **34**:54-60.

Burton, J.F., 1979 The Essex Skipper (*Thymelicus lineola* Ochs.) at Blackheath and elsewhere in south-east London. *Entomologist's Rec. J. Var.* **91**:294-295.

Burton, R.M., 1983 *Flora of the London area.* London Natural History Society.

Buxton, E.N., 1884 Epping Forest: its moths and butterflies. in *Epping Forest.* Epping

Chalmers-Hunt, J.M., 1960-1961 *The Butterflies and Moths of Kent: A Critical Account. Part 1: Introduction and Rhopalocera.* West Wickham. (Originally published as Supplements to *Entomologist's Rec. J. Var* **72-73**).

Chalmers-Hunt, J.M., 1961 *Ochlodes venata* B.& G. (Lep., Hesperiidae) in Kent. *Entomologist* **94**:284.

Chalmers-Hunt, J.M., 1966 *Colias croceus* Fourc. (Clouded Yellow) in 1966. *Entomologist's Rec. J. Var.* **78**:238.

Chalmers-Hunt, J.M. 1968-1981 *The Butterflies and Moths of Kent. Volume 3: Heterocera and Supplement.* West Wickham. (Originally published as supplements to *Entomologist's Rec. J. var.* **80 - 93.**

Chalmers-Hunt, J.M., 1972 *Polygonia c-album* L. in Kent. *Entomologist's Rec. J. Var.* **84**:111.

Chalmers-Hunt, J.M., 1976 *Nymphalis antiopa* (L.) in 1976. *Entomologist's Rec. J. Var.* **88**:269.

Chalmers-Hunt, J.M., 1977a The 1976 invasion of Camberwell Beauty (*Nymphalis antiopa* L.). *Entomologist's Rec. J. Var.* **89**:89-105.

Chalmers-Hunt, J.M., 1977b Post hibernation appearance of the Camberwell Beauty (*Nymphalis antiopa* L.) in 1977, and some additional records for 1976. *Entomologist's Rec. J. Var.* **89**:248-249.

Chalmers-Hunt, J.M. 1979 An albino *Maniola jurtina* L. and other curiosities. *Entomologist's Rec. J. Var.* **91**:219.

Clarke, C.A., 1971 The Holly Blue in London. *Entomologist's Rec. J. Var.* **83**:394.

Classey, E.W. 1935 *Argynnis paphia* in London. *Entomologist* **68**:183.

Cockerell, T.D.A., 1891 A preliminary list of the insect fauna of Middlesex, 2. *Entomologist* **24**:29-33.

Cook, R.R., 1964 *Colias hyale* in Essex. *Entomologist's Rec. J. Var.* **76**:243.

Cooper, Mrs, 1943 *Nymphalis antiopa* at Edgeware. *Entomologist* **76**:170.

Couchman, L.E., 1924 *Limenitis sybilla* on Wimbledon Common. *Entomologist* **57**:283.

Courtney, S.P., 1982 Coevolution of Pierid butterflies and their cruciferous foodplants. V. Habitat selection, community structure and speciation. *Oecologia* **54**:101 - 107.

Craske, R.M., 1951 *Lampides boeticus* at Wimbledon. *Entomologist* **84**:47.

Cribb, P.W., 1962 The Essex Skipper Butterfly in Middlesex. *Entomologist's Gaz.* **13**:15-16.

Curtis, J. 1824-27 *British Entomology*. London.

Dallas, W., 1917 *Euvanessa antiopa* in 1917. *Entomologist* **50**:235.

Danreuther, T., 1935 Migration Records, 1935. *Entomologist* **68**:209-212.

Danreuther, T., 1946 Records of the Bath White Butterfly (*Pontia daplidice*) (L.) observed in the British Isles during 1945. *J. Soc. Brit. ent.* **3**:1-7.

Danreuther, T., 1946a Records of the Long-tailed Blue Butterfly (*Lampides boeticus* (L.)) observed in the British Isles in 1945. *J. Soc. Brit. ent.* **83**:8-9.

de Worms, C.G.M., 1950 The butterflies of London and its surroundings. *Lond. Nat.* **29**:46-80.

de Worms, C.G.M., 1959 A Supplement to the butterflies and moths of London and its surroundings. *Lond. Nat.* **38**:33-50.

de Worms, C.G.M., 1962 A review of the Macrolepidoptera of the London area, 1960 and 1961. *Lond. Nat.* **41**:60-65.

de Worms, C.G.M., 1964 A review of the Macrolepidoptera of the London area for 1962 and 1963. *Lond. Nat.* **43**:26-33.

de Worms, C.G.M., 1965 An analysis of the Macrolepidoptera recorded from the garden of Buckingham Palace. *Lond. Nat.* **44**:77-81.

de Worms, C.G.M., 1966 A review of the Macrolepidoptera of the London area for 1964 and 1965. *Lond. Nat.* **45**:89-97.

de Worms, C.G.M., 1969 Résumé of the Macrolepidoptera of the London area for 1966 and 1967. *Lond. Nat.* **48**:121-124.

de Worms, C.G.M., 1970 A review of the Macrolepidoptera of the London area for 1968 and 1969. *Lond. Nat.* **49**:82-89.

de Worms, C.G.M., 1972 A review of the Macrolepidoptera of the London area for 1970 and 1971. *Lond. Nat.* **51**:28-38.

de Worms, C.G.M., 1974 A review of the Macrolepidoptera of the London area for 1972 and 1973. *Lond.Nat.* **53**:86-99.

de Worms, C.G.M., 1975 *Danaus plexippus* (Linnaeus) (Lep., Danaidae) in the outskirts of London. *Entomologist's Gaz.* **26**:38.

de Worms, C.G.M., 1976 A review of the Macrolepidoptera of the London area for 1974 and 1975. *Lond. Nat.* **55**:48-57.

de Worms, C.G.M., 1977 Purple Emperors and other butterflies on Bookham Common, Surrey, in 1976. *Entomologist's Rec. J. Var.* **89**:88.

de Worms, C.G.M., 1978 A review of the Macrolepidoptera of the London area for 1976 and 1977. *Lond. Nat.* **57**:81-90.

Dixey, F.A., 1874 *Notes on the Entomology of the Highgate District.* London:Highgate School.

Doubleday, E., 1836 Remarks on the entomology of Epping and its vicinity. *Entomologist's Mag.* **3**:147-159, 283 - 292.

Dutfield, J., 1748 *A new and complete natural history of English moths and butterflies* 1. London.

Edelsten, H.M., 1911 *Papilio machaon* in Middlesex. *Entomologist* **44**:365.

Emmet, A.M. Pyman, G.A. and Corke, D., 1985 The Larger Moths and Butterflies of Essex. *Essex Nat.* **8**(*new series*): 1:135.

Evans, K.G.W. and Evans, L,K., 1973 A survey of the macrolepidoptera of Croydon and north-east Surrey. *Proc. Croydon nat. Hist.sci.Soc.* **14**:273-408.

Fenn, C.,	1895	On the gradual disappearance of Lepidoptera from south eastern London and its neighbourhood. *Entomologists Rec. J. Var.* **6**:228-232.
Firmin, J., *et al*,	1975	*A Guide to the butterflies and larger moths of Essex.* Fingringhoe:Essex Naturalists' Trust.
Fitch, E.A.,	1891	The Lepidoptera of Essex, 1. Butterflies. *Essex Nat.* **5**:74-108.
Ford, E.B.,	1945	*Butterflies.* London:Collins New Naturalist.
Foster, A.H.,	1937	A list of the Lepidoptera of Hertfordshire. *Trans. Herts. Nat. Hist. Soc. Fld. Club* **20**:157-279.
Frazer, J.F.D.,	1961	Butterfly populations on the North Downs. *Proc. Trans. S. Lond. Ent. Nat. Hist. Soc.* **1960**: 98-109.
Frazer, J.F.D.,	1977	The Chalk Hill Blue butterfly *Lysandra coridon* at Burham Down, 1955-74. *Trans. Kent Fld. Club.* **6**:71-74.
Frazer, J.F.D.,	1981	Roosting Sites of Blue Butterflies. *Trans. Kent Fld. Club.* **8**:149-151.
Freebry, A.M.,	1964	*Colias hyale* L. in Essex. *Entomologist's Rec. J. Var.* **76**:243.
French, R.A.,	1957	Migration Records, 1956. *Entomologist* **90**:227-238.
French, R.A.,	1968	Migration Records, 1965. *Entomologist* **101**:156-161.
Frohawk, F.W.,	1905	*Vanessa antiopa* in Middlesex. *Entomologist* **38**:283.
Frohawk, F.W.,	1921	On the appearance of *Anosia plexippus* in Britain. *Entomologist* **54**:145-146.
Frohawk, F.W.,	1928	*Euvanessa antiopa* at Dulwich. *Entomologist* **61**:236.
Frohawk, F.W.,	1930	*Euvanessa antiopa* in Kent and Surrey. *Entomologist* **63**:14.
Frohawk, F.W.,	1934	*Polygonia c-album* in the London area. *Entomologist* **67**:205.
Frohawk, F.W.,	1934	*The Complete Book of British Butterflies.* London: Ward Lock.
Frohawk, F.W.,	1945	*Argynnis lathonia* at Sutton. *Entomologist* **78**:21.
Furneaux, W.,	1894	*Butterflies and Moths.* London: Longmans, Green and Co.
Garland, S.P.,	1981	*Butterflies of the Sheffield area.* Sorby Record Special Series number 5.
Gibbs, A.E.,	1902	Lepidoptera. *Victoria County History of Hertfordshire* **1**:110-168.
Goater, B.,	1974	*The Butterflies and Moths of Hampshire and the Isle of Wight.* Faringdon:Classey
Goodden, R.,	1978	*British Butterflies: A Field Guide.* London: David and Charles.
Goss, H. & Barrett, C.G.,	1902	Lepidoptera. *Victoria County History of Surrey* **1**:109-150.
Goss, H., & Bower, B.A.,	1908	Lepidoptera. *Victoria County History of Kent* **1**:178-208.
Greenwood, J.A.C.,	1971	Butterflies in the City of London. *Entomologist's Rec. J. Var.* **83**:346.
Haines, T.T.,	1934	*Polygonia c-album* in East London. *Entomologist* **67**:9.
Hammerson, M.J.,	1965	Butterfly Records. *Entomologist's Rec. J. Var.* **77**:227.
Harper, E.,	1868	*Argynnis lathonia* at Darenth. *Entomologist* **4**:131.
Harris, M.,	1766	*The Aurelian, or Natural History of English Insects; namely Moths and Butterflies together with the plants on which they feed.* London.
Harwood, W.H.,	1903	Lepidoptera. *Victoria County History of Essex* **1**:136-177.
Hawes, F.W.,	1890	*Hesperia lineola*, Ochsenheimer: an addition to the list of British butterflies. *Entomologist* **23**:3-4.

Hawkins, C.N., 1924 *Limenitis sybilla* at Wimbledon, etc. *Entomologist* **57**:282-283.

Haworth, A.H., 1803-29 *Lepidoptera Britannica*. London.

Heath, J., 1981 *Threatened Rhopalocera (butterflies) in Europe*. Strasburg: Council of Europe, Nature and Environment Series.

Heath, J., Pollard, E. and Thomas, J., 1984 *The Atlas of the Butterflies of the British Isles*. London:Viking.

Helps, J.A. 1891 Lepidoptera of Dulwich. *Entomologist's Rec. J. Var.* **2**:140-141.

Heslop, I.R.P., 1959-60 Revised, indexed check-list of the British Lepidoptera. *Entomologist's Gaz.* **10**:179-187; **11**:55-66,169-178.

Holdaway, P., 1979 The Monarch, *Danaus plexippus* L., in 1978. *Entomologist's Rec. J. Var.* **91**:27

Holdaway, P., 1980 The White-letter hairstreak: *Strymonidia w-album* Knoch. *Entomologist's Rec. J. Var.* **92**:153.

Howarth, T.G., 1971 *Nymphalis antiopa* (L.) at South Harrow, Middlesex, in 1970. *Entomologist's Rec. J. Var.* **83**:153.

Howarth, T.G., 1973 South's British Butterflies. London:Warne.

Ing, A.K., 1918 *Eugonia polychloros* at Kingston. *Entomologist* **51**:161.

Jackson, A.C., 1965 The Macrolepidoptera of the south Herts. plateau. *Lond. Nat.* **44**:73-76.

Jones, A.W., 1955 Notes on the butterflies of Wimbledon Common. *Lond. Nat.* **34**:108-114.

James, R., 1940 *Limentis camilla* and other butterflies in London. *Entomologist* **73**:213.

Kelly, E.N., 1949 *Papilio machaon* at Hayes, Middlesex. *Entomologist* **82**:184.

Kloet, G.S. and Hincks, W.D. 1972 A check list of British Insects (edition 2), Lepidoptera. *Handbk. Ident. Br. Insects.* **11**(2).

Lewin, W., 1795 *The insects of Great Britain*. London.

Lobley, J.L., 1889 *Hampstead Hill*. London.

Marshall, J.E., 1978 *Polygonia c-album* (L.) (Lep., Nymphalidae) feeding on hops (*Humulus lupulus* L.). *Entomologist's Gaz.* **29**:16.

Meldola, R., 1891 The Lepidoptera of Leyton and neighbour hood; a contribution to the county fauna. *Essex Nat.* **5**:153-170.

Mendel, H. and Pietrowski, S.H. 1986 *The Butterflies of Suffolk*. Suffolk Naturalists' Society.

Mera, A.W., 1929 Stray Notes on the Butterflies of Epping Forest. *Essex Naturalist* **22**:201-202.

Minnion, W.E., 1953 An introduction to the butterflies and moths, with special reference to the Ruislip district. *J. Ruislip & dist. nat. Hist. Soc.* **2**:19-22

Morley, A.M. and Chalmers-Hunt, J.M., 1959 Some observations on the crimson ringed butterfly (*Parnassius apollo* L.) in Britain. *Entomologist's Rec. J. Var.* **71**:273-276.

Morris, F.O., 1895 *A History of British Butterflies* (eighth edition). London:Nimmo.

Morris, G.M., 1954 *Euvanessa antiopa* in the City of London. *Entomologist* **87**:220.

Mouffet, T., 1634 *Insectorum sive minimorum animalium theatrum*. London.

Newman, E., 1869 *An Illustrated Natural History of British Butterflies and Moths*. London.

O'Keeffe, D., 1970 *Celastrina argiolus* L. in Kent. *Entomologist's Rec. J. Var.* **82**:243-244.

Owen, D.F.,	1953	The ecology and distribution of the Satyridae in West Kent. *Lond. Nat.* **32**:13-44.
Owen, D.F. and Owen, J.E.,	1950	The Butterflies of Greenwich Park. *Entomologist's Rec. J. Var.* **62**:15-16.
Owen, G.V.,	1951	*Danaus plexippus* (L.) (Milkweed Butterfly) in Kent. *Entomologist's Gaz.* **2**:75.
Payne, R.G. and Skinner, J.F.,	1981	*Provisional distribution maps of butterflies in Essex.* Essex Biological Records Centres Publication Number 1.
Peachey, C.,	1980	*The Conservation of Butterflies in Bernwood Forest.* Foxhold:NCC.
Petiver, J.,	1699	*Musei Petiveriani Centuria quarta rariora naturae.* London.
Petiver, J.,	1703	*Musei Petiverani centuria nona & decima.* London.
Petiver, J.,	1704	*Gazophylacium naturae et artis* 3. London.
Petiver, J.,	1717	*Papilionum Britanniae.* London.
Plant, C.W.,	1981	A review of the Lepidoptera of the London area, 1978-1980. *Lond. Nat.* **60**:100-104.
Plant, C.W.,	1983	A review of the Lepidoptera of the London area for 1981 and 1982. *Lond. Nat.* **62**:116-125.
Plant, C.W.,	1984	The Clouded Yellow butterfly *Colias croceus* Geoffroy in the London area in 1983. *Lond. Nat.* **63**:94-96.
Plant, C.W.,	1985	A review of the Lepidoptera of the London area for 1983 and 1984. *Lond. Nat.* **64**:45-62.
Plant, C.W.,	1986	Migratory Lepidoptera in the London Area: (Presidential Address-9 December 1985). *Lond. Nat.* **65**:7-29.
Plant, C.W.,	1987	A review of the Lepidoptera of the London area for 1985 and 1986. *Lond. Nat.* **66**:
Pratt, C.B.,	1946	Some butterflies in Epping Forest in 1945. *Essex Naturalist* **27**:306.
Ransom, D.P.,	1957	*Parnassius apollo* in London. *Entomologist* **90**:297.
Ray, J.,	1710	*Historia Insectorum.*
Richardson, N.A.,	1940	*Nymphalis antiopa* at Hendon. *Entomologist* **73**:161.
Riley, N.D.,	1945	*Pontia daplidice* in North Devon. *Entomologist* **78**:143.
Sabine, E.,	1893	*Polyommatus boetica* near Dartford. *Entomologist* **26**:300-301.
Samouelle, G.,	1819	*The entomologist's useful compendium.* London.
Saville, C.,	1915	*Vanessa antiopa* in Surrey. *Entomologist* **48**:267.
Scott, E.,	1950	*A list of butterflies and moths (Macro Lepidoptera) occurring in the neighbourhood of Ashford, Kent.* Ashford:Headley Bros.
Sellon, R.S.,	1891	The Fauna of South London. *Entomologist's Rec. J. Var.* **2**:164.
Sheldon, W.G.,	1934	*Papilio machaon* in Surrey. *Entomologist* **67**:205.
Showler, A.J.,	1962	*Papilio machaon* L. in Kent. *Entomologist's Rec. J. Var.* **74**:246.
Smart, P.E.,	1955	The Brimstone butterfly, *Gonepteryx rhamni* L. at Cripplegate. *Lond. Nat.* **34**:12.
Smith, B.H.,	1912	*Vanessa antiopa* in Kent, 1911. *Entomologist* **45**:209.
Smith, R.,	1981	The Camberwell Beauty: *Nymphalis antiopa* L. in 1981. *Entomologist's Rec. J. Var.* **93**:241.
Smith, W.,	1905	*Vanessa antiopa* in Surrey. *Entomologist* **48**:91.
Sokoloff, P.A.,	1976	*Nymphalis antiopa* L. in north-west Kent. *Entomologist's Rec. J. Var.* **88**:293.

South, R., 1906 *The Butterflies of the British Isles*. London: Warne.
Stainton, H.T., 1859 *A Manual of British Butterflies and Moths*. London.
Steel, C. and Steel, D. 1985 The butterflies of Berkshire, Buckinghamshire and Oxfordshire. Oxford:Pisces Publications.
Stephens, J.F., 1828-44 *Illustrations of British Entomology*. Haustellata. i - v. London.
St. John, W.G., 1968 Butterflies in the London area. *Entomologist's Gaz.* **19**:32.
St. John, W.G., 1972 Lepidoptera Records. *Entomologist's Gaz.* **23**:166.
St. John, W.G., 1975 *Nymphalis antiopa* (L.) (Lep., Nymphalidae) in London. *Entomologist's Gaz.* **26**:66.
Sutton, F.R., 1964 *Vanessa atalanta* L. in Central London. *Entomologist's Rec. J. Var.* **76**:200.
Swete, C.J., 1860 *A Handbook of Epsom and District*. Epsom.
Symes, H., 1965 Where have all the butterflies gone? *Entomologist's Rec. J. Var.* **77**:271-273.
Talbot, G., 1909 *Apatura iris* and *Vanessa antiopa* in Essex. *Entomologist* **42**:282.
Thomas, J. and Webb, N. 1984 *The Butterflies of Dorset*. Dorset Archaeological & nat. Hist. Soc.
Thompson, P., 1937 Some tenants of banana-crates. *Essex Nat.* **25**:208-209.
Turner, G.C., 1917 *Eugonia polychloros* in West London. *Entomologist* **50**:142.
Tutt, J.W. 1899-1914 *A Natural History of British Lepidoptera*. i-v, viii-xi. London:Swann Sonnenschein.
Tutt, J.W., 1907-08 *British Butterflies* 1-2. London.
Tyssen, R., 1857 Captures in Epping Forest. *Entomologist's Wkly. Intell.* **2**:115.
Waller, J., 1957 *Danaus plexippus* in South London. *Entomologist* **90**:307.
Weal, R.D., 1946 Camberwell Beauty at Chingford. *Essex Naturalist* **27**:305.
West, B.K., 1981 *Rorippa sylvestris* [Cruciferae] as a larval foodplant of *Pieris napi* L. *Entomologist's Rec. J. Var.* **93**:179.
West, B.K., 1982 *Pieris rapae* L. and *Cardaria draba* [Cruciferae] as a larval foodplant. *Entomologist's Rec. J. Var.* **94**:72.
West, B.K., 1982 The Brimstone *Gonepteryx rhamni* L. apparently imbibing at *Hydrangea* flowers. *Entomologist's Rec. J. Var.* **94**:172.
West, W., 1868. *Colias hyale* at Brockley and Lee. *Entomologist* **4**:131.
West, W., 1906 The Lepidoptera of the south-eastern district of London. *Entomologist's Rec. J. Var.* **18**: 141-143.
Wheeler, A.S., 1955 A Preliminary List of the Macro-Lepidoptera of Bookham Common. *Lond. Nat.* **34**:28-36.
Wheeler, A.S., 1962 *Adopoea lineola* in Surrey. *Entomologist's Rec. J. Var.* **74**:51.
Whittingham, W.F., 1894 *Vanessa antiopa* in Epping Forest. *EssexNat.* **8**:88.
Wilkes, B., 1741/42 *Twelve New Designs of English Butterflies*. London.
Wilkes, B., 1749 *The English Moths and Butterflies*. London.
Wilkinson, R.S. 1975 The scarce swallowtail *Iphiclides podalirius* (L.) in Britain. *Entomologist's Rec. J. Var.* **87**:289-293.
Wilkinson, R.S. 1977 The great Cornhill fire and the demise of the first Aurelian Society. *Entomologist's Rec. J. Var.* **89**:250-251.
Wilkinson, R.S. 1981 The first records of *Papilio machaon* L. in England. *Entomologist's Rec. J. Var.* **93**:4-6.
Williams, E.F. 1953 Butterflies in the Brentwood area in 1952. *Essex Nat.* **29**:110-111.
Withers, B.G., 1975 Among the British Lepidoptera. *Entomologist's Rec. J. Var.* **87**:37-44.
Youens, C.T., 1891 Variety of *Gonepteryx rhamni*. *Entomologist's Rec. J. Var.* **2**:36.

THE LONDON NATURAL HISTORY SOCIETY

The Society is organised in Sections for Botany, Ecology and Entomology, Geology and Archaeology, and Ornithology. There is also a Ramblers section which includes places of historical interest in its programme, and one local section which has its indoor meetings in Hounslow. The Ecology and Entomology Section also provides for those interested in mammals, reptiles, amphibians, fishes and all invertebrate groups. All meetings are open to every member whatever their specific interests may be.

The Society is governed by a Council which includes both elected members and representatives of all the Sections. The principal officers and elected members of Council are elected at the Annual General Meeting of the Society in December or thereabouts. The Sections also have their own AGMs at which their officers are appointed.

The London Natural History Society offers you . . .

INDOOR MEETINGS These average one a week and vary from first-class illustrated lectures to informal discussions. They are held in meeting rooms in central London.

FIELD MEETINGS These too provide opportunities for members to increase their knowledge and to get to know one another. Experienced leaders act as guides and offer help to beginners.

PUBLICATIONS *The London Naturalist* and the *London Bird Report* are published annually and sent free to all members. They contain articles on natural history subjects relevant to London, compilations of recent records and details of the Society's affairs. Members also receive a *Newsletter* and *Ornithological Bulletin* every other month.

LIBRARY The Society's library is housed at Imperial College, South Kensington. A large selection of books and journals on most aspects of natural history is available to members for reference or on loan free of charge. Some journals are circulated to members who pay a small annual subscription, much less than the cost of buying one's own copy.

PROGRAMME Full details of all the events planned for the coming half year are sent to members.

CO-OPERATIVE ENQUIRIES Many members contribute individually to enquiries into various aspects of natural history, while Sections organise local teams to play the Society's part in national enquiries. Mapping the breeding birds and the flora of the London area have been carried out by the Society's ornithologists and botanists respectively. A continuous survey of Bookham Common in Surrey is conducted by the Society.

The LNHS and YOU

We welcome every new member and hope that you will be amply rewarded for joining a Society catering for so wide a range of natural history interests. London's transport system makes it easy for the naturalist to reach a variety of habitats – the Surrey hills, the Essex marshes, the Thames valley – heaths, woods and waters, all rich hunting-grounds for your enjoyment. The LNHS will show you how you can make the very most of these opportunities.

Family membership is available to members of the family of an Ordinary Member living at the same address. Family Members enjoy all the benefits of the Society and are entitled to vote, but do not receive any publications except Programmes.

Junior Membership is available to all under 18 years of age, or under 25 if in receipt of full-time education.

Subscriptions fall due on 1st January each year. The first subscription of Members enrolled on or after 1st October extends ot 31st December of the following year. Such members do not receive the Journals published in the current year. An Entrance Fee of 50p is payable to all new Members.

Application forms are available from the Membership Secretary,

P.C. Holland
Flat 9, Pinewood Court
23 Clarence Avenue
Clapham
London SW4 8LB

Back numbers of both *The London Naturalist* and the *London Bird Report* are available for certain years. For full details please write to the Publication Sales Secretary at Upper Flat, 65 Arthur Road, London SW19 7DN.

INDEX